VOICES
OF THE
PACIFIC

VOICES
OF THE
PACIFIC

★ ★ ★

UNTOLD STORIES FROM THE
MARINE HEROES OF WORLD WAR II

Adam Makos

with Marcus Brotherton

BERKLEY CALIBER, NEW YORK

THE BERKLEY PUBLISHING GROUP
Published by the Penguin Group
Penguin Group (USA) Inc.
375 Hudson Street, New York, New York 10014, USA

USA I Canada I UK I Ireland I Australia I New Zealand I India I South Africa I China

Penguin Books Ltd., Registered Offices: 80 Strand, London WC2R 0RL, England
For more information about the Penguin Group, visit penguin.com.

This book is an original publication of The Berkley Publishing Group.

Library of Congress Cataloging-in-Publication Data

Makos, Adam.
Voices of the Pacific : untold stories from the Marine heroes of
World War II / by Adam Makos ; with Marcus Brotherton.
p. cm.
ISBN 978-0-425-25782-1
1. World War, 1939–1945—Campaigns—Pacific Area. 2. World War, 1939–1945—Personal
narratives, American. 3. United States. Marine Corps—History—World War, 1939–1945.
4. Marines—United States—Biography. I. Brotherton, Marcus, author. II. Title.
D767.9.M35 2013
940.54'59730922—dc23
2012046253

FIRST EDITION: April 2013

PRINTED IN THE UNITED STATES OF AMERICA

10 9 8 7 6 5 4 3

Jacket design and interior maps by Bryan Makos of Valor Studios
Jacket photos (front): soldiers: USMC; tropical tree background: Bryan Makos; WWII
Marine uniform: Adam Makos; (back): Eugene Sledge: courtesy of Eugene Sledge;
Robert Leckie: courtesy of Vera Leckie; John Basilone: courtesy of Richard Greer
Book design by Tiffany Estreicher
Title page photo courtesy of the United States Marine Corps

ALWAYS LEARNING   PEARSON

*Dedicated to the American and Allied servicemen
and -women whose voices were forever silenced while
fighting for freedom in the Pacific.*

CONTENTS

FACES BEHIND THE VOICES

(IN ORDER OF APPEARANCE)

 SID PHILLIPS

 JIM YOUNG

 ROY GERLACH

 ART PENDLETON

 RICHARD GREER

 R. V. BURGIN

 T. I. MILLER

 JIM ANDERSON

 CHUCK TATUM

 CLINTON WATTERS

 CLARENCE REA

 DAN LAWLER

 STERLING MACE

 WAYBURN HALL

 HARRY BENDER

INTRODUCTION

Meet the survivors.

The World War II veterans of this book endured unspeakable horrors, came home to America, and more than sixty-seven years later are still alive today. These men—Marines who fought in the Pacific—are national treasures.

This book could not be written ten years from now. Not five. Maybe not even two. All the book's contributors are in their golden years. Some are eighty-eight years old, others ninety. Richard Greer, our oldest contributor, is ninety-five. But the men shared their stories as if World War II happened yesterday.

In the following pages, these veterans will take you back in time. You'll experience the shock they felt as boys when Pearl Harbor was bombed. You'll feel the jolt of boot camp as civility is thrown out the window to turn boys into men. You'll sail with them to the island of Guadalcanal for their harrowing first battles as Marines as they square off against a seasoned and vicious foe. The journey does not stop there. They'll take you to Australia for a raucous R&R, then back to the sound of gunfire, to the rain forests of Cape Gloucester, the coral ridges of Peleliu, the black sands of Iwo Jima, and the mud of Okinawa. In the end, they'll bring you home, as they once returned, triumphant, joyous, yet tormented by the loss of so many friends.

Today these men are fathers, grandfathers, and great-grand-fathers in our communities, our neighbors, the guy at the grocery store, the man in church. Yet what they experienced was so graphic, so horrible, it seems astounding that they are among us. And normal. And so humble.

Many books exist about the Pacific War. What sets this book apart is its oral-history style. In this type of book, the author presents the "voices," then steps back into the shadows. This is a conversation between you—the reader—and the men. Imagine for a moment it's late at night and you've walked into the kitchen for a drink and you find your father or grandfather and his old war buddies around the kitchen table. They're swapping stories. You listen and what you hear you'll never forget. That is this book.

★   ★   ★

After Tom Hanks, Steven Spielberg, and Gary Goetzman produced their award-winning HBO miniseries, *Band of Brothers*, viewers wanted to know about the battles that took place on the other side of the world. This led to the production of the 2010 miniseries *The Pacific*.

The Pacific brought to life the names, places, and battles of the legendary 1st Marine Division. This unit fought in the first American offensives against Japan and was still in the theater of war when the shells stopped flying. The HBO series followed three principal veterans, the quirky Robert Leckie, the sensitive Eugene Sledge, and the larger-than-life John Basilone. These men deserved the spotlight they received. Basilone wore the Medal of Honor for good reason, and after the war, Leckie and Sledge documented their experiences in epic books for the world's education. Each appears as a character in *Voices of the Pacific*, but not as "voices," simply because none of the three are now living.

The power of this book comes from its freshness. We swing the spotlight over to living heroes who served alongside these icons. The "new voices" in this book are veterans with their own breed of heroics. Some are hometown heroes. Some, like Sid Phillips, R. V. Burgin, and Chuck Tatum are already known by their books or from the silver screen. And many of the men in this book are speaking up for the first time. A reader need not have seen *The Pacific* to appreciate *Voices of the Pacific*. The heroism in these pages stands alone.

★   ★   ★

For many years now I've worked closely with the Marines whose stories follow. I met Chuck Tatum a decade ago and edited his book *Red Blood, Black Sand* for him. I also had the privilege of working with Sid Phillips, on his lighthearted memoir, *You'll Be Sor-ree!*. Sid had more stories in him—dark, violent stories he did not put in his own book. I asked him why he was hesitant, and he said he didn't want his grandkids reading about the raw, rotten, savage side of World War II. So instead he focused on the humor and camaraderie that he found amid the horror.

There's a time and place for everything, and this book is about last words from living men. The veterans are not getting any younger. None of us are. So in this book, the gloves come off—for Sid Phillips and all our contributors. They agreed to participate because we made them a promise: *In this book, you can tell it as it was.*

What follows is not a sanitized version of the war. It's the last survivors talking to you, digging deep and pulling out painful memories, gut-busting humor, and rousing accounts of American bravery, sacrifice, and old-fashioned goodness. Here they give us one last tale, one last time.

★   ★   ★

So where did we find the men who loaned us their voices? Our recruiting efforts were like a snowball. One veteran agreed to participate then told us where to find his buddy, then his buddy told us how to find *his* buddy. Before we knew it, we had the fifteen heroes whose voices you will hear.

Time was of the essence, so I enlisted the help of journalist Marcus Brotherton, who had profiled the men of Easy Company for his bestselling oral history project, *We Who Are Alive & Remain*. Together we did countless hours of interviews, editing, and shuffling the parts of the book together like a jigsaw puzzle.

We got a little carried away. We interviewed World War II Marine pilots of Wildcat and Corsair fighters who had roamed the skies above the ground-pounders. We talked with Katharine Phillips-Singer, whom you may remember as the Southern lady who stole the show in Ken Burns's documentary *The War*. Katharine shared her colorful memories of the World War II home front. But in the end, we ran out of pages. That material is not lost. In fact, it's available to you on our website, www.valorstudios.com.

★   ★   ★

One question puzzled me at the start of this book, but not at the end. *How did these men return to the world after what they saw, did, and suffered?* How does a man keep his sanity after sleeping in waterlogged foxholes so long his toenails rot away? How does a man tell a joke after having 970 battleship shells dropped around him, each blast sucking the air from his lungs? How does a man keep fighting after seeing his gut-shot buddy be carried away, screaming on a stretcher?

The answer, we invite you to discover, lies on the pages that follow. I'll let you come to your own conclusion, but I've come to mine: The Marines of this book are an extraordinary breed.

Adam Makos
Denver, November 2012

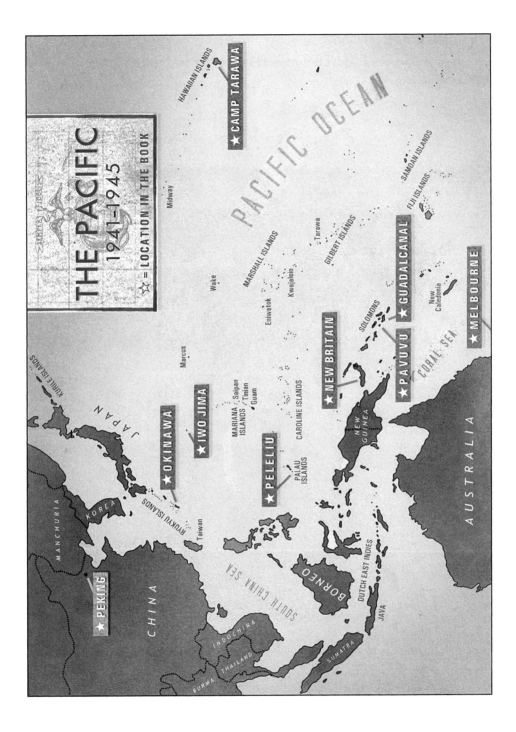

CHAPTER ONE

WE'RE IN IT NOW

★ ★ ★

Pearl Harbor

On Sunday, December 7, 1941, the Japanese Navy launched an aerial sneak attack on the American military at Pearl Harbor and across the island of Oahu. On that day, the Japanese killed 2,400 American servicemen and fifty-seven civilians in an act of undeclared war.

SID PHILLIPS

December 7, 1941, was a Sunday afternoon, and I didn't have anything to do. I went by the Albright drugstore in my hometown of Mobile, Alabama, where my friend W. O. Brown was the soda jerk (soda fountain attendant). I was sitting at the counter talking to W.O., and there were about twenty people in the drugstore. This lady burst through the side door and said, "Turn on the radio!" W.O. had a small radio and he turned it on. The news commentator didn't give any specific information other than we'd been attacked and the casualties were heavy. Evidently he'd been instructed to give only that amount of information and nothing else. We switched from station to station, and they were all talking about the attack on Pearl Harbor. There was no music. Nothing but news. We just sat there and listened, shocked.

Everyone was puzzled, asking where Pearl Harbor was. I was the only one in the drugstore who knew it was in Hawaii and told everyone this. Pearl Harbor wasn't a household name then. But my uncle Joe Tucker had been stationed there, and my mother had received letters from him.

After half an hour, I got on my bicycle and rode on out to my house on Monterrey Place. Everyone had heard about it by then. The news had traveled through the neighborhoods.

I went to enlist the day after Pearl Harbor. W.O. and I thought we'd be the early birds and get there before a crowd assembled. Our initial plan was to join the Navy. We got to the Federal Building about eight in the morning, and boy—the line for the Navy recruiting office was at least three hundred yards long.

I had to go to work, and W.O. needed to go to school, so we walked to the head of the line to see what was going on. I was seventeen but had graduated high school and landed a good job down at the U.S. Engineers office in downtown Mobile. My job was to carry maps over to the Federal Building, about two city blocks away, where the maps were duplicated and made into blueprints. It paid $90 a month, which was far more than I ever made in the Marine Corps (when I joined, I made only $21 a month in the Marines).

A Marine recruiter came up and started talking to me and W.O. "Do you boys want to kill Japs?" he said.*

---

* The Marines of WWII had grown up seeing a steady stream of newsreels and reports from China where the Japanese had brutalized the population—burying prisoners alive, beheading them, and even tossing babies in the air and catching them with bayonets. The image of a Japanese citizen—once thought to be someone who loved poetry, calligraphy, and gardening—changed into that of a brutal soldier with a penchant for sadism. The Japanese—both civilians and soldiers—became derisively known as "Japs" even before America entered the war.

"Yeah, that's the idea," we said. "But we're going to join the Navy."

"Nah," he said, "you don't want to do that. You can't get into the Navy if your parents are married. And anyway, all you'll do in the Navy is swab decks. But I guarantee that if you join the Marine Corps, we'll put you eyeball to eyeball with the Japs."

There wasn't any line at his office. So that's the big reason why we joined the Marines—because the damn line for the Navy was too long. We were so stupid. We didn't know anything about the Marine Corps other than what was on the recruiter's posters. Years later, W.O. and I compared notes and we figured that just about everything that Marine recruiter told us was a lie—except meeting the Japs eyeball to eyeball.

What was our predominant motivation for enlisting? It was anger. Even more than duty, I'd say. The only information we had was that it was a sneak attack on Pearl Harbor. No warning at all. So the American people were really angry. It's something that almost can't be put into words—how infuriated we were as a country.

JIM YOUNG

On Monday morning, December 8, 1941, the day after Pearl Harbor was attacked, I was at work at the shoe factory in Mount Joy, Pennsylvania. I was twenty years old. I shut down my machine. The boss said, "What the hell are you doing?" and I said, "I'm sorry, but I'm leaving to join up." It was then that I heard other machines being shut down and guys saying, "We're going, too."

I hitchhiked to Philadelphia and arrived at 1 P.M. at the recruiting offices. The sidewalks were lined up for blocks with guys wanting to enlist. I had decided to go in the Navy. After waiting in line for hours I finally got in the naval office, only to be turned down because some of my teeth needed to be filled. I had some cavities. When the war broke out, the military outfits had certain codes; you had to be in this and that shape. The war was so new they hadn't had time to lower their standards.

Across from the naval office was the U.S. Marines office. As I started to walk away, some guy in the Marine line said, "Hey, Mac, what's the matter?" I told him the Navy had turned me down. "Why don't you try the Marines?" he said. I told him the office would be closed by the time I went out and got in the Marine line. He told me to just keep talking to him and keep moving with the line and that no one would even notice. Then when we got to the door we would just pop in. Well, it worked, and I became a U.S. Marine! They never even said anything about my teeth. I was told I could leave the next day or wait until after Christmas. I chose the latter so I could say my good-byes to my mother and friends.

My mother was sad to see me go. She was my role model. I worked for her in her little mom-and-pop store—groceries, fruit, and produce. I peddled the fruit to other towns for her. My stepfather was a state policeman and he wasn't a good guy. He was very mean to my brother Phillip and me. I was kinda glad to be leaving.

ROY GERLACH

My parents were both Mennonites, pacifists, and didn't approve of war. We lived on a farm in Lancaster, Pennsylvania, and I had the choice of staying out of the service two ways, either by being a conscientious objector because of my parents' religion, or by getting an agricultural deferment for working on a farm. But I didn't quite agree with my folks about being pacifists. I can't say I was right or not about it. I was twenty-one years old and it was my decision.

I went from work to Lancaster, and there was a big long line to join the Army. I didn't have time for that. I found another long line, and that was to join the Navy. I didn't have time for that neither. So I went down the hall and found the Marine Corps office. I went in there.

"What do I have to do to become a Marine?" I asked.

"Can you hear, talk, and see?" the sergeant said.

"Yes," I said.

"Okay, you're in."

So I became a Marine because they had the shortest line.

They had a group leaving the 29th of December. So I thought, "Good, that will give me Christmas at home." I didn't tell my parents I had signed up until I was set to go.

Parris Island Boot Camp, December 31, 1941

SID PHILLIPS

We were so stupid, we'd never heard of Parris Island. I think that recruiting sergeant told us we'd have a short training program at a beautiful resort on the beach in South Carolina. When we arrived at the Marine Corps Recruiting Station at Parris Island, we soon realized it wasn't even an island. There's a causeway that connects it to the mainland. It's just a name—Parris Island. That boot camp was rugged. Before Pearl Harbor, it lasted twelve weeks. But after Pearl Harbor they shortened it to just six weeks. Everything was intensified and sped up. It was wintertime when we arrived, December 31, 1941. And it was cold.

As you arrived, there with civilian clothes and long hair, all the guys who were already there would holler, "You'll be sorry!" We were rapidly sorry within the first few hours that we were there. They had that pegged just right.

JIM YOUNG

A big Marine sergeant started yelling at us to line up so he could take roll call. When he finally called "James F. Young!" no one said a word, not even me. One of the guys I'd met said, "Didn't you tell me that was your name?" I finally yelled, "Here, Sir!" The sergeant said, "Boy, we got us a real dumb ass here! Don't even know his own name." I was very embarrassed. My stepfather had always made me use his last name, which was Wolfe. No one had ever called me anything different, so my mind went blank when the sergeant called "James Young." Anyway, it was my first goof in the Marines and I hoped it was the last.

Parris Island was something to see. Marines were drilling, and we wondered if we would ever be able to march as well as they could. The first night was kind of scary. The base was near to the ocean and open to attack from the sea so everything was under "blackout." The drill sergeant made us take turns at guarding the area (with no guns). I guess we looked funny standing at the door of our Quonset hut wearing civilian clothes.

The following day we got our Marine clothes. When we got back to the barracks, there was a civilian with a Marine captain. The captain told us that the man wanted to purchase our civilian clothing. He said that we might as well sell because by the time the war is over, nothing would fit us anyway. Most of us sold everything we had. I think I got about $3 for the works, which included a suit, topcoat, shoes, and everything else.

We moved into a two-story barracks on the top floor. There was a zigzag stairway to come down to the drill field. Each day we were up at 4 A.M. to drill all day until we got it right. In the morning the drill instructor would stand down there and yell *"Fall out!"* Then he would time us. If we didn't do it fast enough, he would make us do it again and again until it suited him. Well by the time we got it right, we were leaping over each other and over the stair rails. Those who were too slow ended up doing mess duty. We also got our rifles and were told that if we ever dropped ours then we would have to sleep with it.

SID PHILLIPS

They never let you wear enough clothing to be warm. We wore khaki pants and a sweatshirt. You didn't complain about it being cold, because all that did was bring on more push-ups, more double-time jogging, and whatnot. So there wasn't anything you could do except endure it, and gripe under your breath. But Parris Island was rough, and still is, and should be. And I'm glad it was. It teaches discipline to young men, and you need that to survive. You learn not to do anything except take orders, take orders, take orders. Do what you're supposed to do.

JIM YOUNG

One Sunday afternoon while sitting on the barracks steps, a Marine was walking by eating ice cream. I asked him where he got it. He told me to just go straight across the drill field to the PX (base store). After thanking him, I went over and got a pint of vanilla-and-chocolate ice cream. I returned and had no more than started eating it when my drill sergeant came out of the barracks. He said, "Private Young, that looks real good, can I have a bite?" I said, "Yes, sir" and handed him the ice cream. He opened the pint box. "Wow, that's really good," he said. He then told me to take my hat off, and when I did, he took the whole box and set it upside down on my head and told me not to move. He mashed my hat down real hard and told me not to move until all the ice cream was melted. By this time, all the guys in the barracks were laughing. The sergeant then told me that no one was allowed to go anywhere—even if it was a Sunday—and especially not to the PX.

On another day the drill sergeant was upset with one of the guys because he was always getting out of step. He called the guy out of ranks and told him to hold his rifle over his head and run around the drill field until he was told to stop. Well, the sergeant stopped him after the third lap. The Marine was just a kid, about seventeen years old, and looked like he was about to cry. The sergeant told him that now he will think twice to stay in step. The sergeant asked him if he was all right and feeling better and the Marine said, "Yes, sir, I do." The Sergeant then said, "Well that's just great. Now get that rifle up and give me a couple of more laps."

SID PHILLIPS

After finishing boot camp at Parris Island, we went to Camp Lejeune, North Carolina, for more advanced training. It wasn't even named Camp Lejeune yet. It was still called "New River." Thousands of acres. All the buildings were just framed, brand-new. Nothing was paved. It was far from any town and just a giant mud hole when it rained. The 1st Marine Division was being assembled there on the East Coast while the 2nd Marine Division was being formed along the West Coast.

W.O. and I were assigned to the 1st Marine Division. They called our division "the Raggedy-Assed Marines" because we were stationed out in the boondocks. We took pride in that name—it made us sound macho. The division had three regiments, the 1st Marines, 5th Marines, and 7th Marines. The regiments each had three battalions and each battalion had four companies—the company was what mattered. That was your home. Your friends. Who you identified with. A Company, B Company, C Company, and so forth. And, of course, there was a headquarters company of support people—clerks, cooks, messengers, and intelligence people.

They put W.O. and me in H Company of the 1st Marines. H Company was a heavy weapons company. Three platoons of .30-caliber machine guns. A platoon of 37mm anti-tank cannons. A platoon of .50-caliber machine guns (for anti-aircraft purposes), and a platoon of 81mm mortars. I wound up in the mortar platoon with W.O. and fellows like Jim Young and Roy Gerlach.

JIM YOUNG

Initially we trained with sticks because we had not received any real weapons yet. Maybe this was because the war came so fast. Real weapons arrived soon, and we were separated into riflemen, mortar men, or machine gunners. There were about seventy-five of us in H-2-1's mortar platoon, all to service and defend four guns. "Hip pocket artillery" they called our mortars. We were all schooled on how the mortars were set up and fired. The sergeants told us they would see who could set up the gun the fastest and he would become the gunner and in line for promotion to corporal. Those with the second fastest time would be promoted to PFC. Well this was a big deal to all of us and also a lot of fun. Each man got three tries. The sergeants got a big kick out of watching us stumble over each other. As luck would have it, I was one of the four fastest guys.

A gun squad had six men. Being the gunner meant I carried the bipod, which weighed 46.5 pounds, and the gun sight. My sidearm was a .45-caliber automatic pistol, which was easier to carry than a rifle. The assistant gunner carried the mortar tube, weighing 44 pounds, and the third man carried the base plate that weighed 45 pounds. The others served as ammo case openers and carriers.

Battle training was now in high gear. We started to fire the real ammo and the noise was very loud and scary. To fire a mortar, a man added or subtracted bags of gunpowder (called increments) to the base of the shell, depending on how far he wanted the shell to go. Then, he dropped the seven-pound shell into the mortar's 81mm-wide mouth. The shell slid down the mortar tube until it hit a firing pin at the bottom that triggered a loud explosion and fired the shell up and out, like a bullet. A man's head was right alongside the tube after he dropped the shell. He would flinch. We always stuffed cotton in our ears, but it didn't help much. There was a scary thing we had to do called "Remedy Misfire." This took place if a round of ammo failed to go off and was still in the tube. You had to remove the mortar's tube and slide the "hot" shell out from the bottom. But we got it down.

When we weren't training, the nearest town was Jacksonville, and we were allowed to go to town every night unless we had duty watch. Jacksonville was a small town, but it did have a USO and pretty girls to dance with.

ROY GERLACH

We got $21 a month. Then the overseas pay was $5 more per month. That's what all of us privates got, anyway. But you didn't spend it on much except on cigarettes and gambling. They signed us up for life insurance, and that cost $11 per month, a big chunk of our pay. But you didn't have a choice. You signed up whether you wanted to or not.

SID PHILLIPS

People ask me how well I knew one of our machine gunners, Bob Leckie, who later wrote a famous book about our time in the islands. I explain that H Company was a large company. There were sixty-five men in our mortar platoon alone. Nobody ever called him Leckie, he was "Lucky." I'm not sure if anyone even knew his real name. Back then, Bob was not a famous writer. He was just another PFC like anybody else. I saw him all the time at roll call, and we'd say hi to each other. But, since we weren't in the same squad, we didn't have a whole lot of close time together, like you did with the men in your own platoon.

JIM YOUNG

One day the sergeants came to our Quonset huts and said, "This is it. We are moving out tomorrow. All leaves are canceled, no phone calls, and everyone is confined to their barracks." We were all excited. No one had a clue as to where or how we were going. A lot of guys were upset because they could not contact their parents or girlfriends to say good-bye. We realized that many of us had seen our loved ones for the last time. Everything was frenzied, and no one got much sleep that night.

We were awakened about 4 A.M., ate chow, and marched a few miles to a railroad siding where a train waited for us. The train took us in Pullman cars from North Carolina and headed southwest. Someplace in the Midwest we stopped for coal and water. On the other side of the tracks was a large factory where a lot of girls waved at us and wished us luck. Soon a truck pulled alongside the train with box after box of sweet cider for the Marines on the train. The girls at the factory had all chipped in to buy us the cider. We all yelled our thanks to them, and they waved their hankies out the window at us as we pulled out of the station.

The train stopped in San Francisco. The sight of the Golden Gate Bridge was just awesome. While in San Francisco, I turned twenty-one years old on June 12, 1942. At the docks in San Francisco we boarded a ship called the *George F. Elliott*. It was a real old scow. The bunks were stacked five high. You could hardly move without hitting the bunk above you. We steamed out of San Francisco Bay.

While passing under the Golden Gate Bridge, I started to get seasick and so did many of the others. Guys were all along the rails of the ship throwing up. The wind from the ship's forward motion would blow vomit over everyone in back of them. The forward decks were getting very slippery and it stank to high heaven. After we were out at sea, they finally told us where we were headed. Our destination was Wellington, New Zealand.

SID PHILLIPS

Life on a troop ship is miserable. As privates, our accommodations were just fold-up spring beds stacked up five high like loaves of bread. You chose one, and that was your space. You put all your gear on that rack. Even today I marvel at the fact that we all found our way around that ship. Nothing was marked or had any signs. In the military, you just learn to make the best of a lot of bad situations. To me, much of the misery of war is not the fighting. It's the living conditions. On board ship, we were in a confined area with hundreds of other men. You're shoulder to shoulder with other men all the time. There were no fresh water showers, only salt water, so you're sticky all the time. We did everything by the numbers, whenever our unit was told. We went on deck and stood in a line four hundred yards long to wait two hours or more to get to the galley for a meal. Then we went down into the galley, which was hot, and got a steel tray and went through the line. They gave us a very small amount of food, which we ate standing up. A sergeant checked you off, so you couldn't go through the chow line again. It was so hot in the galley, we were relieved when we got back on deck.

They made me captain of the officer's head, which meant I cleaned the officer's latrine. It actually turned out to be pretty good duty. I had freshwater facilities, and could take a freshwater shower and wash my clothes in freshwater, so it turned out to be a good thing.

JIM YOUNG

The trip was a nightmare for me because I was so seasick. To top it off, a Marine named Al Schmid (a real pain in the ass) had the bunk below me and would keep kicking the bottom of mine. He thought it was funny. He was a bully and was always picking on guys. Well, one day he pushed "Indian" Johnny Rivers, a former Golden Gloves boxer, a little bit too far. I guess he was an American Indian. He was dark and scrappy. But someone said he used to drive an Indian-brand motorcycle, too. Johnny told the lieutenant that he had had enough of Al. The lieutenant told Johnny to put up a boxing ring on the forward deck and to put an end to this bickering once and for all.

Al was pretty tough, but Johnny just cut him to pieces. Every time Al was knocked down, he would just get up again. Well, the lieutenant stopped the fight, and Al had a little better attitude after that, but not much.

After eighteen days at sea I started feeling a little better when we saw Wellington, New Zealand.

SID PHILLIPS

When we got to New Zealand, we were put into work parties. All the ships had to be unloaded completely, and then reloaded, because they had not been combat loaded (where the most essential equipment goes on top) when we left San Francisco. Work duty went on twenty-four hours a day—four hours on, four hours off—around the clock. You never did get a good night's sleep. It was July, but that was New Zealand's winter. It was sleeting most of the time, or drizzling, and we didn't have any good winter clothing. So we were freezing and cussing and grumbling while loading mountains and mountains of ammunition and barbed wire and the like.

JIM YOUNG

Once loaded, we were under way again, this time to practice beach landings in Fiji. The captain wanted to send me and six other

Marines back to the States because of our seasickness. We all re-
fused. He said, "Well, it's up to you boys if you want to stay." On
Fiji we began landing exercises. Several guys fell off the nets and
broke arms and legs. It seemed to me we needed lots more practice.
Everything that could go wrong, did. Some of the landing craft
broke loose from the lines and hit the water. We made a run for the
beach. No one had thought about coral reefs, and many of the boats
ran aground. Some had the bottoms ripped open. The general called
it a disaster and called the whole thing off. We never did get ashore
on Fiji.

We were supposed to go back and train at Wellington, New
Zealand, for three or four more months, but Washington got word
that the Japanese were building an air base on one of the Solomon
Islands. From there, it would be possible for them to bomb Australia. The island needed to be taken before the airstrip was completed.
The island was named Guadalcanal, and we'd all soon get to know
it really well.

CHAPTER TWO

EYEBALL TO EYEBALL

★ ★ ★

Guadalcanal

On August 6, 1942, the Marines watched from the railings as the U.S.S. *George F. Elliott* steamed into the waters north of Guadalcanal. They had come to seize the island's semi-completed airfield from the Japanese before it became operational. With Guadalcanal's airfield, the Japanese could bomb the shipping lanes to Australia and choke the continent, putting Australia at risk for enemy invasion.

JIM YOUNG

We were awakened around three in the morning on August 7, 1942, the day we were to fight the Japs. Breakfast was at 5 A.M. The food was steak and eggs. After eating, which was hard to do, we went up on deck to watch the bombardment of Guadalcanal. It was unbelievable, and the noise was horrendous! Most of us were scared and bewildered. We couldn't even hear each other without yelling.

We received orders to go below and get everything ready to disembark. The sea was rough and dangerous. Due to the waves, boats were dropping six to ten feet, just as men were ready to get in

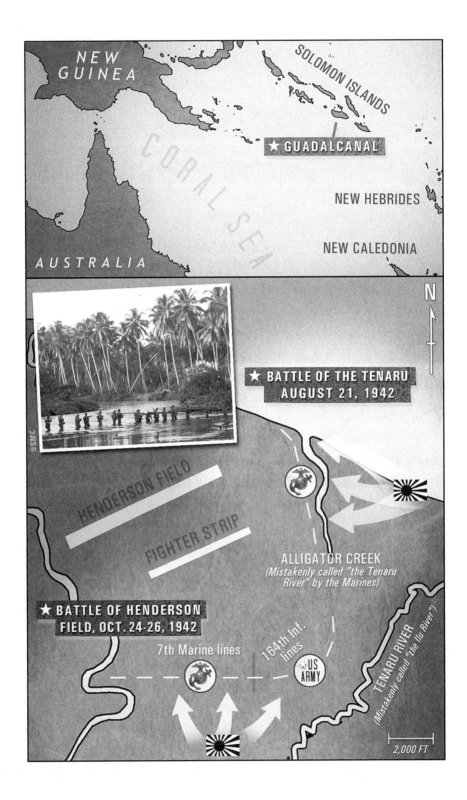

NEW GUINEA

SOLOMON ISLANDS

CORAL SEA

★ GUADALCANAL

NEW HEBRIDES

NEW CALEDONIA

AUSTRALIA

N

USMC

★ BATTLE OF THE TENARU
AUGUST 21, 1942

HENDERSON FIELD

FIGHTER STRIP

ALLIGATOR CREEK
(Mistakenly called "the Tenaru River" by the Marines)

★ BATTLE OF HENDERSON
FIELD, OCT. 24-26, 1942

7th Marine lines

164th Inf. lines

US ARMY

TENARU RIVER
(Mistakenly called "the Ilu River")

2,000 FT

them. Or if the boat didn't drop, it came roaring up. A man was crushed between the landing craft and the side of the ship. Lots of guys were hurt that way. One of the men from my gun crew, a Marine PFC, had made it into the landing craft and had his hand on the craft's rail when our wiremen stated to lower metal coils of communication wire from the ship. A line broke and the heavy coil of wire hit his arm and snapped it. They hoisted him back aboard.

It was go time. The engines on the landing crafts were all roaring at full throttle. We were on our way in and everyone was nervous.

SID PHILLIPS

There was a flag flying on the stern of every landing craft. I looked over the side at the flags, and my friend Carl Ransom was doing the same thing. You could see a whole line of them. It looked like they reached to the end of the world. I got a lump in my throat. Ransom did, too. As he wiped his eyes, he said, "That salt spray makes your eyes water, won't it?"

We had never had that happen before, never in training, and I never saw it happen again after that. They were too good a target. A big old red, white, and blue thing like that shouts, "Here I am! Here I am!" Our Colonel Cates was a very patriotic Marine. If there was an order given to fly a flag on every landing craft, I'm sure Cates gave that order.

I noticed that morning how everybody's cartridge belt was full and bulging. You could see the shiny brass cartridges here and there in the belt. You had two clips of five rounds in each of those pockets. When we had made practice landings in the Fiji Islands, they never issued any live ammunition. We made the landings with empty, flat, cartridge belts. They didn't want some idiot firing his rifle into someone. Things were different now. This was the real deal.

When we came ashore at Guadalcanal, we were in that landing

craft where the front end would drop down. Some of the riflemen were in old Higgins boats that didn't even have the front ramp. We had the front ramp because otherwise we couldn't get that mortar out of the boat. We were expecting a life-and-death struggle with hand-to-hand combat on the beach. When the ramp went down, we found our guys on the beach laughing at us and opening coconuts. We came out of the landing craft ready to fight and they just laughed. They had done the same thing a few minutes before. There were no Japs in our vicinity at all.

ROY GERLACH

I didn't go in on the first wave. I was a mortar man assigned to the mortar platoon, but I spent a lot of time as a cook. In the Marine Corps, you were assigned to the job you were supposed to do, and then if you could do something else, you did that, too. Whenever there was action, I was on the mortars. But if they needed a cook, well, I did that, too.

The first week when I was aboard the ship, my name came up for mess duty. So I went down and did that for a week. After that was over, a fellow says, "How was it down there?" I said, "Oh, not too bad." He didn't want to be a mess man and wash dishes and so forth, so he says, "I'll give you five dollars if you'll take my week of mess duty." So I took his five dollars, and I took his week. At the end of that week, another man asked me the same thing. After two or three weeks of being down in the galley, the head cook said, "Well if you're going to be down here, you might as well cook." That's how I started cooking. There was maybe four hundred to five hundred guys I cooked for.

I don't remember much about coming in to the beach. There were no Japs there. They'd all taken off to the hills. Right away we found all these coconuts. They fell out of the trees. We took our bayonets, bored holes in the coconuts, and drank the milk. But it made the guys sick. Too much fresh milk, I guess.

SID PHILLIPS

All the first day we struggled through the jungle to reach a hill called the Grassy Knoll, a mile inland. We had no good maps for Guadalcanal at all. They had some maps drawn up by some Australian people who had been on Guadalcanal. These crude maps were named by the Australians. They even had the names mixed up for the Tenaru and Ilu rivers.

So the game plan was to go to the Grassy Knoll and get the high ground. The thing that stands out so clear in my memory was the heat, the incredible heat in the jungle, with no breeze. And we had just come from winter in New Zealand, so it was a severe climate change. We just griped and bitched. In that jungle, it's so hot, and you're carrying a sixty-pound pack when you come ashore. Extra ammunition, packs of food for four days, a change of clothing. You drop your bedding, and keep going. The heat was so oppressive.

We were issued one canteen then. We'd been taught water discipline. You were only supposed to take small sips of water and roll the water around in your mouth before you swallowed. You were never supposed to guzzle water. Everybody nearly died of thirst that first day. We ate crackers, cans of hash—there was no water in the food; it just dried you out more and made you more thirsty.* At the end of the first day, we were exhausted, halfway up the Grassy Knoll. They told us to lie down where we were, dig a foxhole, shut up, and go to sleep. So we did.

---

* After Guadalcanal, Marines would be issued two canteens that they would carry behind their hips on a belt.

JIM YOUNG

When morning came, we were ordered back to the beach to set up defenses in an effort to repel any Jap attempt to land. One of our lieutenants was bitten in the face by a scorpion during the night. He had swollen up so much that he was completely blind and had to be led by the hand on the long march back to the beach. As we approached the beach, about ten Japanese Torpedo bombers skimmed the water and headed for the convoy. They were so low we could see the faces of the pilots and the big red meatball on their wings. They did not care about us on the beach. They went straight for the convoy of ships. One plane headed directly for our ship, the *Elliott*. It crashed into the water first and bounced up and slammed into the ship.

ROY GERLACH

We didn't have no galley [kitchen] for the first three or four weeks because our cooking equipment sunk with the *Elliott*. I wasn't on the ship then, but I saw it all. Most of the troops were on shore by then. But the unloading of the ship wasn't done yet. There was one shipman I knew on the *Elliott*, he always used to say, "I'm gonna be here when you go, and I'll be here when you get back." He wasn't.

SID PHILLIPS

People ask me when we first contacted the enemy. We were strafed by enemy planes almost immediately on Guadalcanal. You dig a foxhole and try to dig it as deep as you can, just try to bury yourself with the earth. The strafing never ended on Guadalcanal. They were always coming in, bombarding us. We considered that contact with the enemy.

JIM YOUNG

The Jap Zeroes would come swooping over us. I could actually see the pilots, the faces in those airplanes. You could see them turn their heads and look down at you. Sometimes they were grinning.

SID PHILLIPS

The day after we landed, we captured the airfield. When I first saw the airfield, I was surprised that there weren't many buildings except for this pagoda-looking thing. That served as the tower. The runway wasn't very visible unless you were up in the air. There were no wrecked Japanese planes. The place was empty. We went over there and looked at the pagoda. We were some of the first Americans to walk into that building.

The first American planes we saw come in there were the B-17 Flying Fortresses. Sometimes two, sometimes three. They would stop, refuel, and leave. The Flying Fortresses came in before we had any Navy or Marine planes at all.

On August 9, from their bivouac on a hilltop over the beach, H Company witnessed a violent naval battle between the U.S. and Japanese navies. This, the Battle of Savo Sea, produced so many sunken ships off the island's shore that the waters gained the name "Iron Bottom Bay."

SID PHILLIPS

The Savo Sea battle was like watching a summer storm from a beach. You would hear this rumble of naval gunfire and see what looked like flashes of lightning. You've seen distant lightning where the sky lights up? It was that sort of thing. You couldn't see any real details of the naval battle, but when a ship would blow up, we cheered. We assumed it was our boys doing the whipping. The next morning we saw one American cruiser creep slowly by, right off-shore, with part of its bow blown off. Somebody said it was the *Chicago*.

We were then told about the disaster. We lost four cruisers that night. You could maybe see a ship smoking, three miles away. Our supply ships were still in the harbor, but they were pulling out. Leaving us. They hadn't even unloaded half our supplies. But they had to get the hell out of there.

At that moment we felt that we might be considered "expend-able." It had occurred in the Philippines. It had occurred at Wake Island. It had occurred at Guam. It had occurred at every stage of the war in the Pacific up to Guadalcanal, so yes, we felt expendable.

JIM YOUNG

Without our ships, we were alone on the island. There was no food except for what we had in our backpacks, K rations. After sending out search parties to look for food, we found stores of Japanese rice and oats which would hold us over until the Navy could return with more supplies. It took a strong stomach to eat this because the rice and oats were crawling with maggots and worms. We found that if we dumped the rice and oats in water, then all the bugs would float to the top where we could skim them off.

We bivouacked at the end of a coconut plantation, near a meadow with a patch of trees. The trees were lime trees and we made lime-ade. We used warm water and we had no sugar. This stuff was ter-rible, but it was something different to drink. This meadow had the oddest plants I've ever seen. If you took a walk through them, it looked like a well-worn path, but twenty minutes later there was no trace of where you'd walked.

In the days that followed, we still hadn't seen the Japs up close, but the air raids continued. We had an old gunnery sergeant, fifty years old, real nice guy and a real Marine. We called him Gunny Dixon. Gunny told us to dig foxholes. When we were finished, he took one look at them and started to laugh. "Well, well," he said. "They don't look deep enough to me. I bet by the end of the week they will be deep enough to stand in." How right he was! Bombers flew over us, and we couldn't do a thing about it. We had no guns that could reach them and we had no airplanes. The bombs falling had a whistling sound as they came down.

One day the Jap bombers came from a different direction. They had always bombed the airstrip from the takeoff point to the liftoff point, but this day they came straight from the sea toward our tree grove. This time they were after us, and not the airstrip. I was watching them with field glasses, and I could see the pattern of bombs exploding and knew it would surely hit us. I yelled a warning, and we just made it to our foxholes in time. It was impossible to stand in the foxhole. The earth was shaking like an earthquake. Big chunks of earth filled the air and the smell of cordite was overpowering. It's hard to believe that no one was killed.

We found a Jap bunker near us that held about twenty of us. It was very dark inside, and while using it during an air raid one day, one of the guys let out a loud scream. It scared all of us and we scrambled for the exit, even though the air raid was still in progress. A six-foot-long lizard was up on the roof of the bunker, and its scaly tail had flopped down and touched the Marine's face. He thought it was the guy next to him so he reached up to brush it away. When he felt the tail, he went ape. We all got a kick out of it when it was over.

At night the Japs sent a lone bomber that kept flying around for hours before he decided to drop his bombs. They did this to keep us from getting any rest. We called him "Washing Machine Charley" because of the sound of his engine.

The bombing raids never ceased. After a while, we were shelled from Jap cruisers and subs as well. What made us mad is that we could see the Japs scurrying around their decks and manning the guns. But we had nothing that we could reach them with. All of our long-range guns were on the ships that took off when the naval battle took place.

SID PHILLIPS

The rifle platoons, they had daily patrols. Fifteen to twenty men would go out with an officer, scouting, trying to find out if there were any Japs in a particular area. In the mortar platoon we seldom went on patrols.

But we did go out after a Marine patrol had been ambushed and the survivors came back to our lines. So they put together a three-hundred-man patrol to go back out there to recover our dead. They wanted one 81mm mortar to come along, so they came to the mortar platoon and said, "Number four gun is going." That was me. Lieutenant "Benny" Benson, he was the lieutenant for our gun, he went with us.

The riflemen were on the point, watching for the enemy. In the mortar squad we trudged along behind them with that damn heavy stuff. We went about five miles out, carrying that mortar the whole way. You either carry part of the mortar or the ammunition. If you were an ammunition carrier, you carried a cloverleaf of ammunition on your shoulder. It was a strenuous march in the tropics. There were no roads. To be on the ground in a dense jungle, you did not even need to see combat to have a miserable time. You might have hiked way out and way back, and had to ford several streams, and walked through water waist-deep where your clothes got soaked and your feet didn't dry out and your pants chafed your crotch. You just can't convey that misery in words.

When we reached the area where the ambush had occurred, the mortar platoon stopped 150 yards from the site and set up our mortar. If the Japs were gonna ambush this big patrol, we were gonna give our guys mortar support. You could just look where our guys were and we would have fired beyond them. But the Japs had vacated the area.

We never did get up to the actual site of the ambush, but this old Marine sergeant came walking back, and Benny knew him real well because Benny was an old Marine, too—thirty years old was ancient in our minds. Benny said, "What's the scoop up there?" and this sergeant said that all the Marines had been beheaded and had their genitals stuffed in their mouths. They brought our dead back on canvas stretchers, their bodies covered by ponchos.

Our hatred for the enemy burned from early on. We had heard about the Bataan Death March, where they bayoneted American prisoners who fell exhausted by the roadside. We had talked to the 90mm anti-aircraft battery that was near our bivouac—they were a defense battalion that had been at Pearl Harbor. Then there was the Goettge patrol. A few days after we landed on Guadalcanal, some Jap prisoner told Colonel Frank Goettge that the Jap's buddies wanted to surrender five miles west of our lines, where the Matanikau River met the sea. Goettge took a patrol of twenty-five men out to take their surrender. But it was an ambush. Goettge and his men were butchered. Only three of them escaped by swimming back to our lines.

Was he an idiot for thinking the Japs would surrender? No, we just didn't really understand the enemy yet. Surrender was out of the question for a Jap unless he was knocked unconscious. But even then, if you saw an unconscious Jap, you'd be very cautious, because he might be only pretending. He might try to kill you. Japan soon proved a brutal enemy. They ignored the Geneva Convention. They tortured prisoners of war then killed them. Hell, they would torture a body and mutilate it even after a guy was dead. A hatred between the Marines and the Japanese rapidly developed. We never took a prisoner, never in my battalion, that I know of.

On August 20, bad news came to the Marines, word that the Japanese were landing fresh troops to retake the airfield. That same day a new armada of planes was heard in the sky.

SID PHILLIPS

It was late in the afternoon, and we were at our mortar position when we heard airplanes circling the field. We ran for cover. They came in from the south over those ridges. The roar of all the airplanes was deafening. They were loud by themselves, but when you have the sky full of them—wow! Someone screamed that they were our planes. We just went wild. I looked up and saw a blue-gray SBD dive bomber with the letters USMC painted on the underside of the wing. We flung our helmets way up in the air. We were beating on each other. Some of the guys were crying with joy they were so happy. We hadn't had any friendly planes except those two or three Flying Fortresses that came in. We had been strafed regularly by the Japanese Zeroes. Seeing our planes told us that Uncle Sam had decided we were going to fight for this miserable island.

On August 21, 1942, the Marines and the Japanese Army would meet in the first major battle of Guadalcanal. The Japanese had landed nine hundred soldiers of the elite Ichiki Regiment, who marched west along the beach, toward the airfield. The Marines of H Company waited for the enemy along the west bank of a small river they called "Alligator Creek," or "the Tenaru."

JIM YOUNG

We took turns manning defense lines at night. It was scary. The jungle was thick in front of us and the nights were black. We heard all kinds of noises, and some of us would fire a few rounds in front of us just in case Japs were sneaking up on us. The trouble was that everyone got jumpy when someone fired, and the whole line would open up. You would think a hell of a battle was going on. Well, the general got fed up with all the shooting and nothing to show for it. He issued an order that if any more of that wild firing happened, he wanted to see dead Japs, or that unit would catch all the working parties. Let me tell you, the next night the whole island seemed to be deserted. It was so quiet. The only sound came from "Washing Machine Charley."

SID PHILLIPS

The Battle of the Tenaru was the first real fight on the island. Our lines ran north and south from the ocean back to where the airfield began. We did not have a perimeter around the airfield. We didn't have that many men.

We were stretched out in these holes, every seven yards, two men with rifles, two men with rifles, then maybe six men with a machine gun, their position covered with logs and dirt, then two men with rifles, and two men with rifles, and so on. The jungle around you was so thick, you didn't know who was where, or what was where. You would lie there and listen to all those different damn jungle noises. One of those iguanas, three feet long, could be scurrying around, wrestling and making noise. You would wonder, *Is that a damn Jap or is that an iguana?* So you stayed awake. You didn't want to give a false alarm. After a while, you would get used to it, and you begin to take pride in the idea that you could tell a land crab from a creeping Jap, you know.

The mosquitoes were eating us alive. There was no repellant or anything. We just lay in those holes and fed those mosquitoes all night long. We'd been living on rice and nothing else for a long time there. Everybody was wore out, exhausted before long. Every two hours you were supposed to switch off on watch with the guy in your foxhole. We were always on edge.

Because things were so spooky, they would take our squad leader, Sergeant Carp from Brooklyn, and put him up on the perimeter. He carried the BAR (Browning Automatic Rifle) and they wanted his firepower up there. Plus, he had been in the Marine Corps about three years and was an old-timer that they considered much wiser than we kids. They put him up on the perimeter every night with that BAR.

On the H Company line, a Marine named Art Pendleton led one of twelve machine gun squads.

ART PENDLETON

I was a corporal. I had joined the Marine Corps in January 1942 in Worcester, Massachusetts. Before that I was a pretty ordinary guy. A country boy from central Massachusetts—horse-and-buggy country. I enjoyed school. Never had any such thing as an affair with a girl (until I got into the Marine Corps). Never would touch a drop of alcohol. Never even heard of drugs. It was a whole different way of life. Women were also much different. If you ever saw a woman in the barroom in our town, it would be a story to tell.

That all impacts your character I suppose. When I boarded the train in Boston to go to Parris Island, there were lots of other men there, from all over New England. One fellow who ended up in H Company with me, came from Southborough, Massachusetts, which was just a short distance from where I lived. His name was Whitney Jacobs. Jacobs was a hairy little guy and powerfully strong but not the kind of person that you would think of being a Marine. The rules and regulations for joining at that time were stringent. You couldn't be an African American, which was sad.* You had to

---

* Not until June 1942 did the Marine Corps accept the first black recruits. By the war's end, more than 19,000 black Marines would serve with distinction.

have all of your teeth except for two, you had to be a certain weight, a certain height, you had to have certain education, and the list goes on and on. You wouldn't think that little Whitney Jacobs would have ever made it, but he did.

The night of our first battle with the Japanese, our machine gun emplacement was on the beach looking out at the ocean while others were on the riverbank. There was only one likely place that the Japanese could breach our lines—the sandspit. The sandspit was part of the beach that separated the river from the ocean. The sandspit was like a dam. The river trickled over it all the time. The only time the river would run freely over it was when, I suppose, there was a heavy rain. Right behind the sandspit the river got deep. We knew the Japanese could walk across that bit of sand if they attacked, so we strung some barb wire on some poles there. It was like a ninety-degree angle. We were about the only gun that was that close to the sandspit.

Whitney Jacobs, who was a rifleman, was near the river. Riflemen and the machine guns and BARs were right up front. Whitney thought that he heard something out of place in the night. He fired without waiting for orders.

That one shot started the battle because the Japanese were there, trying to cross the river.[*]

JIM YOUNG

Around 1:30 A.M. on August 21, a few shots were fired up on our defense line at the Tenaru River. The tempos of firing increased with a few machine gun bursts. Then all hell broke loose.

---

[*] Art Pendleton would remember, "Whitney got the Navy Cross for shooting the first shot of the battle. Why? He didn't know why and neither did I."

SID PHILLIPS

The Japanese unit had come marching down the beach, moving west, and when they got to the Tenaru River, they spread out and formed a front. Some of them waded through the creek quietly. It was black as dark. When the Japs hit, Sergeant Carp and his fox-hole companion, a Marine named Beer, had fallen asleep. They were just so exhausted and so tired. A Jap officer jumped in their hole and hacked them up, killing them both, until someone shot him. When the firing started, the darkness became almost as bright as day. A wall of fire poured from our lines. A real roar. We knew the real enemy was here. They were disciplined and vicious.

ART PENDLETON

The Japanese had landed nearly a thousand men of the best that they had from the Ichiki Regiment. They tried to come across the sand first, but ran into our barbed wire, so they had to cross the river. It was neck-deep in spots. The Japanese put themselves to a big disadvantage from the start.

JIM YOUNG

A screaming horde of Imperial Japanese soldiers tried to cross. They came in waves of fifty and a hundred men at a time. We had about ninety men on the defense line.

Japs who could speak English were screaming, "Marine, tonight you die!" and "Blood for the emperor!" We started yelling back at them, "F—k your emperor!" and "Go to hell!" Anything we could possibly think of.

The Japs threw coconuts in the river. That way, it was hard to tell if you were shooting at a coconut or a Jap's head. Then they charged across the water. Some of them got through our line and were bayoneting our men.

On the front lines, one of my close friends, Crotty, from New York, was in a two-man foxhole. A Japanese officer had snuck through the line and came at him from the back of the foxhole. The other Marine in the foxhole with Crotty had put a bandolier of ammo across the back of the foxhole and rolled on to his back to reach for it. When he looked up he saw the Jap officer with his saber raised over his head. The Marine drew his knees to his chest to protect himself. The Jap's saber hit him in the kneecap and split his knee down through the shinbone. Crotty heard his buddy scream and turned around. He shot just before the Jap could bring the blade down for the second hit. The bullet went up through the Jap's rib cage and came out under his armpit. He fell on them.*

Our lieutenant, Benson, was yelling for us to prepare to move the mortars into action. We were powerless for the moment. A mortar required light to see where you're aiming, so we just waited, watching the flashes, praying for the hint of dawn. I thought to myself . . . *You wanted to see Japs, well, here they are.*

ART PENDLETON

My gun was on the beach when the battle started. John Rivers and Al Schmid's machine gun emplacement was on the bank of the river. John Rivers was a very nice guy and very tough. A former boxer. He had given up a chance to be a champion lightweight

---

* Jim Young would remember, "Crotty kept the Jap's saber. I remember him taking the saber along to Melbourne. He made a mistake and he gave it to a girl there and never got it back."

prizefighter to enlist instead. We had four heavy machine guns in our platoon and his happened to be right in the spot where the Japanese came across the river. John was right in the middle of it.

The Japanese never should have hit us there. They were in water up to their neck getting across the river. Hell, they were fodder for us.

JIM YOUNG

John was the gunner and Al was his loader. Even though they had boxed one another on the deck of the ship, they worked together well. Their gun was in a sandbagged pit on the riverbank, and the Japs were attacking them like herds of cattle. Johnny was mowing them down until he was shot in the face and killed. Al took over as gunner and kept fighting until the Japs threw a grenade into his gun pit and wounded him and his ammo bearer. Blinded, Al resumed firing with the ammo bearer shouting in his ear, directing his fire.

A guy from North Carolina named PFC Steve Boykin, a very nice gentleman, he got hit up there on the line. His one leg, the whole back of it was almost blown out. His men slid him back off the line and set him against a tree. One of the Japs got through and got to him and stuck him with a bayonet but didn't kill him. The Jap was killed. Somehow Boykin survived.

ART PENDLETON

As the battle raged on, Whitney realized that one of our machine guns had stopped firing, the one that had been devastating the enemy. You can't fire a machine gun steady because if you do the enemy will zero in on you. But when you're in that kind of a situation, you don't use common sense. You're firing for your life.

Whitney crawled a few feet to the silent gun emplacement. He stayed on his stomach and peered into that emplacement and called out. Inside, John Rivers was dead, and Al Schmid, who was blinded and in bad shape, answered him. Whitney shouted, "Don't shoot—I'll go get help." So he backed off and reported to the officer in charge. Right away our lieutenant called my gun in because I was about one hundred feet from that point.

We rushed to move. The gunner carried the gun and the assistant gunner carried the tripod. When running up to the line to get a look at where we're going, a hand grenade, I believe, went off between my legs. It lifted me up in the air a little bit, but it didn't touch me. I thought, *Wow! How lucky can you be?*

Everything seemed so confusing. We were directed to Rivers's gun position. No one was in it. I don't know where Rivers's body went or where Schmid went. They were destined to get knocked out because they were firing so heavily. Rivers's gun was totally destroyed, so I just threw it out of the emplacement. That machine gun killed many, many, many Japanese. I put my gun in its place. We were in the middle of it now.

The Jap officers had these fancy sabers and were swinging them in the air trying to scare the hell out of us. Our guys were way beyond being scared. They were there to kill everybody. You forget about being scared when your life is at stake. There's no such thing as scared.

I started firing as soon as I got the gun set up. If you didn't, you were going to get killed. Rivers's position was the focus of the whole Japanese attack. The Japs were all over the place.

SID PHILLIPS

As the battle raged, our 81mm mortar platoon was facing the beach in case there was a landing coming in from the ocean. All four guns. So the attack was coming from our right flank. Our lieutenant moved us towards the battle, up parallel to the river. Our foxholes were all over. Our machine guns were so well dug in you could hardly see them at all in the dim light. As we moved up in the dim light, we kept falling in foxholes. To fall in a foxhole with a mortar tube or base plate can be painful as hell. It could kill a man if it fell on him.

JIM YOUNG

We set up the mortars in the coconut grove parallel with the river. We had no defensive cover for protection. It was like being in the middle of a football field. We had to work fast because the Japs spotted us and started shelling us. The lieutenant was worried that we may not have enough clearance through the coconut leaves. I told him I thought I could get through. I fired the first round and knocked a palm leaf off a tree, but the shell didn't explode so the lieutenant gave the order to "fire for effect." This means to fire as fast as you can.

SID PHILLIPS

There was a pile of Japanese dead right out in front of our new mortar position. About thirty yards away. They had killed them before we got up there.

We were trying to hit an area about the size of six football fields on the other side of the river. We just kept blanketing the whole area over there.

ROY GERLACH

Our front lines kept the Japs backed up in the river. I was with the 81mm mortars; I carried shells to the guns. Our mortar fired a three-inch-wide shell that you dropped down into the tube and it shot up into the air. It reached out over our lines and came down and killed anyone for thirty yards. No, it never bothered me being a Mennonite and being in the war. I guess I was more broad-minded.

ART PENDLETON

The thing that impressed me more than anything were the flares. When they would shoot a flare in the air, you could hear it pop when it lit. When they ignited, it was a very bright light. Then the parachute opened and the flare would very slowly float down to earth. No matter what you were doing, everybody stopped. You didn't move a hair. If you dared to move, you were going to get shot. We lit flares and so did they. It was just to check positions and see who was where. Those flares were probably one of the most danger-ous things in the battle.

SID PHILLIPS

We were firing heavy, fifteen-pound shells. It is a deafening explo-sion when that thing goes off. You just can't believe it. If you shot the biggest firecracker ever, it was a thousand times louder than that. We were actually awed by the results of that fifteen-pound shell. At Camp Lejeune we had one day of firing live ammunition, but the range was over two thousand yards away. We had never had any close-up firing until that battle.

JIM YOUNG

We saw Japs, their clothes on fire from our mortar bursts, running to the sea and river to put the fire out. Our number four gun had a misfire and had to be taken out of action. Corporal Mugno's ramrod for cleaning the mortar tube had a sock wrapped around the end of it that came off and fouled the gun.* It was utter chaos.

ART PENDLETON

At one point they tried to flank us at the sandspit. My gun wasn't shooting at the sandspit at all since that was covered by another gun on our left. That was also covered by the 37mm cannon. The 37 was a lightweight cannon, but they had canister shot for it, the same as you would shoot game birds with. It was not one bullet; it was many pieces of metal flying through the air, like a giant shotgun. It was firing again and again.

I wasn't worried about the sandspit. I wasn't even thinking about it. We had our hands full just taking care of what was in front of us. They had to cross the river and climb up the bank in order to get to us. We slaughtered them.

SID PHILLIPS

During the battle, Colonel Pollock came running over to our gun and said, "Who is the gunner here?" I held my hand up and he said, "Well boy, use me as the range stakes. He ran out about forty feet in front of the gun and held his hand up. I put the sights on zero deflection, and we dragged the gun so that we had him lined up. Then I noticed beyond him through the trees was an abandoned American amphibian tank on the enemy side of the river. The Japs had gotten a machine gun into that thing and were firing from inside it.

Pollock said to try three hundred yards. Our shot was right on,

---

* Jim Young would remember, "After the battle was over, Lieutenant Benson really chewed him out."

but it was a little bit beyond the target. We lowered our mortar down and our third round landed right in the tank. Everybody along the line cheered like a touchdown in a football game.

ART PENDLETON

Near the end of the battle, Colonel Pollock, who was a great man, came to me and said "Stop firing." I said, "I'm trying to take out couple of guys that I'm seeing running there." He said, "Don't. We don't know what's over there and we might open up another Rivers situation here." He knew the fight was over and didn't want us getting ourselves killed or the other Marines who were surrounding the enemy from different directions at that time. He was our colonel and I respected him a lot.

SID PHILLIPS

The Japs tried to pick us off with a 75mm howitzer cannon they had wheeled up. It had iron wheels on it, and they drove us away from our mortar once. They also fired those grenade launchers, those knee mortars, at us. When those things went off, it sounded like you had slapped two pieces of two-by-four together. A *crack!* and if it hit close it would scare the hell out of you.

JIM YOUNG

The battle wound down and it grew light. In the end, the Jap dead were piled three to five feet high. There must have been a hundred or more bodies in front of our 37mm cannon that was located on the sandspit, which was the only way the Japs could attack without going through the creek.

ART PENDLETON

I can remember looking at these Japanese soldiers who were caught in the barbed wire, and their heads were blown open and the brains and innards was dripping out of their heads. That scene is still with me nearly every day, seventy years later.

The Japanese soldier was very different from what you would consider the Japanese population. They're a kind, generous, easygoing nation of people who love nice things and are very delicate in their artistry, music, and everything else. Their soldiers, however, were brainwashed to the point where suicidal attacks were nothing for them nor were acts of unspeakable brutality. We were a bunch of American kids. Our social system was different, and we were brainwashed in as much as you do what you're told to do and don't question orders, but if someone told us to throw our lives away we weren't ready to give it up. There's a big difference.

JIM YOUNG

Two hundred bodies were piled up in front of the gun position of Johnny Rivers and Al Schmid. Schmid survived the battle, although he was blinded.*

I could hardly believe I was seeing so many dead enemy soldiers. Some just looked like they were sleeping. Others were mangled. Some were burnt.

---

* Jim Young would remember, "Al was awarded the Navy Cross and regained only partial sight in one eye. In 1944, a movie called *Pride of the Marines* was made featuring actor John Garfield playing Al's part. Garfield even went to stay with Al in Philadelphia as he recovered and visited a veterans' hospital to study the lives of blinded veterans. The movie came out in 1945 and was a hit."

SID PHILLIPS

General Vandegrift and his staff came right up behind our guns. Vandegrift was the top dog on Guadalcanal. He was within ten feet of us. A corporal followed behind General Vandegrift with a twelve-gauge pump shotgun, and he kept the shotgun at port arms; I don't even know if it was on safety, but all he had to do was point that thing and fire it. He stayed right with the general, and that's when my buddy Ransom said, "Phillips, if you want to get your ass kicked, just go over there and stand between the general and that corporal."

Our tanks didn't come up until maybe ten o'clock in the morning. They passed right down the beach right there. You could have walked over and touched them. When the tanks got through, our whole 1st Battalion, A, B, C, D companies of infantry, had circled around from the south, and they came around and drove all the Japanese survivors ahead of them out into the ocean. About thirty Japs ran out and jumped in the surf. Everybody kept firing at them until no more heads were visible.

JIM YOUNG

At about two in the afternoon the next day, the temperature was around ninety-five degrees. We walked among them looking for ones that were still alive. Several of our men had been shot by Japs who were only playing dead. The colonel issued orders to shoot any one of them that might be alive. The smell of death almost took your breath away. The chaplains were taking the dog tags off the dead Marines. They said we lost forty men. It was one hell of a night and we were glad it was over.

ART PENDLETON

I can't even begin to tell you how many bodies were in the river floating around after this battle. You could hardly see the water. We killed nine hundred of them. They were some of their best men that used to train on Mount Fujiyama. They'd put up full marching gear and run up the mountain and run down the mountain. We never would have won that battle if we didn't have the advantage of the river.

Their bodies were all over the place for two weeks. The crocodiles were ripping them apart. There were a few of them that survived and escaped back on their fast ships to the other side of the island. These men fought again, but they were all annihilated in the end.

SID PHILLIPS

After it was over, Colonel Pollock came over and told us we had done real well and shook hands with everybody.

This Japanese unit that hit us there was half of the Ichiki Regiment, an elite unit. They first went ashore at Guam and captured our Marines there. Evidently they had gone through all the Marines' personal gear, because the Japanese packs were full of snapshots of American people—Marines and their girlfriends. We found about a hundred of these snapshots after the battle.

We collected up all the pictures of Americans and decided that the best thing to do was burn them. You wouldn't want to send them to the families, even if you could identify them. We kept all the Japanese pictures. You'd never burn them. You could trade them to sailors on board ships for almost anything—clothes, chewing tobacco. Money had no value, but you could do a lot by trading souvenirs. I opened one Jap pack that had three Marine Globe and

Anchor emblems in it. My friend Deacon Tatum got stuck with Carp's BAR and had to clean his blood off of it.

ART PENDLETON

I remember two riflemen, who were my friends, a big shell landed beside them and killed them both. It didn't just kill them, it blew them to pieces. Their names were Barney Sterling and Arthur Atwood. They would both receive the Navy Cross, posthumously. Our lieutenant gathered me and a couple of guys and we got ponchos and picked up their body parts. We carried them up through the coconut grove and dug their graves right near the end of the Henderson Field airstrip. That was the beginning of the Marine cemetery on Guadalcanal. From that time on there were a lot of graves in there. I never cared about going back to Guadalcanal, but a friend told me it's a big cemetery now.

CHAPTER THREE

THE TEST OF WILLS

★ ★ ★

Guadalcanal

SID PHILLIPS

Not long after the Battle of the Tenaru my eighteenth birthday came along, on September 2. I walked over to the beach, sat down, and had a five-minute meditation, all alone.

We'd had a lot of action by then. The C rations had run out. There was no real food, just that damn Jap rice to eat twice a day. You went through the chow line and there were no seconds. The flies got so bad you finally almost didn't notice them, they were simply always around. If you took out your spoon to eat a meal, they'd be on your spoon. If you went through the chow line, the flies would be all in the food. It had some sort of bugs in it. After a while everybody ate the bugs, too. As a nation, we were poorly prepared for war. To get a task force at sea, ready to fight, is not something you could do except with a great deal of preparation. Or even to issue rifles to all the men in your military. You've got to have ammunition for the ships. That all takes time. When the war began for us, I'd say Japan was probably twice as strong in the Pacific as we were.

I remember looking at the ocean and thinking, *This water goes all the way to my front door in Mobile*. I wished I could walk on water and go home.

ART PENDLETON

We still had virtually no navy. The Japanese were kicking our ass for a long time out in the ocean. When my gun was on the beach, we often watched the Japanese come cruising along the coast with submarines and ships, just a few hundred yards out. Because there was no competition for them, the subs would surface and their crews would walk the deck.

We would all stand on the beach thumbing our nose at them, dancing around, and doing every obscene gesture that we could think of because we were half-naked anyways. They couldn't do anything except unplug the deck gun and shoot at us. The coconut trees would get knocked down and everything would go to hell. We'd jump in our holes, and then as soon as they stopped we'd come out and start the whole thing over again.

Eventually, we brought up a 75mm cannon on a half-track to shoot at the sub. It was going to be a heck of a surprise for them. But before we could fire, Colonel Pollock rushed in and gave the gunners hell. He did not want them to fire that 75mm gun. He was afraid it would reveal some of our firepower. We didn't know at the time what the Japanese had coming our way, so he didn't want to tip our hand. I can understand his point. I thought, *What a disappointment!*

Shortly after that an Australian two-engine bomber flew in for reconnaissance; he was taking pictures. He saw the sub, circled around, and dropped a bomb on the fantail of the sub. The bomb messed them up. The sub couldn't dive. It was going around in circles. We were having a blast cheering, adding insult to injury.

JIM YOUNG

The Navy tried to supply us with ammo and food. They would sneak in as fast as they could, and we'd help unload so they could get away before the Jap air raids began again. I never understood why the Japs always came at the same time every day. It got so you could set your watch by them.

A destroyer brought gasoline for our airplanes. We were towed out to the ship on a barge, which was then tied to the ship. We had put about fifteen drums of gas on the barge when we got word of a Jap air raid coming. The destroyer had to get under way. It started to leave and was dragging the barge with it. We were yelling our heads off for them to cut us loose. We ended up having to use our own knives. Right about that time the Jap planes arrived, and we jumped into the sea and started to swim for shore. The Japs went after the ship, but they didn't hit it.

The next day I was put on another working party. A destroyer took a chance and brought in more gas. We had almost unloaded it when we got a surprise air raid. A Jap plane must have flown in from a Jap cruiser. It went into a dive and released one bomb, which struck the ship on the fantail, where its racks were full of depth charges. There was a tremendous explosion. The ship's bow rose straight up, and the ship slid under the water with almost all hands still aboard.

SID PHILLIPS

Every day the machine gunners would come to eat at the battalion mess tent. They would walk right by the mortar platoon. The story got out that Leckie's father back home had asked if he needed his dress uniform, his dress blues. It was such an absurd idea that anybody would have a dress uniform there in that nasty, filthy, dirty situation we were in. It made everybody laugh.

When Leckie would come walking down, we would ask him, just about every day, "Hey, Lucky, has your dad sent your blues yet?" and he would say, "I'm looking for them tomorrow. I'm pretty sure they'll be here tomorrow." Leckie had a good sense of humor.

ROY GERLACH

We had a galley near the Tenaru in a coconut grove. There was no place for the men to sit down. We served whatever we could find. Mostly corned beef and cabbage, although we didn't have too much cabbage. We had plenty of corned beef though, because we were close to Australia and they were known for their corned beef. So that's what we cooked. Corned beef patties. Corned beef hash. The troops would get to chattering because they didn't have anything else. Cans and cans of corned beef. We didn't even have any bread, because we had no bake shop set up. We discovered where the Japs had stored a barn full of rice. So we took that, too. Then we ate corned beef and rice.

The troops had this joke. They always wanted to know what kind of corned beef we were having today. They'd make up a sign and put it where we fed everybody. Today's menu: Corned beef without catsup. Corned beef without pickles. Corned beef without catsup or pickles. Jap rice without raisins. Jap rice without peaches. Rice pudding without pudding. And so on.

ART PENDLETON

One time, a torpedo that missed its target floated in. I don't know whether that was American or Japanese. It must have been about twenty feet long. One of the fellows said, "Oh, I know all about those torpedoes. Let's go down and get it." So we swam in and brought the thing to shore. This thing was monstrous you know. One of the fellows got to the nose of it and unscrewed the nose cone. He knew what he was doing because inside the nose cone was alcohol. Alcohol kept the firing pin in good order I guess. So we got the alcohol out of the torpedo and fifty of us drank one gulp apiece.

JIM YOUNG

I had come down with a bad case of hemorrhoids. Of all times, the lieutenant told me to take twelve men down to the beach to help unload a destroyer that was sneaking in. I told the lieutenant that I could barely walk, much less unload a ship, so he called for the corpsman to check me out. The corpsman confirmed there was no way I could handle the work party. So the lieutenant called another corporal, Clifton Barter, to take over my job. Corporal Barter asked if he could use my .45-caliber pistol so he wouldn't have to carry a rifle. I said, "Sure," and off they went. While they were unloading, the air raids started. The men all jumped on the truck and tried to make a run back to our area. It was too late. Bombs were raining down on them. They stopped at an old bomb crater and all jumped in. Damned if one of the bombs didn't fall right on top of them.

One of the Marines, a sixteen-year-old boy who was later sent home, survived the blast and ran back to our company with the news. The lieutenant, a few other guys, and me jumped into a jeep and raced to the spot. It was awful. At least five were dead and others badly wounded. You could hardly tell who was who.

I finally located Corporal Barter. He was badly wounded and asking for water. A fragment about the size of a softball had hit him. It had gone through the bottom of his rib cage and was sticking out the other side of his chest. The corpsman told me to give him whatever he wanted. There wasn't anything more we could do for him. As we were loading the truck with the wounded, Corporal Barter died. The lieutenant told me to go get my .45-caliber pistol from Barter's body. It wasn't easy for me to do that. It was my fault that he was killed instead of me. That's how I felt about it then. That's how I feel about it today, too.

SID PHILLIPS

We had no medicine. Everybody had diarrhea, dysentery. Some had it worse than others. W.O. had it worse than others. There was a chance that he might not survive. He became emaciated, couldn't even stand up. We had one boy in the hospital, it was a big tent. No cots. No beds. They just had the boys lying on the ground. Nobody wanted to go to the hospital. They didn't have any medicine anyway.

W.O. and maybe two others were bad. I didn't think they were going to live. They looked like they'd just been released from Dachau. Everything went right through them. It got so bad, they couldn't even sit on our pole head. They just lay on the ground in their own diarrhea. It was a real medical nightmare for the corpsman, because they didn't have anything to give them.

We had some little Jap pushcarts that the Japanese had used, like a cart on two bicycle wheels. Every day I pushed W.O. over to the ocean so he could get clean. His clothes were full of crap. We washed those out. We just told him he was pretending to be sick. We wished to hell he'd quit pretending and get well. We just told him he was a pain in the ass. Nobody gave anybody any sympathy or compassion—ever! It was good-natured ribbing, yeah. But that was typical of the military all through WWII. It was a way of showing camaraderie. It didn't really help a person to sympathize with him. It would depress him if you did. But if you kidded him, it would make him smile, and he'd fire back some wisecrack at you.

So we nursed our sick right there where we were. We had them stretched out on the ground. We could give them water. But it was just bad. I really didn't think W.O. was going to survive. Our corpsman got ahold of some Japanese paregoric and gave it to W.O. and to another boy, and they improved a little bit. And then when they began to eat a little bit, they began to improve more rapidly.

ART PENDLETON

I was wounded twice on the 'Canal. The first wound I got was during a patrol when I got hit in the ankle with shrapnel. I was treated in the field by a corpsman since we didn't have hospitals.

The second time, I had a case of diarrhea. When we went to the toilet, we had slit trenches that we dug. The trench was twenty-four inches wide, probably four to five feet deep, and maybe eight feet long. You would set a pole across and place your behind on the pole. This was our toilet facilities.

During one of the bombings, which were constant every day and night, I got blown off the pole along with what clothes I had on. I didn't land in the waste but woke up on the ground beside the trench. My clothes and a shoe were blown clean off. A wild pig was laying beside me, dead. That wasn't a good thing—we didn't eat those animals because they were full of worms. After that I went to my gun emplacement, which was a hundred feet away on the river. I was so ill from the blast that I couldn't move for two or three weeks. My back never fully recovered from that.

SID PHILLIPS

You were always filthy. The only way to wash was to go to one of the rivers and take a bath. We loved that. Whenever we could, we would get permission to go and take a bath. This was once every ten days or two weeks.

General Vandegrift was the leader of our division. He was kind of a dumpy guy, not very handsome. Everybody knew him on sight.

On one of my bathing episodes over there, he was on a log maybe twenty yards upstream from us. We didn't know he was there. This bar of perfumed cashmere bath soap came sailing by in the current. That was most unusual, because none of us had any soap, except the occasional bar of GI soap—it came in square brown blocks and you could cut off a hunk of it, if the galley had any. So when this bar of fine-looking soap came along in the stream, I snatched it up and hollered, "Who lost this?!" This hand went up, upstream. It was General Vandegrift, naked as the day he was born. His orderly came down and I gave it to him. All the guys wanted to smell my hand afterward. They joked that I must be having a date that night, to be using that fine stuff.

On September 18, a glimmer of hope landed on Guadalcanal's shores. The 1st Marine Division's 7th Regiment—the 7th Marines— arrived as reinforcements with support units. Some four thousand men strong, they had been preparing the island of Samoa to resist a Japanese invasion until the call for reinforcements came from the 'Canal. One of the 7th Marines was Sergeant Richard Greer . . .

RICHARD GREER

When we arrived on Guadalcanal, I heard word that Colonel Edson, the leader of 1st Marine Raiders, said to his men, "Here comes some competition, boys." He was right.

I'll be ninety-six on my next birthday. When Pearl Harbor occurred I was twenty-four, older than a lot of new recruits then, and had a decent job working as office manager for Burlington Mills. We had 496 looms and were making parachute cloth. Due to my job being considered essential services, I had a deferment from the war. But I just ignored it. Right away the next morning I called the office and said, "I won't be in this morning. I have some business to take care of."

I knew the Marine recruiter in Roanoke, and when he opened the office I walked in and said, "Well, I'm ready to sign up."

"It'll take you a while to get to officer's school," he said.

"No, I don't want to be an officer," I said. "I've thought about this. I want to be a mud Marine. I want to go, and go now. I'm not going to stay with the Corps forever. I've got the rest of my life planned. But I'll go and fight as long as the enemy's out there."

Pretty soon I was in Parris Island. That went real easy for me. Besides holding a job with a multinational company, I was also an outdoorsy guy. I used to spend time on the rivers, creeks, and mountains. Every night I was out fox hunting or coon hunting for half the night, along the river. Boot camp didn't matter to me any more than going around the block.

In late February 1942, I was sent to Camp Lejeune, and was assigned to D Company, 1st Battalion, 7th Marines, a weapons company, the heart of the battalion in those days. The company had 278 men in it, and we had 81mm mortars, a 37mm cannon, and twenty-four water-cooled machine guns spread across three platoons.

John Basilone and I had gotten to be friends pretty early on. He was a sergeant and I was a corporal but we were really close. John was happy-go-lucky and easy to get along with. He was absolutely a nut about teaching people machine guns. He knew a machine gun like damn few people ever did. When he put his duty belt on, he was totally duty. But otherwise he was always having a good time and carrying on.

He used to practice taking his .45 out of his holster, seeing how fast he could do it. He was always practicing his quick draw. We used to walk out of the movies on base and he'd throw his left hand down, grab his .45, and draw it out of his holster. He said, "Greer, you don't ever practice that. You better start." I said, "John, don't worry. I'm going to have my .45 in my hand the whole time."

I was a machine gunner, but I could also read naval regulations and understand them because I had studied business administration in college. So they often used me for administration duties. I could write reports, court-marshals, muster rolls, and stuff like that. I don't know how they'd found out, but they would pull me off the line to do those things.

Lieutenant Colonel Chesty Puller was our battalion commander. I was a runner for him part of the time. I took messages from the D Company commander to the battalion commander, who was Puller, many times. I played ball on the same team as Puller when we weren't in combat. He was a catcher. He seemed to know everybody, even if he knew our names or not. He had fought bandits in Nicaragua and called people by Spanish names like "hombre."

We went through five first sergeants on Guadalcanal for one reason or another. Off and on, I was acting first sergeant. It was because of maturity. I was older and knew what the hell was going on. They would call me out of the first platoon and say, "Come on down to the first sergeant's tent, something's happened to him." That's when I saw Puller on a regular basis. Gunnery sergeants and first sergeants set up the defenses or FPLs [final protected lines]. As acting first sergeant for D Company, I would tell Colonel Puller, "Sir, Captain Rogers said we're ready for your inspection. The defenses are set up." Before inspection I would go through and talk to those platoon sergeants and tell them, "If any of you damn right move anything with this setup, I'm gonna damn well see that you get court-marshaled." After inspection, Colonel Puller always said, "Beautiful job, boys. Beautiful job."

But when combat would start, Puller was always screaming at his platoon leaders, his lieutenants, and anyone who wasn't performing like he wanted them to. He would pop up here, disappear, and pop up ten feet over there. He did it all time. He told us later that was how he learned to fight as a Marine down in Nicaragua and Haiti. He won two Navy Crosses down there and would soon win a third on Guadalcanal.

SID PHILLIPS

People sometimes ask me what the worst part of Guadalcanal was. During those weeks and months on end when everybody had dysentery—there was no toilet paper. Here we were, all with diarrhea, some of us had it worse than others—but we all had it, and there was no toilet paper! The living conditions were just awful. Flies were everywhere. Flies. Flies. Flies.

But, seriously, ask any Marine what the worst part of Guadalcanal was, and they'd say the night the battleships bombarded us.

On October 13, the American Army landed 2,800 reinforcements from the 164th Infantry Regiment on Guadalcanal to aid the Marines. At 1:30 A.M. the next morning, the Japanese battleships *Kongo* and *Haruna* anchored offshore with smaller warships.

JIM YOUNG

I had the midnight watch with William Howard Brown, my ammo carrier and good buddy. I called him "Brownie." He was eighteen and I was twenty-one. Everyone else was asleep. We were sitting along the beach, looking out to sea when we saw what we thought was heat lightning or a storm over the ocean. We both said the same thing. "Great, now we're going to have to be sitting here in the rain." All of a sudden we heard a terrible noise, something like a train going past real close. Then there were more and more flashes out at sea. Two Japanese battleships with fourteen-inch guns were shelling us. Big, fourteen-inch-wide shells were coming in that sounded like train cars flying overhead. The first thing we'd done was start screaming "Condition Red!" which told everyone to run for the foxholes. I doubt they needed the urging.

This turned out to be one of the most frightening experiences we ever had. We had one big dugout that held about eight of us. We had one little candle going in there. Some of the guys were praying through the explosions. Our roof would shake just like an earthquake. I thought, *This is it for us.*

RICHARD GREER

The Jap ships were bold enough to anchor off Lunga Point. They were hitting Henderson Field and the defenses around it. Each one of those damn shells will knock down a city block!

I was in a slit trench at the company command post. Hell, the shells hit so close it'd knock you out of the trench. I'd been tossed out of my damn hole ten to fifteen feet. You would just scramble back like a rat into that hole. It scared the living hell out of you. All I could think of was *Where is our Navy?* Your head was ringing. A lot of guys had concussions, bad concussions, and a concussion can kill you just like anything else. I lost my hearing.

People don't know that it was the worst shelling the Marines took in World War II. If you know anything about World War I, the worst shelling was at Passchendaele in Belgium. This was equal to Passchendaele.

ROY GERLACH

Once again it was really good to be a cook. Our galley was near the Tenaru River, so to hit the airport they had to shoot over our heads. I looked up and saw those shells, red-hot, flying through the air.

SID PHILLIPS

We were on the eastern end of the runway when those two battleships started shelling. There would be a flash of light, when those big shells would burst, that made the outside look like a brilliant, bright light. When those shells would go off, it was like being thrown off of a two-story house and landing on your stomach. It would knock all the air out of you and you couldn't breathe, like you got punched in the gut. It was awful and it went on and on and on and on. Hunks of shrapnel, red-hot, would sit on the ground and glow.

I saw grown men sobbing. You could always tell a Catholic boy because he'd start reciting the Hail Mary. We were pretty well dug in, with dirt-covered logs over our foxholes, but the roof would jump up in the air, up to four feet. The dirt sifted down through the logs on top of us. The concussion was so tremendous that you just sort of became drunk from it, groggy. You stay in your hole for hours with all those shells exploding close by. Our shelter fell down on us and we were chest-deep in dirt. Uh, man. That's scary to me, I mean the idea of suffocating underneath the pile of logs and dirt.

When it was all over, nobody said anything for what seemed like an hour. Your ears—you couldn't hear anything for a while. Finally, Ransom said, "I hope to hell Tojo doesn't get that idea again!" Somebody else joked how those Jap gunners couldn't hit a bull in the ass with a bass fiddle. We started laughing. But we had been really scared during that whole bombardment—even though nobody would admit it out loud. You didn't know if the next one was going to land right in your hole. We had a lot of casualties.

I was praying all the while, just trying to hold on. I was raised in the Christian church and had gone to Sunday school as a boy. You had to—it wasn't optional. But I'd say my faith wasn't really unshakeable until much later in life. The idea of faith is that you *hope* He's real. But faith beyond that is that you *know* He's real. And I now know that God is real.

JIM YOUNG

I smoked my first cigarette after that. Someone said they help calm your nerves. It didn't. Everybody was semi-shocked, I guess. They fired 970 of those huge shells that night. They destroyed airplanes. Gasoline dumps. Everything.

The Japs came in and were unloading thousands of troops, way down the island. We could see them from the top of the hills. We had no way of stopping them now without our planes. We were very low on ammo and supplies.

We were ordered to board trucks and head to the lines closest to the landing. Our convoy of trucks was caught in an air raid, midway across the airstrip. We were like sitting ducks. The trucks stopped and we hid under them. In the scramble my helmet was knocked off and a piece of shrapnel hit the top of my head. I was lucky it hit a glancing blow and just made a minor wound. The corpsman said, "Oh, that isn't much." He put some sulfur powder on it and that was that. I never did get a Purple Heart for it.

We didn't expect a land attack for a few more days because they were about six miles down the beach and had to make their way through the jungles, which were very thick. The general told us the situation was grave and that we could decide for ourselves. We could surrender or take off into the jungle and hope that the USA would finally retake the island.

RICHARD GREER

We didn't think we were gonna lose. We always thought we were gonna win, even when Roosevelt was considering pulling us out of Guadalcanal and hitting the island again later. We got word that we might have to go to the hills to fight as guerillas, but we had known that could happen the whole time.

We knew that a fight was coming. We were preparing our sector for a long time before the Japs got there. We went down there and found every wrecked plane on the airfield and pulled every .50-caliber out and set it up. We probably had 50 percent more ordnance than the table of organization called for.

SID PHILLIPS

There was a radio communicator with us on Guadalcanal. And when the situation looked really hopeless, he'd pick up that field telephone and spin that handle, and he could disguise his voice so it didn't sound like him at all. He'd say, "This is Sergeant *Sacaraoi-uoiasdfasdf*, and I want to inform that the Japanese *blahladfoiuadso-fasf*." He could talk double talk so the guys on the other end wouldn't know what in the hell he was saying. It almost made sense, but it didn't. You knew that if you were on the other end hearing it, it just sounded like static. He'd throw the word "Japanese" in there every once in a while, and "might attack," and "what should we do," and then hang up. The phone would ring in a few minutes, and it would be our major on the other line. Then the communicator would say, "Yes sir, no sir, I have no idea sir, we have not used our phone at all." Then he'd hang up and we'd all howl.

"There ain't no brig," he'd say to us. "What are they going to do to me?"

We'd all almost cry laughing. He was just doing it to be an idiot.

JIM YOUNG

We were moved from the Tenaru area, across the airport, and down south to bolster that line. That night we knew they were coming and waited to see what part of our lines would be attacked.

The climactic battle of Guadalcanal, the Battle for Henderson Field, reached a crescendo just after midnight on October 25, 1942, when the Japanese emerged from the jungles south of the airport, located the Marine lines, and charged with fixed bayonets.

JIM YOUNG

We were lucky. They didn't attack H Company but instead hit the regiment that was tied into our line to the west—the 7th Marines—Chesty Puller's outfit.

RICHARD GREER

About 1 A.M. it was like the hordes of hell were turned loose. The Japanese were all over the damn place. They were hopped up on some kind of damn drug, throwing dynamite, throwing hand grenades, wielding swords and rifles. They were screaming and yelling "Banzai!" "Kikiboo!" "Marine you die!" "Blood for the emperor!" and derogatory things about Eleanor Roosevelt, Babe Ruth, and all that kind of crap. We would yell back, "Eat shit, Jap!" It was a little low, but some Jap screamed at us, "Screw Eleanor!" and some Marine yelled back, "You screw her! I don't want it!"

The Battle of Henderson Field had begun. They loaded the machine gun belts as fast as they could, and we took them to the line where all hell was breaking loose. You know a twelve-hundred-yard front line is not a big front, and you got seven thousand Japanese attacking it. You couldn't hear yourself think!

Our company had three machine gun platoons and so you got twenty-four guns there and they were spread out to support the other companies—A, B, and C. John Basilone's guns were attached to C Company at the time. I had to travel about a thousand yards to get the ammo to John's guns. About three-fifths of a mile. It was a good old trek, in the jungle. I could see it pretty good, especially when the flares were floating down. Otherwise you had to feel your way in the black night. We had cleaned out seven hundred yards of jungle in front of the guns, but it was still thick as hell. We had been in there about a month, and in a month you get to know every tree.

I got to near Basilone's gun, and I handed him a belt of ammunition or two. He was strong, so he could easily carry the 250 rounds in one belt. That belt's a long and heavy son of a gun. At one point I carried five belts plus my Springfield rifle, and that really just about tore my legs off! Basilone said, "You don't have to bring them to the guns." I said, "Hell, I can bring it to the guns." John had his .45 on him, and I remembered the times he used to practice his quick draw. That night he killed a bunch of Japs with it. He took the ammo from me and went back to keeping the machine guns hopping.

I carried ammo to all three platoons of D Company that night and the other companies in the battalion. The guns were arranged with fields of fire that crossed each other so that a damn rabbit couldn't get through. You'd sit behind your gun, and even in the black of the night if something crossed in front of it, it'll register in your sight. You'd squeeze off a burst of three or five rounds. There's none of that Hollywood shit where you burn up a belt.

The Japs they kept coming and we kept firing. There was mortars and there was artillery, there were any number of machine guns. The sky was flashing with color from the tracer ammo and the blasts of the artillery. It's something that you never dreamed you'd ever live through. I give the Japs one thing—they were sure as hell bold in their attacks. They were crack troops of the 17th Army, which had swept all the way down the China coast and cleaned out Singapore.

JIM YOUNG

We could see and hear all the guns firing. We could hear the Japs screaming their heads off. We were all expecting to get hit, too. The word was that a few had broken through and were within fifty feet of the Colonel's command post! That's when John Basilone done his thing. He ended up saving the day by running guns up to the line and firing a machine gun from the hip.

RICHARD GREER

I have no idea how many ammo runs I made during the first night of battle. On one trip going up to Basilone I had three belts of ammo around my neck—750 bullets—which was pretty damn heavy. But he needed them. John was burning through them. Those belts are long, so I had to double them up around my neck. I was really being constricted. I came around a corner and a flare went off and there was a Jap colonel sitting right there against a tree. I threw my rifle up and then another flare went off and I noticed somebody had taken half the top of his head off already.

D Company's old Master Gunnery Sergeant Fowel was the best mortar man on Guadalcanal. He had four 81mm mortars and was dropping those 81mm mortar shells right smack on the Japs, right smack in front of the lines. He was short and stocky and he had gotten pretty fat, but damn did he know mortars. The company command post was no more than twenty-five yards behind the line, the battalion command post was another fifty yards back, and that's about where the mortars were. Man I tell you what, they put out some ammo that night. Old Gunnery Sergeant Fowel had cancer and the guys really loved him. If we had a can of milk, we'd save the milk and give it to the Gunny.

The breakthrough came during the early morning, between two of the rifle companies, right near the D Company command post. The Japs broke through and stopped to rest between the front lines and the mortars. A few of us from the command post—me, Gunny Farrel, Sergeant Sanner, and one other Marine—and about ten guys from the mortar platoon went and wiped them out. It didn't amount to a hill of beans. I'll tell you, I'm almost 100 percent sure that when we reached them the Japs were all asleep.

After that, one of the Marines who was with us, why, he blew his stack. He mentally lost it. The only Marine I ever saw lose it. The guy was raving and waving his rifle with that long bayonet on the end. Puller came up and ordered me to disarm him. I laid my rifle down but then thought he was going to cut me. I took the bayonet off my rifle and moved in on him. I hit him, not too hard, with a butt stroke on the side of the head. It knocked him right out. By that time, two MPs came up and they carried him off. I got no sleep that night. I would never dream of it.

After a day of scattered fighting, Greer, Basilone, and the 7th Marines rebuilt their defenses and prepared for another round.

RICHARD GREER

That night they came again. They came out of the jungles throwing grenades, dynamite, and shooting their guns. It was kinda hairy. There was a little breakthrough, but it was pretty quickly sealed up. It was basically a repetition of the first night. I was doing the same thing again, running ammo. Basilone was on the line, working the machine guns, as was everybody. The Japs made pass after pass. Suicide attacks. But we held.

After that second night, I looked at the pile of dead enemy bodies in front of our lines and said to my old buddy, Tom Boyle, "Tom, I wonder what killed all those dead Japanese—small arms fire, artillery, or mortars?" So we went out there and took a look at the Japanese dead. We were curious. They were piled up several feet high. In some places they were as high as the barbed wire. We turned them over and looked. Small arms fire. That's what got them. Basilone's section killed an entire company worth. I know one damn thing, there were even more dead Japs in front of A Company than anywhere. You never hear about that. They were in a more vulnerable position, but they had the benefit of cross fire from an Army cannon.

After the battle they brought a bunch of bulldozers, dug a long trench, and buried those Japanese in there, around 3,500 of them. To this day, I can't believe the slaughter. It was an expensive campaign for them.

I don't know who relieved us, but we went up on Bloody Ridge. It was quiet up there. Just about at dark, I lit a cigarette and some Jap across the ridge opened up on me with one of those Nambu machine guns and shot the hell out of the gun emplacement around me. I damn near got killed. Never did that again.

After the Marines and Army defeated the Japanese in the Battle for Henderson Field, the Navy scored a follow-up victory at sea. The tide turned and supplies flowed regularly in to the Marines—food from Australia, ammunition from the States, and mail from home.

JIM YOUNG

Everybody had a comic book. I don't know where we got hold of them but that's about all we had. I read lots of them. *Superman, Dick Tracy*, and that kind of stuff.

SID PHILLIPS

In the Pacific, you got a detached feeling, like you were all alone, way out in the middle of nowhere. We received mail on Guadalcanal when ships came in. You just loved to get mail. I mean, our morale would shoot way up. Often you didn't receive any mail at all for weeks and weeks on end, then you might get ten letters all at once. This was before the era of civilian travel. Back then, Hawaii, in our minds, was about as far as the moon is today. It took days by ship to get to Hawaii in 1941. There was no air service to any part of the world.

All the guys would sit around and everyone would read their

mail. Someone would holler, "Betty got married! Son of a bitch." The faithful writers to me were my mother, my sister Katharine, and my best friend back home, Eugene Sledge.

Eugene and I were in grade school together, in high school together. We both played snare drum in high school band. We both had the same hobbies—history and hiking in the woods. So we had thousands and thousands of experiences together. My sister has nailed down his personality—if you just think of the movie *Gone with the Wind*, and think of Ashley in the movie—he's an exact reproduction of Eugene Sledge's personality. Always polite, always a gentleman, always sincere, never rude, that's Eugene exactly.

In high school Eugene had an old car, and we used to travel all around the county. We had a prank that we would play. In those days, Mobile still had streetcars, and the streetcars were on fixed tracks. We found if we could pretend to break down on the street car track we could block all traffic—literally hundreds of cars—up and down Government Street. Eugene would stop the car, and with a straight face I would get out and lift the hood and tinker with the engine while the traffic backed up. Eugene would hand me a screwdriver, and I'd say, "Try it again." On the old six-volt system you could ground the starter with the ignition turned off. We'd act like we'd be trying to start that car for five or ten minutes, or until the police arrived. Finally, he'd turn on the ignition and the car would start. I'd exclaim, "You got it!" and we'd jump in and drive off. Nobody ever caught on that it was all just a hoax to tie up traffic.

I remember writing Eugene a letter, warning him not to join anything. "Stay out of the Boy Scouts, the Salvation Army, and particularly the Marines. Don't join anything!"

ROY GERLACH

Right in the camp where we stayed, there was this Japanese tractor. A couple of the fellows and me got it running, and we'd drive down to the beach, to the food depot. You were supposed to have a voucher to get supplies. Well, you had to have a mess sergeant to get a voucher. But we didn't have any mess sergeant. So no vouchers for us! How were we supposed to eat? You did a little lying and fibbing and got it the best way you could. We only took the good stuff, the fruit and whatnot, then drove back. When that routine stopped working, we tried something else.

We were bivouacked right along the road to the commissary, where they stored food. They used to go by us in trucks, piled up high with food. They'd have to go slow because the dirt road was rough. So we'd go down on the road, stop the truck, and grab a case of stuff off it. But they got wise to the idea and improved the road, smoothed it out so they could go faster. So we'd go down there and dig ditches across the road so the trucks couldn't go so fast. Big ruts. That gave us a chance to get more food.

ART PENDLETON

We kept going on patrols, every day. That never stopped. I used to warn my men before we went out, "Don't be a hero! You don't win a war by getting yourself killed." I would tell them, "If someone throws a hand grenade and you see it, don't throw your body on it like the heroes do. If you wanna kick it out of the way, okay. If you wanna pick it up, okay—you might lose an arm or you might get killed, but whatever you do, don't throw your body on it. You're not gonna help win the war if you get dead."

At first I carried a tommy gun, the same as what the gangsters used to use, complete with the drum magazine. We quickly gave up those guns because when you walked in the jungle you had to be very quiet and with every step the bullets would slide forward and hit the steel drum. You would get that *bump, bump, bump* all the time. We threw those away and then used Reising submachine guns, which were made with a wood stock and had a straight magazine that held a dozen rounds. They were okay except when you got into real firefight. The spring in the magazine would jam and the cartridge wouldn't go into the chamber. So it didn't take long for us to throw those things away either.

The Japanese were excellent at the jungle fighting. They were everywhere. You could be eating and you could have a Jap creeping up on you. I remember being worn to a frazzle just looking for them. We were out there every day. Eventually your shoes would rot from going in and out of the water. Your clothes were a mess. You wanted to get rid of them. We used Japanese sandals eventually.

One time there were about twenty of us on a patrol. We were out to capture Japanese alive, which was not a good job, believe me. We were on a mission to collect prisoners of war to exchange for Americans. This was what we were told at least.

We surprised some Japanese and took them at gunpoint. One of the Japanese turned to me and he said in perfect English, "You know I went to the university in New York." Now if that wouldn't blow you away, I would like to know what would? What I said to him was totally stupid. I said, "It doesn't make any difference. You're my prisoner." That was the end of the conversation. He never spoke after that to me.

In early November, Chesty Puller led Greer, Basilone, and their battalion against Japanese troops at a place on the coast, east of the airfield, called Koli Point. Many of the Japanese gathering there were survivors of the Battle of Henderson Field.

RICHARD GREER

On November 1, we were sent out to Koli Point. We must have had ten thousand men, Marines and Army. And the Japanese had a large concentration of troops there, too. On November 8 we could see the point up ahead. While everyone else encircled the Japs, we attacked up the beach. They saw us coming.

The enemy artillery fire opened up. It was an absolute surprise to us, but the Japs had landed a few field pieces by ship. The first round hit right beside our new first sergeant, a guy named Potts. He got hit in the back and cut in two. We ran for the trees. I got into the trees when a second round hit and knocked me unconscious, but not before shrapnel went through my shoe and stuck in my ankle. The same round put a hunk of shrapnel in Colonel Puller's leg and killed another Marine.

When I came to, a "chancre mechanic" [slang for "corpsman"] was bandaging up my ankle. I was lucky as hell because that damn Marine shoe caught some of the shrapnel. I said, "Hell with that ankle!" I was more worried that I was spitting blood. Blood was coming out of my eyes and nose and ears. The corpsman said, "It's a concussion. You'll be all right since you're healthy as hell." It never bothered him. He fixed my ankle and I went back to duty.

We reorganized and headed back out on the offense. The day after I got hit, George Cooper, who was from my hometown of Rocky Mountain, Virginia, got five rounds from a machine gun right in the belly. I saw him going out and George said, "How bad is it?" I looked and I said, "If the medics get you on the boat in time, get you to a hospital ship, you'll be all right." They got him out of there, but they couldn't find the damn boat. He died. I went to see his folks when I got back and that wasn't easy. I still think about it a lot.

Before the Americans could encircle the Japanese, they escaped into the jungle toward the island's center. An American Army sergeant would later remember, "The Americans learned once again that offensive operations against the Japanese were much more complicated and difficult than was defeating banzai charges."

RICHARD GREER

They slipped away, but we tracked those jokers for thirty days out there in the jungle. They were all over hell and half of Georgia, but they didn't have anywhere to run. Basilone called it "the Great Jap Hunt." We had them good.

With Guadalcanal irreversibly in American hands, fresh Marine and Army units relieved the 1st Marine Division, whose men prepared to rotate out of the combat zone.

SID PHILLIPS

Finally, after weeks and weeks of fighting, they brought us off the line and down to the beach. Tex and I got put on a work detail, unloading a shipment of some canned food. Supplies in quantity finally had begun to arrive. The Navy pulled a couple steel barges in there, and you could unload off a ship onto that barge, easier than you could onto a landing craft. They put us in working parties, and we worked all the time. We soon had stacks and stacks of food, as high as a man could reach. You could create alleyways out of the food.

We had been starving to death for so long. Just hungry all the time. We couldn't imagine having all this food. Tex and I got back there in one of those alleyways, and we each opened a can of sliced pineapple. We didn't have anything to eat with, but we each ate a whole gallon can of it. We couldn't keep it down. We just lay down on that barge and vomited overboard until we got rid of it. He would vomit and laugh, and then I'd vomit and laugh. He'd say, "That was too much, wasn't it?"

JIM YOUNG

After five months of fighting on Guadalcanal, we were all in bad shape. Everyone was sick with malaria, dysentery, and jungle rot. The Army arrived and relieved us. The ships to take us away gathered just offshore. It was a great day. We had won the first major land campaign of the war, and Australia would never be threatened again.

On December 22, 1942, H Company would depart the island. Two weeks later, Greer, Basilone, and D Company would follow them.

SID PHILLIPS

After we left the beach, we got to a troop ship, and some of those were very high-sided. The only way to get aboard was to climb up the side on a big rope net, a long, long ways, to the top. We got about halfway up that thing, and we couldn't go anymore. We were just too weak. I'd never seen a bunch of men weaker than we had become.

A man was afraid he was going to lose his grip and fall back into the boat, which could've killed him. The sailors soon realized we were that bad off, and they'd come down and grab you by your collar and give you a little help so you could get up another couple rungs. They'd reach down from the deck and pull you up. You were just completely exhausted at the top. I was five-ten and weighed 175 pounds when we started the campaign at Guadalcanal. I weighed 145 at the end.

Ransom lay on the deck in a heap. He looked up to the sailors with a grin and said, "Swabbies, Uncle Sam's tough Marines are a wreck!"

CHAPTER FOUR

REST AND RESPITE

★ ★ ★

Australia

After a stopover at the island of Espiritu Santo, the sick, battered men of the 1st Marine Division arrived in Australia, their home for the next nine months and a place of needed respite.

SID PHILLIPS

First we sailed to Brisbane and dropped anchor. Our 5th Regiment had already been there for a week, but they were so full of malaria and mosquitoes that medical crews decided it was too much of a hazard for the Australian population. We never went ashore at Brisbane. After a few days, we sailed for Melbourne. None of us had a map in our pocket and we didn't know where that was. It took us about a week to sail there.

JIM YOUNG

On arrival at the docks in Melbourne, we were rushed to trucks as fast as possible. The Marine Corps didn't want the people to see how dirty and grimy we were. Our clothes were in tatters. Pant legs

GUADALCANAL

CORAL SEA

AUSTRALIA

BRISBANE

MELBOURNE

N

USMC

WARBURTON

★ MELBOURNE

PORT
PHILLIP
BAY

DANDENOG

PHILLIPS

5 Miles

had rotted away, and some of the guys' private parts were showing. There were a lot of ambulances lined up to take the sick and wounded to area hospitals.

RICHARD GREER

Within the first two weeks of arriving in Australia, there were ten thousand cases of malaria in the hospital. Any hospital anywhere was full of Marines. We went into Guadalcanal with the strength of twenty thousand men, lost around seven thousand one way or another; that dropped us down to about thirteen thousand. When we got to Melbourne, malaria broke out and we had three thousand men effective at one time if you can believe that. Slowly, with good food, good veggies, and plenty of quinine [the treatment for malaria], we got better. I had malaria then and I had it off and on for the next forty-five years.

ART PENDLETON

I had malaria when we went to Australia. At first I was in a confinement area with a big barbed wire fence patrolled by men with rifles loaded with ammo. They didn't want anyone infected mixing with the local populace. Then I was placed in an Army hospital filled with Marines with dysentery and malaria, Oh boy! They said in a good climate it takes twelve to fourteen weeks to get rid of malaria but mine lasted off and on for fourteen years.

SID PHILLIPS

I came down with hepatitis A. A lot of guys had it then. Most of us were in terrible physical condition. When I went over to sick call, the doctor just took one look at me, nodded, and said, "Stand over there." A whole floor at the hospital was set up with nothing but hepatitis cases. Fortunately, I got better.

JIM YOUNG

Our battalion was billeted in the Melbourne Cricket Ground. It was a stadium, something like the Madison Square Garden in New York City. Bunks were placed over the bleacher seats. Our mess halls were where concessions stalls were. The front facing the game field was enclosed with plywood up to about eight feet from the top. When it stormed, the guys up there got wet.

After a week, we were still not allowed to go on the town because we had no uniforms. Ours went down with the ship at the 'Canal. But finally the Aussies donated us army pants and jackets. They had to be dyed green before we could wear them on leave. After that we had a ball.

The 1st Marine Division decided to issue shoulder patches, two per Marine, to commemorate their victory at Guadalcanal.

RICHARD GREER

Ah hell, everybody had the patch on in little or no time. I had at least five of the originals—you could buy them in Melbourne. We had a lot of pride in that patch, absolutely. The patch actually bore kinship to the flag of Victoria, the Australian state where we stayed. Their flag is blue with red elements and theirs had five white stars in the same pattern.

The stars on the patch are in the shape of the Southern Cross, which represents the southern hemisphere of fighting. You could make out that star formation all over the South Pacific. Everybody could pick that out. The word Guadalcanal was written on the patch. That was a little unusual, to define your division around one battle. It was a good deal for us who were at Guadalcanal because it became world famous.*

When I look at that patch, I think of two nations fighting our asses off over a ninety-mile strip of land that wasn't worth a damn, but strategically whoever held it held Australia. It cost all told fifty thousand lives, forty-eight warships, two thousand warplanes, and it was one of the most savage battles of World War II. That's what that patch brings to my mind.

SID PHILLIPS

We were ordered to assemble on the Cricket Grounds for an award ceremony. General Vandegrift, Colonel Edson, Sergeant Mitchell Paige, and Sergeant John Basilone were all to receive the Medal of Honor. Basilone was what we called an old Marine. He'd been in the service in the Philippines before Pearl Harbor. They called him "Manila John." We were in different regiments, so I never met him. Remember, back then I was an eighteen-year-old private in the rear rank of the Marine Corps. I was an absolute nobody.

I remember it was a bright sunny day. We were standing there at rigid attention during the speech making, and Ransom kept mumbling, "Hurry it up, c'mon, hurry it up, let's get this over with, hurry it up!" I've often thought of the humor of that. Here we were at this auspicious event, and we were all wishing it would hurry up and be over so we could go on liberty.

---

* Richard Greer would remember, "When I came home, I never took my patch off. No one had a problem with that, but if they did it would have taken a pretty big deal to get that patch off me. Back home you would go in a bar and people would recognize you were a Marine. Then they would see 'Guadalcanal' and everybody knew about Guadalcanal since it had been in the papers so damn long. That patch got us a lot of free drinks. I had people come up and thank me, over and over, but I can't say whether it was the patch that did it or the Marine uniform. It happened."

RICHARD GREER

By the time we got to Australia, I was invited to move into the staff NCO tent, and that's where I lived with Basilone and the other sergeants. Basilone and I never really discussed that night he turned back the Japs in the Battle of Henderson Field. We lived together and hit the town together, but we never discussed that. I don't know who wrote Basilone's Medal of Honor citation, but they brought it to me to type up. I typed it up and kept a copy for myself.*

I knew Mitchell Paige. He was a professional Marine, a platoon sergeant in F Company. He always thought he should have had the first Medal of Honor given to an enlisted Marine [in WWII] instead of Basilone—but Basilone's action happened a day before his. John never paid any attention to that. They both deserved the medal, John just earned it first, so he got more of the glory.

JIM YOUNG

Pretty girls were everywhere. There were dance halls, amusement parks, and beer parlors. Artie Shaw's Navy Band came to the USO, and when they started to play, the music was heard outside on the busy street. All of a sudden the sidewalks and streets were jammed with Aussies listening to the music. The city ended up closing off the whole block to traffic. It was something to see all those people singing and dancing in the street.

The division put on a big parade for the people of Melbourne. There were about seventeen thousand of us. It was just like a New York City ticker tape parade. The Australians loved us! They said if it weren't for us, the Japs would be bombing them by now. They took many of us into their homes and treated us like their own.

---

* Greer would remember, "I got John to sign my copy of his citation and it's now in the World War II museum in New Orleans."

SID PHILLIPS

I can't quite express the joy and jubilation the Marines felt to be back in civilization. We had been so far away from all that, then to suddenly be around streetcars and grocery stores and restaurants, it was just a wonderful feeling, it really was.

RICHARD GREER

Basilone, J. P. Morgan, and me made a lot of liberties together. J. P. Morgan was Basilone's best friend. They were the closest of all. Morgan had been in the Marines since at least 1940. He was a sergeant. He and Basilone were down in Cuba together.

When we got a three-day pass, Basilone, Morgan, and me, we'd catch a train and go about ten miles outside of the city to some nice little town that had a good hotel and a good kitchen and a good bar. We would make our arrangements—we just had a flat price on everything—and we'd spend our time there, the three of us. We didn't bother anybody or anything. Mealtime would come and we'd hit the kitchen. Otherwise we'd hit the bar. Basilone was our bartender. That's the way we spent most of our liberties.

ROY GERLACH

We lived high on the hog. We'd go off base and get steak and eggs and ate a lot of that. Pretty good stuff. Now, I'd never eaten lobster, and didn't know anything about it. One time another fellow and I went into this busy restaurant. The Australians ate lobster. So I said to this fellow, "I'm going to get a lobster tail."

"You get your lobster," he said. "I'm going to get steak and eggs."

When the lobster came, they set a bowl of melted butter in front of me, and salt and pepper, and all this stuff you're supposed to pour over the lobster. But I didn't know that. I just dove in, tore a chunk out of it, put it in my mouth, and chewed and chewed and chewed. It didn't appeal to me. I pushed it back and ordered steak and eggs.

We were in a booth. In the course of time, two Australian Air Force men came in and sat on the other side of our booth, because it was so busy. One guy pointed at my lobster and said, "You going to eat that?"

"You're welcome to it," I said.

So they both dove into it, dipping it into the melted butter and salt and pepper, and saying, "Oh, it's good, good, good. Try some."

So I did. I liked it better then. So that's how I learned to eat lobster.

RICHARD GREER

Australia was full of absolutely beautiful theaters and what threw me about the theaters was you could smoke inside them during the movie.

Everybody was pretty calm in the city and in the streets, but there were still bar fights from time to time. Morgan was a middle-weight boxing champion at one time, so he wouldn't back away from a fight. When he and Basilone were together, Morgan would get in a brawl and Basilone would get in it to back him up or pull him out. That's the way it goes.*

Best of all, Melbourne was also full of women who had not been properly chaperoned around since 1939 because all the Australian men were in North Africa because of the war. Of course we Marines were half-dead with malaria, but we still had a wonderful

---

* Richard Greer would remember, "Basilone, Morgan, and me, we was in a brawl back at New River a time or two. I was about six-three, two hundred pounds, and in absolutely wonderful shape. We did just fine."

time down there. I doubt if there are a half dozen Marines in the whole division that didn't have some kind of serious girlfriend during that eight months.

SID PHILLIPS

Deacon Tatum was a good friend of mine. He and I and W. O. Brown did everything together. Deacon was about five years older than I was, maybe twenty-three, and mature for his age. I was still a kid. Deacon had been preparing to become a minister before the war and was always trying to straighten me out. He said I was a "bad case." I kidded him back, because he smoked, chewed tobacco, and dipped snuff all day long. He was a great friend and took me under his wing.

There were two girls in Australia that Deacon and I took up with—sisters. Deacon found the older sister first. When he took her home, her mother told him that her daughter could not date one-on-one with a Yank. It always had to be a double date. So Deacon had to find somebody to date the girl's sister. He came to me and said, "I've got a blind date for you." And I said, "I don't need your help." But he said, "Come on there, just one date. You will not be sorry."

So we met the girls, and the sister, my date, was really pretty. I mean, really pretty! She was as gorgeous as Elizabeth Taylor. Shirley was her name. She was sixteen years old. I was eighteen then. The girls' mother was a widow—her husband had died from effects of being gassed in WWI, and right away the mother gave us a talking to. If we Yanks were to date her daughters, we always needed to stay in a group. Neither Deacon nor I was ever to take either sister off by herself. Most of the time, we'd go to the movies with the girls. Or we'd go to this amusement park they had there with merry-go-rounds and Ferris wheels and whatnot. Or we'd go to historical sites in Melbourne. So we had two nice girls who remained nice girls. People let their imaginations run wild when they think of us Marines romancing the Australian girls. I'd say most of the relationships were old-fashioned and nonsexual. They were good girls and we respected that. Every relationship I ever had with a girl in Australia was chaste.

The first month we had liberty almost every day, and we loved going out to these girls' house. The girls' grandmother lived with them, too. The family worked but were really poor. They didn't have a refrigerator or even electricity. But they were very kind, and we got to be close with the whole family. There was no food rationing in Australia except for tea, and we didn't give a damn about tea, so Tatum and I would go by the grocery store and get great big steaks and potatoes and go by the house, and the mother would prepare the food for all of us. We did not want to be an expense to the family. At least once or twice a week we ate in their home. We had a wonderful time.

ROY GERLACH

I never had malaria, but I got yellow jaundice in Australia. I turned yellow. I was in the Army hospital there for about thirty days. They said I got it from going from eating a poor diet to a high diet too quickly. On Guadalcanal there wasn't much to eat of course. When you have jaundice, it can make your eyes weak. They got my color straightened out then they gave me liberty. It was great.

RICHARD GREER

Despite all this fun we were having, we were training all the time. We got new supplies, including semiautomatic M1 Garand rifles. We'd been fighting with the old bolt-action Springfields. Replacements came in from the States, and our division began to get back on its feet. It would take months and months.

Among the Marine replacements arriving to Australia that spring 1943 was twenty-year-old Romus Valton Burgin who went by the name "R.V."

R. V. BURGIN

I grew up on a farm in east Texas, a town called Jewett. I picked cotton from age three or four on up. After school. Weekends. Whenever. In high school, I was involved in everything—I played basketball and football. When we played basketball, we played at night. The bus wouldn't wait, so after each game I'd walk home, all eight miles of it. I did that a lot. Football games were played in the afternoons because we didn't have a lighted field. I played both sides of the field, defensive end and cornerback. My senior year, the team voted me captain of the football team. That meant a lot to me because it came from the other players. Lord no, I wasn't a big kid. I weighed 140 pounds. But I was fast and I could hit hard.

I wanted to go to college, but I didn't have two quarters to rub together, so going to college was not something I could do. When Pearl Harbor hit, I was working in Dallas and living with my sister. I got a job as a traveling salesman for the Columbus Stationery Company, selling personalized, engraved stationery door to door. I was enjoying myself out on the road, so I kept postponing enlistment as long as I could. There was a general expectation throughout the country that all young men would do their duty and enlist. People I met on the road would often ask me why I wasn't in uniform. No matter what day of the week, I always told them I was going to enlist "next Friday." That became my standard answer.

I stayed with the stationery company until September 1942, when the draft board got to pushing me. I wanted to make my move first and enlist before I was drafted. Enlisting wasn't the easiest decision I ever made. I knew I had to do my duty, but I also knew that war is hell. My uncle had told me stories of WWI, and I had seen short films of war. So all along I had a mind-set that eventually I was going into battle, but I didn't rush headlong into it like some guys did.

My draft notice said I was to be drafted into the Army on November 13, 1942. But I did not want to be a dogface in the Army. I didn't like the Army's uniforms, and I didn't like the sloppiness you sometimes heard about in the Army. So on November 10 I went to Houston, thinking I'd join the Air Force or Navy or Marines. The Air Force had a long waiting list, same as the Coast Guard. The Navy recruiter was a smart aleck. That left the Marines. I officially joined the Marine Corps. I was twenty years old.

Boot camp was normally twelve weeks, but we were rushed through it in six. Everything was sped up because they needed troops overseas as soon as possible. I got to Australia on March 31, 1943, and was put in the mortar section of K Company, 3rd Battalion, 5th Marines or "K-3-5." When I got to K Company, it was right after the Guadalcanal campaign, so they merged us raw recruits in with the old-timers. We were welcomed, but a Marine still needs to prove himself.

At the rifle range I shot "Expert" designation on my M1 rifle. The commander commended me, and shortly after I was promoted to private first class. Then we had a recreation day where a competition was held between companies. We broke down machine guns, field-stripped weapons and put them back together again—things like that—to see who could do the task the quickest. From out of the whole battalion, I was the fastest in setting up a 60mm mortar and getting on target with it. That was the first time anybody recognized me as being anything more than a new recruit. After that competition it was like I became one of the family—the United States Marine family—and there's no greater feeling in the world.

After the veterans of Guadalcanal rebuilt their health, the Marine Corps kept them busy. The Corps had a habit of keeping a Marine fighting fit by keeping him discontent.

SID PHILLIPS

In the Marine Corps you were always being put on guard duty or "brig duty." Brig duty was the duty we hated more than any other. You were armed with a weapon and live ammunition. You were told to kill these damned prisoners if they didn't do what you told them to do. The Corps didn't like them any more than we did. Our thinking was *If these goofball Marines would have just obeyed orders, I wouldn't be guarding them on brig duty!* So you really had no compassion towards the prisoners.

These people made it hard for the rest of us. We were guarding them instead of out on the town. You really had no good feelings for them at all. Our thinking was *I wish the son of a bitch would try to make a break for it because I'll shoot him* (laughs).

One time I was put on brig duty at the Fourth General Hospital, the same hospital where I had recovered from my hepatitis A. About fifteen of us pulled this duty—W. O. Brown was one of them, and we were all stationed in beautiful quarters there, stucco one-story buildings with wide wooden bunks with clean sheets. Beautiful meals were served by Australian middle-aged women. We called them all "Mother." Our job was to guard Marine inmates in a restricted area on the hospital's top floor. They were real bad hombres and were shackled to their beds, being held for trial while they recovered from malaria.

I was guarding the hospital's main entrance one morning. That was better than guarding the prisoners on the top floor. All you did was stand there at parade rest. You came to present arms, to salute an officer when he or she went in or out of the hospital. All of the nurses were officers, so there were no boring waits. Every few minutes a nurse would come in or go out, and all you'd do is come to present arms, and they'd return the salute if they wanted to.

About five American staff cars pulled up to the curb. There was very little traffic in Melbourne. Most of the people didn't have any gasoline, so the streets were practically empty. All these American Army generals and Navy admirals began to get out of these cars. I thought, *What in the hell is this?* And then the President's wife, Mrs. Eleanor Roosevelt, climbed out of the first car in line. Then I realized what it was all about.

She walked straight to the hospital door and saw me standing there. I came to present arms. The thing that startled me was how tall she was. She was the same height as me, and she had on low heels. She walked right up to me and said, "Young man, are you a Marine?" I thought that was a strange question because here I was in uniform with the insignia on it, but I said, "Yes, ma'am." You're really not supposed to talk to anybody when you're on sentry duty, but of course if the First Lady came up to you like that, it would be proper to answer. She said, "Were you on Guadalcanal?" I said, "Yes, ma'am." She said, "Are you being well fed?" I said, "Yes, ma'am," because by then we were. She said, "Are you being well cared for?" I said, "Yes, ma'am." She said, "What state are you from?" I said, "Alabama, ma'am." She said, "I should have known that." She smiled and walked on into the hospital.

That was my encounter with Mrs. Roosevelt.

ROY GERLACH

After I got out of the hospital from my yellow jaundice, I was walking up the street and something hit my eye. It just felt like a cinder. I tried rubbing it out, but it got worse. Pretty soon my eye swelled shut. So I went back to the hospital. The eye doctor didn't know what it was. The doctor called in different doctors for a consult. They kept putting drops in it. They started getting concerned that

I was going to lose my eye. Finally they concluded it was a strained nerve. They got it straightened out, but I ended up in the hospital for another thirty days.

RICHARD GREER

Basilone and I went on our last liberty together around the 4th of July 1943. He came up to the first sergeant's tent and said, "You know some nice gals, don't you?" I said, "Of course." He said, "Well, let's get a couple of nice girls to go into the mountains."

Morgan didn't want to come along. He didn't make as many liberties as we did. I don't know what old Mo did instead. When we would go to some country motel, Mo was always up for that. But taking some gals to the mountains, he wasn't too interested. He was married; we weren't. When we went on liberty, we thought, *Hell, forget about tomorrow.* We knew we were going back in combat.

We picked up two girls. Those poor young Australian gals were really suffering. Their men had all been in the war since 1939, and a lot had never had a date. They were good gals, just like back home. I can still remember both of their names—Hazel and Jeanne. I got a hell of a mind.

We went to Melbourne and caught the train up to Warburton in the Australian Alps. It was snowing up there, with two feet of snow. That was the first time those gals had seen snow. We played around in the snow all afternoon and took a bunch of pictures.

During that weekend John said, "I'm going to the States. They want me to go back and sell war bonds." He had been ordered home. He didn't think the plan was worth a dang, but he always obeyed his orders, whatever they were.

That was the last liberty we made together. Pretty shortly after that he went to the States. John hated to leave D Company but was a good Marine and went where the Corps needed him.

R. V. BURGIN

I don't remember ever being kept in camp on a weekend. We showered, got dressed, and headed for downtown Melbourne. We had to be back by midnight Sunday night. All the first couple months, my buddy Jim Burke and I always went on liberty together. He and I had met on the ship coming over and got to be real good friends.

We'd often get into Melbourne on the train about ten o'clock in the morning when the pubs first opened up. Jim would head straight into the Young & Jackson Hotel, right across from the train station, and start drinking right away. On the wall of the bar they had a huge pink painting of a naked lady named *Chloe*. That painting was famous all over town, at least as far as the GIs were concerned, and every Marine in Melbourne that I ever knew walked into that bar at least once to pay his respects to *Chloe*. Jim could really hold his liquor. I never did see him drunk. He'd still be there at six o'clock at night when the bar closed. But he could come out of the bar after being there all day and still walk a straight line. Me? I'd get out and go see a movie, or go walk the gardens. They had some of the most beautiful gardens in Melbourne I'd ever seen. In those days you could buy a beer for about twelve cents. A good meal would set you back fifty cents. That was really living.

After about two months of being stationed in Australia, Jim and I spotted two very pretty young ladies walking down the street, a blonde and a brunette. They turned into a candy shop. I turned to Jim and said, "I'll take the brunette." He said, "Okay, I'll take the blonde." We followed them in and talked to them. Their names were Florence and Doris. They said they were both eighteen. They offered to show us the Melbourne Museum, a few blocks down. So we went. The main exhibit featured this famous racehorse named Phar Lap, which had died while in the States. Doris said, "You Yanks poisoned him." I guess that was the big joke—that the Americans had done in their famous racehorse. Everything in the museum was stuffed and mounted, and we walked around a bit until Jim finally said, "Let's get the hell out of here, everything smells dead."

We went to the train station where Florence's mother was coming into the city along with Florence's four-year-old brother. Jim and I met them then took turns running laps up and down the train platform, making train noises, with Florence's little brother on our shoulders. When Florence's mother and brother left, the girls and Jim and I took a boat ride on the river. We agreed to meet under the clock at the train station the next Saturday. We did. After that Jim and I double-dated with the girls every weekend.

I liked Florence a lot. She was tall, about five-nine, with dark hair. She was witty and beautiful and very intelligent. We just kinda gelled. I discovered she was only sixteen at the time, even though she'd told me she was eighteen. I guess she needed to lie about her age to go to work at the biscuit factory. She was already supervisor in her department. Her father operated a steam shovel at a coal mine, but he was a disabled veteran—he had been gassed by the Germans in WWI. We saw movies and shows and took carriage rides around the city and often just found a park bench and talked all afternoon.

JIM YOUNG

Most of the division soon got back in shape, and we started training for battle again. A bunch of generals and senators arrived to check us out. We did a live fire demonstration, and the bigwigs were out in front of us in a big bunker. My number one gun was the first to fire using the range data that was phoned to me. I let the mortar round go and lo and behold the shell landed on top of the bunker. Well, all hell broke loose.

The bigwigs came running out of the bunker, coughing and

wheezing, covered with dust. I knew I was going to get hell because Lieutenant Benson was also in the bunker and had given me the range distance. He was all dirty and raving like mad. The first thing he did was kick me right in the ass. I guess he really knew that he was the one who made the error, because I'd repeated his order back to him twice to make sure he knew what he was doing. I guess he didn't realize that the distance he gave me was from the bunker to the target and not from the gun to the target. He had me removed as gun corporal, but later on he realized his mistake and put me back in charge.

SID PHILLIPS

We had a camp outside the city in a suburb called Dandenong. When we were there it looked like Dodge City in *Gunsmoke*. They took us out in the outback, gave us a little cloth bag of rice and a bag of raisins, and told us to walk back to town—one hundred miles in three days. If you made it, you got a seventy-two-hour pass into Melbourne. Everybody made it, nobody collapsed.

R. V. BURGIN

PFC Merriel Shelton and I were in the same mortar squad and became friends. He had this thick Louisiana Cajun accent and always talked through his teeth. When he got excited, you couldn't understand him. He was a little man and a character all right but not as goofy as everyone thinks. He came to the company about two months before we left Australia. He was a bartender for the officer's club for a long time; the company had loaned him out. That was his profession by trade when he came into the service.

We were getting ready to go on liberty and go into Melbourne on a Friday night after four o'clock. Shelton's bunk was right next to my bunk. He had his money lying out on his bunk, and I said to Shelton, "How much money do you have there?" He picked up the bills and counted them and said, "Oh I gots ten or twelve pounds." Then he picked up the change and rattled it and shook it around in his hand and said, "I mus' have ten or twelve ounces here." Here he thought the currency a weight thing when really Australian money was called "pounds," "schillings," or "pence."

I said, "I'll tell you what, Shelton, you're just a SNAFU waiting to happen."* Everybody else was getting ready, and they heard it and laughed. From then on he wasn't "Shelton" he was "Snafu."

ART PENDLETON

They issued us the little .30-caliber carbines. They're neat little guns but have no range on them. They wouldn't knock the man down like a .45 would. But they would stop you if they hit you in the right spot.

SID PHILLIPS

I liked the carbine. It had fifteen rounds, was semiautomatic, so we felt well armed with it. With a pistol you would be doing good to hit a telephone pole at ten feet. You didn't feel well armed with a pistol. With a carbine you could hit a telephone pole at a hundred yards.

At the end of September 1943, the Marines prepared to depart Australia.

---

* SNAFU is the military acronym for "Situation Normal, All Fouled Up." (Other words are sometimes substituted for "fouled.")

JIM YOUNG

After many months, *surprise!* We were called to formation and told to pack up our gear and prepare to move out in two hours. We were not to make any phone calls. This came as a shock to everyone. Two hours later we marched right through the main street of the city. The Australians were going crazy. People were running into the buildings yelling, "The Marines are leaving!" and before you knew it the streets were filled with screaming and crying girls.

R. V. BURGIN

I saw Florence for the last time on September 25, 1943. We spent enough time together in the short time we had for me to know she was the one. I wanted to marry her, then and there, but had the good sense not to. I knew what was ahead and didn't want to leave her a widow. We agreed to correspond and pick things up again, someday.

SID PHILLIPS

Shirley and me, we just had a friendly warm good-bye. We knew we were not going to get married. We lived worlds apart. Back then to go to Australia was a one-month trip on a steamship, and you would spend every penny you could get to make the trip. I was a teenager at the time, so it just wasn't very feasible. But we had an agreement that we would always be good friends and write to one another.

JIM YOUNG

All seventeen thousand of us Marines were marching five abreast like a green snake winding for several miles through the street. We were heading straight for the city waterfront. The girls were crying and screaming whenever they saw their boyfriends. They would run right through the ranks and try to drag their boyfriends out of the line. The sergeants would have to pry them loose from the guys.

One of our sergeants, Marty Grogan, had gotten married and his wife spotted him. When she did, she got hysterical. Lieutenant Benson came running back from the front of the line and allowed Sergeant Grogan to fall out of ranks until he got his wife calmed down. He was to catch up to us as soon as he could. We thought it was very nice of the lieutenant to allow that.

When we arrived at the docks, ships were waiting for us to load. The piers were crowded with people. We were marched onto the ships right away. Once we were on the ship, we saw that the women had come right down to the beach, to the waterline. Many of the guys were writing messages, putting them in blown-up condoms, and floating them in to the beach. We watched as the girls picked them up and yelled the guy's name on it in an effort to locate the right receiver. It was quite a sight! Then we were on our way again with no idea of where we are going.

CHAPTER FIVE

THE GREEN INFERNO

★ ★ ★

New Britain

On December 26, 1943, the Marines landed on the western tip of the island of New Britain, at a place called Cape Gloucester. On the opposite end of the island lay Japan's South Pacific battle capital, the fortress port of Rabaul. The Marines were not there to attack Rabaul but instead to seize the island's western airfield, isolating Rabaul so it would die on the vine.

ART PENDLETON

On the way to Cape Gloucester, I can remember more than once that we discussed how we're not gonna make it this time. The odds were against us. Everyone was saying, "This is my address. Be sure and get in touch with so and so."

JIM YOUNG

We landed the day after Christmas, December 26, 1943. The main body of the 1st Marine Division landed fifteen miles north of us, near the airbase that they wanted to take. Our battalion landed

NEW GUINEA

Cape Gloucester

Talasea

Rabaul

★ NEW BRITAIN

SOLOMON ISLANDS

Guadalcanal

AUSTRALIA

C O R A L   S E A

2 MILES

N

USMC

USMC

Airfield

K-COMPANY
(K-3-5)
LANDING

H-COMPANY
(H-2-1)
LANDING

CAPE GLOUCESTER

Suicide Creek

Aogiri Ridge

★ BATTLE OF COFFIN
CORNER, DEC. 30, 1943

Mt.
Talawe

★ BATTLES OF SUICIDE
CREEK & AOGIRI RIDGE
JANUARY 2-11, 1944

further down the beach to establish roadblocks to stop any retreating Japs.

SID PHILLIPS

The monsoon season had just begun. It rained and rained and rained. That summed up New Britain. It rained as soon as we landed, and it rained the whole damn time we were there. Day and night, it rained. It was just a miserable place.

ART PENDLETON

The mud was ankle-deep where we landed. We found an open space to set up our bivouac, a spot our Navy had cleaned out during their shelling. There was still trees standing; however they were barren, like in the middle of a swamp.

The jungle on New Britain was so thick that if you walked a hundred feet off the trail, you would be lost. No question about it. The trails were only wide enough for one person to walk through at a time. Because of the terrain, you could not just walk or move troops where you wanted to. You had to stay on that trail.

SID PHILLIPS

Our job was to block the coastal trail. Really, the trail was nothing more than a footpath cut by the natives that wound up and down the coast.

ART PENDLETON

A ridge overlooked the coastal trail. The ridge was extremely steep and narrow at the top. That's where we set up, with the ocean and the trail to our backs. We only had to worry about what was out in front of us. We didn't block the top of the ridge with barbed wire; we left that open so they would come along the top of the ridge and into our sights. There were footpaths there that led from ridge to ridge.

The foxholes were spaced apart, separated by thick underbrush. That was part of our defense—it's stuff so thick you can't see a person five feet away from you. We had only one gun on the ridge; there wasn't room for more. My squad was probably ten guys with the one machine gun. We had other weapons, too. We didn't have sandbags at our position. We did have a chance to dig a hole and put the gun in place.

Behind our gun position we dug a depression that a couple of guys could lay in. That depression would fill with water, and at nighttime, when you wanted to take a nap, two guys would crawl in that water and their bodies would keep it warm. There was a drawback to that because your skin would all shrink up.

SID PHILLIPS

We expected the Japs to retreat down the trail from the main fight where the division was or to try to get reinforcements up there. Our lines were like a half circle arcing in from the beach. The front lines were up on the hill so we fortified a spot for our mortars behind them, maybe fifty yards in from the beach. We unrolled barbed wire and set up our mortars in the center.

JIM YOUNG

We were right up against the jungle. It was a ridiculous spot. We had a young lieutenant, a new one, and he insisted on overhead cover on the mortar pits with just a little opening for the tube to stick out. The guns were aiming north at the time, up the coast where we expected the enemy to come. I asked the lieutenant, "Suppose they attack from some other way? We can't turn around in a spot like that." He ignored us.

Worse, we heard that the men on the front lines were in hollering distance of each other, not that close together. It was a bad defensive line.

SID PHILLIPS

It was a tricky, spooky situation we were in. A mortar crew has to know what it's doing. As a shell comes out of a mortar, if it hits a tree it would go off and you're dead. The military term for that is "mass clearance," in other words, if you're going to clear everything in front of you. Before you drop a shell into a mortar, you're supposed to flip the top of your site back and look through it, and that will show if you have mass clearance or not. At night, when you were firing in the dark, you needed to have memorized your mass clearance and not go below it.

ART PENDLETON

I strung a strand of barb wire on either side of our gun pit and hung grenades on it. You pulled the pin halfway out and hung the grenade on the barb. Then if someone touched the thing it would fall and go off. The banking was so steep that it would roll down the bank. Usually there would be more enemy coming up the bank, so it would be effective.

That was kind of a dumb thing to do because in the heavy rain—the rain was unbelievably heavy—it would knock those things off sometimes. In the morning, we would have to go out and pick up the grenades and gently push the pin back in. It was not a nice thing to do.

At 1:55 A.M. on December 30, 1943, during monsoon rains and shielded by the crash of thunder, the Japanese would attack, not from the trail but from the east where a land bridge connected the ridges. The ensuing fight would be remembered as the Battle of Coffin Corner.

SID PHILLIPS

The monsoon was wild and howling. The rain was pouring. It was a dark night and you could only see things between flashes of wild lightning. That storm was just raging.

ART PENDLETON

It was a game of wait, wait, and wait. You have plenty of time, you aren't going anywhere. The idea is you stay on guard in order to catch the enemy off guard.

It was raining, so talking was something you didn't do a lot of because it was difficult. You had a helmet on and rain beating on a steel helmet doesn't improve the hearing any. You couldn't see anything. They couldn't see anything either. You can sense it. Don't forget, you're no longer a civilian. You develop senses that you don't think you have. You can tell when someone is close. You were like an animal really. You're in a war area, a place where you can get killed. You have to be on the alert. Again like an animal. You don't even have to speak, all you have to do is touch somebody and they know what you're saying. You're in a whole different world.

The Japs got very close that night. Like I said, the open space I was watching was ahead of me. That would be the obvious place for someone to try to move and that's what happened.

I was at the gun and you could hear them talking. The rain was certainly no help. They weren't aware that we were there.

They were almost close enough to touch you when we opened

fire. They could only come two at a time since there was no room for more on the top of that ridge. Our gun could pump out 250 rounds a minute, so that's a lot of light and a lot of ammunition. You still couldn't see very far, but all you cared about was what was right in front of you. We were firing point-blank into them.

JIM YOUNG

All hell broke loose. Just like I feared, the Japs hit the ridge to the east. So my gun was out of action since we were aiming north.

My group went to another gun and helped them open ammo boxes and load ammunition. The lightning would flash and it was pouring rain, a terrible night, just pouring rain. The sky was full of tracers and the Jap mortars were opening up on us. We fired as fast as we could, getting five rounds into the air before the first one even hit.

SID PHILLIPS

They had given each gunner a flashlight that put out a very dim light that you tried to shield. You could see your sites, but just barely. That night, I was the only one that had a flashlight that worked. The observation post on the hill directed our fire. They had a telephone and would call back to the gun positions. When we would fire, they would observe where the shell would hit and would call back and say, "You're fifty yards too far, drop it in fifty yards closer." They had us bringing in bursts just fifteen yards from our lines.

Talk about sheer terror. You're praying you don't get overrun. You're opening canisters and removing shells during flashes of lightning. You're adding increments to the shells in the dark, just by feel. You're following the range card and checking your sights with a dim flashlight. You know that you're firing just over your buddies' heads and bringing shells down so close they could reach out and catch them.

ART PENDLETON

I would assume there were a lot of Japs. They attacked in several different spots and overran some positions along the ridge. That's where our other guns got involved.

JIM YOUNG

We heard that the Japs were overrunning our machine gun positions. Two of our buddies from the mortar platoon were up the hill on the main line. They were on OP, or observation post duty, when the Japs hit. Dick Carr was in a pit with Sergeant Marty Grogan. They're the ones who would call back and tell us the targets, give us the azimuth [aiming direction], and so forth. Marty was the fellow who married an Australian girl who was hysterical when she saw him leaving.

When the Japs overran our lines, they managed to jump into the pit and knock Marty down. When he fell over, he knocked Dick down, too. The Japs stabbed Marty with their bayonets and killed him, but they didn't touch Dick because Marty's body was over his. Marty's body was bleeding all over him and the blood was dripping on Dick's face, which helped keep him alive because he looked dead.

The Japs set up their own machine gun in the pit and started firing at other Marines. All the while, Dick was there with Marty's body laying on him, afraid to cough or move.

ART PENDLETON

There was a lot of fire coming back at us and grenades. You're down where you could duck and keep the gun going. You have to be careful, though, because that's how John Rivers got killed. You want to shoot in bursts so it makes it very difficult to zero in on you. I was worried all the time.

JIM YOUNG

One of the Japs must have broken through and threw a grenade right down our throats, because all of a sudden a Jap grenade landed in our gun pit. I was just handing ammo to Punchy Legraff when it exploded and took out five of our guys. I was in back of Punchy, who took hits in his face, neck, and arms. Several of the other boys were also hit. Somehow, I wasn't scratched.

In the morning our guys ran the Japs off the hill. When the fighting ceased, it had lasted about five or six hours, but we had won.

ART PENDLETON

There were probably a dozen or more dead Japanese in front of our position. We had stopped them and that's what we were there to do. They just turned around on that ridge and got away as far as they could.

I got wounded, on my leg. A corpsman patched me up.

JIM YOUNG

We could see our wounded being brought down, slipping and falling in the mud. We spotted Dick Carr being helped by two other Marines. They were just dragging him down to the sick bay because he could not use his legs on his own. Carr couldn't walk for a full day, he was that stiff. He was in shock and didn't know me. He just kept staring.

Later, he told me he was breathing so hard under Marty's body he felt for sure the Japs were going to hear him. He was going to risk crawling or moving but decided that would guarantee he'd be killed. So he remained under Marty's body for five hours.*

SID PHILLIPS

I first had the desire to go into medicine that morning on Cape Gloucester. Watching all our wounded being carried in, in the rain, in the mud, and not having a clue what to do to help them. We weren't taught anything but basic first aid to try and stop the bleeding.

When we collected up the range cards—one came in each canister of shells—some of the cards had red lipstick on them. The girls at the ammunition factory had kissed them. Some even wrote notes in lipstick, like "Love you! Betty." It was still raining, but we passed the cards around and kissed the red lip marks.

ART PENDLETON

While on patrol I found an enemy machine gun. It was small and unique. I had never seen anything like it. The gun was made in Czechoslovakia. The way that we figured it had fallen into the hands of the Russians and then into the hands of the Japanese. I was able to take it all apart, clean it up, and put it into my backpack in pieces. After returning to our original area, I went through my pack and discovered that someone had stolen my machine gun. I raised hell about this. An officer came by and said the gun was needed for an investigation. I said to the guys, "Who told the officer that I had this?" They said they didn't know how the word got out. This officer somehow knew and he came and picked it up. That was it. You don't argue with an officer in the USMC.

---

* Jim Young would remember, "Dick Carr died of a brain tumor about ten years after we got back. I think that terrible experience shortened his life, really."

SID PHILLIPS

That was our biggest firefight on Cape Gloucester. The Japs were not there in as much strength as we imagined. Militarily, they didn't have a ghost of a chance. They began evacuating Cape Gloucester and heading east for Rabaul.

We were left to fight the elements. It was the worst jungle. No matter how hard you tried, you could not even get the lay of the land. It never stopped raining. It rained day after day after day, until you thought you would lose your mind. We just bitched and moaned and cursed and groaned.

To the old Marines this was nothing. Nothing was as bad as it was in "the old corps" back in 1927. No outfit was as good as the ones they had been in in the old corps. They were always tougher than you would ever be. They had always seen worse than you would ever see. They were the epitome of everything. Those old Marines would endlessly talk about that. We called it smokestacking. The term was derived from the idea of blowing smoke up our asses (laughs). We would say, "Oh shut up! We're tired of your smoke-stacking. We don't believe any of that shit anyways."

JIM YOUNG

They ordered our battalion to rejoin the main body at Cape Glouces-ter. It was about twenty miles from where we were. We marched to the Cape, finding dead Japs along the trail and a few dead ones hanging from the trees. Snipers harassed us. While on the march, we saw giant bats with faces that looked like foxes. Their wingspan was almost seven feet wide. One of the guys shot one, and the colonel put a stop to that and told us they were harmless and just fruit eaters.

SID PHILLIPS

Every day was gloomy and the jungle was thick, so that jungle became almost as dark as night. I don't remember anything in color in Cape Gloucester; everything is in black-and-white.

One day W. O. Brown and I went roaming about five hundred yards from our bivouac and found an abandoned Japanese hospital tent. All the dead Japs that were in there were reduced to skeletons. They were in uniforms still, with wrapped leggings. Evidently they hadn't had a chance to treat most of them. It was a weird sight. I remember a beautiful microscope sitting on a table.

ART PENDLETON

Once on a patrol we more or less surprised this group of Japanese. I ended up standing less than three feet from a Japanese officer. I had an automatic weapon pointed at his body. We just were staring at each other. I didn't know whether I should shoot him, because he wasn't holding a gun.

Then I saw he was holding a hand grenade to his upper chest with the back of his hand towards me. I just stood there looking at him. It seemed like a long time, but it was probably only seconds. He intended to die. He knew he was going to die and he wanted me to know that. Shooting him was not an option.

As he triggered the hand grenade, I dove out of the way. When the hand grenade exploded it blew all of his body parts on me. I was covered with the blood and stuff.

The others in his group ran and we chased them. We finally eradicated them. These men were starving to death at the time, and we found pieces of dried meat in some of the packs. Then we found a man whose leg pieces had been carved off. They were eating each other.

JIM YOUNG

We joined the rest of the division and set up a camp. Most of the fighting was over for H Company, but the misery had only begun. We were in the midst of monsoon season. From then on it was constant rain and heavy gales. In our outfit we had three men killed and about ten hurt by the storms and falling trees.

ROY GERLACH

Being a cook was not without its dangers. One time, near our camp, we had this big tree. Termites were in the tree. We had a galley set up by then, and we had a corporal by then who was mess sergeant. Well this tree fell apart and crashed on the mess sergeant, right when he was in his hammock. Killed him. He never knew what hit him.

SID PHILLIPS

Everything we owned soon rotted—your clothes, your shoelaces. You couldn't ever get dried out. We all developed all kinds of fungus infections and skin diseases on our extremities. You soon threw away all your socks and underwear. You just lived in your dungaree pants and jacket.

I'd say that the harder a situation got, like on Guadalcanal or New Britain, the more the humor increased, not decreased. We didn't sit down and cry. We cracked jokes about it. There was a lot of joking in spite of all the horror. It went on twenty-four hours a day. Foolishness kept us going.

We saw a bulldozer disappear one day in the mud—they had to throw a line to the driver and haul him, sliding across this pond of mud. That bulldozer went down in this pond of mud with the engine running and the treads turning. The last thing that went down was the exhaust stack. It was still going *pft, pft, pft*, when it finally went under. We laughed at it.

The Marines came to call New Britain "the Green Inferno," after its steamy jungles. To the men of H Company, the island would earn another negative distinction during "Night of the Deluge."

JIM YOUNG

We were issued hammocks with rubber roofs and mosquito-netting sides with zipper entrances. The bottom was also rubber. But the rain was so heavy and the wind so strong that the hammock's "roof" tilted sideways in the wind and the rain came in on you through the mesh sides. We had to cut holes in the bottom to let the rain drain or else we had to lie in six inches of water. There was another drawback: When you zippered up the netting to keep the bugs out, the hammock became a death trap. Jap infiltrators were known to cut the hammock ropes and you would be all tangled and unable to defend yourself.

ROY GERLACH

We set up our galley and we started cooking right away. I never did see any Japanese on Cape Gloucester after they all ran to the hills.

SID PHILLIPS

Les Clark and I were given mess duty, which was undesirable. No Marine wanted to clean up from meals, all that slop. The battalion mess tent was near a small creek that was about twelve feet wide, about one and a half feet deep. Beautiful clear water racing through it. We'd wade into the water with those big Army pots, to clean them.

At night, Les and I couldn't find any more good trees to hang our hammocks from near the mess tent. The cooks had taken all the good spots. So Les and I hung our hammocks on a little ridge, maybe twenty-five yards up from the tent. Japs were no longer a problem. When this unreal, mother of all rainstorms broke on us one night, that little stream turned into a roaring river. The cooks awoke to the water rising up into the hammocks with them. It was pitch-black dark, so they would've drowned if they stayed there. In the dark, they had to climb trees, in order not to drown.

ROY GERLACH

I had the end of my hammock tied onto a tree near a riverbank. In the middle of the night I woke up and my hammock was bouncing up and down. I thought somebody was playing a trick on me. So I rolled over and saw that the water had rose and the stream had washed the dirt away from the tree I'd tied onto. The tree was about ready to go down the stream with my hammock, with me in it. I took my knife and cut the rope my hammock was tied onto. On the ground I got the hell out of that hammock, grabbed my Garand rifle, and scrambled to higher ground. Right as I did that, why, the tree took off and floated down the river.

SID PHILLIPS

When daylight came, Clark and I were high up on our ridge, and no water had gotten to us. We looked down and there were all the rest of the men sitting on limbs of trees, just hanging there, clinging to the trunks of trees, and they were all naked as jaybirds because you slept naked in your hammock at night, since your clothes were wet.

We just burst into tears laughing at them. They'd lost their clothes, their weapons, their hammocks; all the stoves were gone out of the galley, all the food supplies were gone, the mess tent was gone. This wall of water just hit and carried it all downstream. And we wouldn't give them any sympathy. We just laughed at them. The water didn't go down for several hours after daylight, so they were stuck in those trees.

Of course, there was no food for anybody then. The whole battalion went hungry. That wasn't as much fun, but it was so miserable all you could do was laugh about it.

ROY GERLACH

All my gear, the mess tents, and all the cooking equipment washed away, down to the beach. We went and gathered up all the stuff that we could find, pulled up our boots, and started over again. The labels fell off all our cans, so we would open them and separate them by meat, vegetable, or fruit. Then we served it all. The men said it was our best cooking yet and they hoped for another flood soon. That wasn't very nice.

JIM YOUNG

After all that rain I went off by myself to clean my Thompson submachine gun. While doing so, a Marine came by and sat across from me. I had just finished cleaning the gun and was putting the clip in when I tapped the clip to put it in place. The gun fired, grazing the Marine's stomach. Fortunately he recovered in a few days and returned to duty. But I was court-martialed and had to go to trial. The court found that the gun had a faulty sear pin, the reason it had gone off. I was acquitted of all charges. The Marine who was shot said he would never sit in front of a gun again. Needless to say, I was pleased with the verdict.

SID PHILLIPS

We were always wet, always hungry, always dirty, always exhausted, day after day. Weeks went by, and we didn't receive any news from the outside world at all. Then if we did, it might be all just rumors, scuttlebutt. You got so you didn't believe anything. We didn't fear the Japanese by then. Mostly we were just disgusted.

ART PENDLETON

Cape Gloucester was like going to sleep and having a nightmare that wasn't even real. It was way out there. It wasn't even war. You felt like you were sent there to die and that was about the size of it.

On a ship off New Britain's northern coast, R. V. Burgin and the men of K Company, 5th Marines, had been held in reserve. They were called into action after the enemy and the elements proved surprisingly stubborn.

R. V. BURGIN

We didn't go in until New Year's Day, January 1, 1944. We didn't have any resistance at all, because the 1st and 7th Marines had already cleared that out. That first day we moved into the island, while bearing east.

Whenever you're fighting a jungle warfare, it's amazing how close you can get to someone but not be able to see them—enemies as well as your own men. Going through the jungle, you know there's a Marine on your right and your left. But you can't see them. You get to feeling like you're fighting this war alone.

I was a 60mm mortar gunner, but there was no hope of firing the mortars on account of the overhead, the trees and things in the jungle. So we were riflemen, I would say, 75 percent of the time when we were on Gloucester.

We hiked all that afternoon, a few miles, and started to dig in that night. There was a little creek running through there with weeds about waist-high. Everything was pretty quiet for a while. Really tense, though. All of a sudden about fifteen Japs came barreling out of those weeds with their rifles, hollering "Marine, you die!"

You can picture it: a line of enemy soldiers with their rifles in their hands running straight at you. Instead of running like we run, they had a funny fast-paced trot. Leggings. These split-toe shoes. That brownish uniform. That silly looking helmet. That long rifle with mechanical sites. Squint-eyed. Unbelievable determination in his face—like nothing was going to stop him. That was the first time I had ever encountered an enemy soldier.

I was carrying the mortar base plate, so I didn't have any weapon on me except a little .45 pistol. Quick-like I drew it, fired, and killed one Jap—I shot him right through the chest while he was still on the run. Killed him. All around me, other Marines were firing at the enemy and knocked down all but two, who escaped back into the bush. When the firefight was over I thought, *That first Jap got too damn close.* So I picked myself up an M1 rifle and carried that in addition to my pistol. I didn't want one of the enemy ever getting that close to me again if I could help it.

That was the first time I killed a man. I felt relief. I got him and he didn't get me. That was first order of business—to stay alive. To tell you the truth, I was real proud of myself. I did what the Marines had trained me to do—kill the enemy and don't let him kill you. We were put in a situation where you either killed or you were killed. That was the bottom line for us. And me—I preferred to live.

Everything seemed pretty damn scary after that first banzai

charge. That night we moved back up a ridge and dug in. I don't think anyone slept. The land crabs were up there on that ridge and rattling around in the leaves. It was a very nerve-wracking night. You always thought it was the Japs coming for you. But they didn't. Not that night, anyway.

New to island warfare, Burgin and others looked to K Company's 'Canal veterans and Old Breed Marines for leadership, men like Platoon Sergeant T. I. Miller from West Virginia.

T. I. MILLER

Before I went into the Marine Corps, I would never bother nobody, but I worried my parents a whole lot. When you get to around sixteen or seventeen years old, you want to find out who you are. I was pretty independent. Sometimes I would go down there to the railroad tracks and catch me a train and ride down close to Charles Town or Montgomery, West Virginia. Sometimes I would take off and hitchhike down to North Carolina. Just leave and be gone a week. My parents didn't know where I was at so I worried them.

I more or less minded my own business, but occasionally I would get in a fight if someone threatened me. I wasn't one of these bullying kind of guys. But I never was afraid of getting in a fight either. I would stand up and tell them to bring it on.

I'll tell you one thing I did do. I stuck around when my family needed me. I helped my dad get the crops down and stuff like that. When there wasn't any farm work to be done, that's when I did my running. I was a hardworking kid when it was necessary. I never shirked my duties.

I enlisted in the Marine Corps before Pearl Harbor, on September 3, 1940. I was only twenty then but saw the war coming. I liked the looks of the way they did things in the Corps. The Marines were relatively small when I joined. The total strength then was only twenty-five thousand Marines. At the end of the war there were five hundred thousand Marines. I was really one of the first— a bona fide member of the Old Breed.

By the time Pearl Harbor was bombed, I'd already been in the Marines for fifteen months and was a three-stripe sergeant. I fought with K Company on Guadalcanal, the place we nicknamed "the Island of Death." I can't think of any good times we had there. Only the nasty stuff sticks in my mind. Like the Goettge patrol.

We went looking for the Goettge patrol just days after they were lost. We went out with only a reinforced platoon, about forty men. A. L. "Scoop" Adams was our platoon leader. He had orders to see if he could find any remains of the Goettge patrol. We were not to engage in any firefights unless we were fired upon.

We reached the beach where the ambush supposedly happened. There was a sandspit out there. It was low tide so we walked out to it. Only a few of us went across to the sandspit. That's where we came upon the body parts. They were not decomposed at all. There was a head bobbing in the surf. That head was still in the helmet. When the waves would come in, they would pick it up, and down, up and down, all the time we were there. Then there was a shirt that didn't have no head, no arms, no legs—it was just a torso. The Japs cut all the appendages off. A leg was laying there with the boot still on. I asked Scoop, "Do we bury these Marines or just leave them here?" He replied, "My orders are, whatever we find, leave it there and come back and make a report." That was it. What he reported, I don't know if it ever showed up in a report or not. But we all got to know our enemy really well that day.

When I first got to New Britain, I had a little old Reising gun. I didn't think much of it since it was about as useless as tits on a boar hog. They manufactured that little gun where the climate was dry. When they brought it to the humidity of those jungles, every time you fired that thing the mechanism would jam back on the wood since it swelled up. You would have to take your knife out and whittle down the wood to release it. We had to constantly work on that thing to get it to operate. Soon after we landed, me and another fellow were walking on a trail near the ocean. There was a jeep parked. We got to looking and there wasn't anyone in it, but there was a Thompson submachine gun in it, with one of those drum-type magazines. I sneaked up and took it. I put that Reising gun in its place and took off into that jungle. That's how I got my Thompson. But I didn't have any extra ammo for it, but I held on to it since somebody had to give an account of that weapon (laughs).

The next morning we got in a firefight with the 7th Marines, and they wounded one of our men before we got it stopped. Everybody was edgy, and the left hand didn't know what the right hand was doing.

K Company approached a twenty-foot-wide creek with swift-flowing water. One of the first to reach the water was K Company scout Jim Anderson, a new Marine in his first campaign.

JIM ANDERSON

I was the second scout in K Company's 3rd platoon. I carried an M1 Garand rifle. Being a scout was pretty dangerous because you were the first to run into problems. I think I got that job because they knew I would take it. It was my nature to try to get along with everybody—the noncoms, the officers, everyone.

I wouldn't say I ever developed a mean streak in the Marines. I couldn't figure out why they had to be so aggressive or mean to a person in boot camp. The other thing I couldn't figure out was why there had to be so much terrible swearing, every other word. A lot of it was not necessary. Now, somebody like Burgin, I never heard him utter a swear word in his life. I think it came from the guys who were trying to impress their friends or act tough when they were really scared.

All that roughness offended me because I wasn't accustomed to it. I came from a pretty average life. We lived on a farm in Wisconsin. My folks had me go to Sunday school. In high school I played a little basketball and some football, but I wasn't terribly athletic. I enjoyed hunting, but I wouldn't say I was a good shot. We were in good fishing country, but I wasn't terribly enthusiastic about fishing. I won't even talk about how I was with the girls (laughs). But I was a strong farmhand. During the summer, they were raising peas around my home, so I got a job working as a pea viner. Tending boxes and carrying peas, I made good money and I followed orders well.

As Anderson and K Company prepared to cross the creek, Japanese snipers struck and the opposite bank erupted with fire. "It's salted with pillboxes!" a Marine shouted. The swift waters would earn a name that day: "Suicide Creek."

JIM ANDERSON

My first experience in combat was brief and violent. The creek wasn't too wide or too deep that we couldn't wade through it—the fire was just so heavy. As we were moving through the jungle along the bank, trying to find a crossing, a machine gun cut loose. The fellow ahead of me stood up, and *rat-a-tat-tat*, he fell over. I crawled up to where he was lying. I looked at the fellow. He had three or four bullet holes in him. He was dead.

The machine gun was still working. Rifles were still firing. Mortars were falling. It grew heavier and heavier. If I was a little bit smarter about combat, I would have known better than to do this, but I stood up, and of course the same machine gun cut loose, *rat-a-tat-tat*. It felt like a baseball bat hit me in the left side.

Two of the bullets pierced my left side. Others hit my cartridge belt. I knew right away I was badly wounded. I fell over and tried to crawl to the rear. I left all my equipment right there—my rifle, everything. Mortars were exploding on my left and right. I got maybe twenty feet back and stopped to rest or pass out, I'm still not sure. Pretty soon a mortar shell lit up about fifteen feet away from me and put a lot of shrapnel in my left leg. At the same time, a sniper was firing at me. He was missing me by only a foot or so every time he shot. I knew I was a dead man unless I moved.

I kept going and crawled up a hill that was behind our side of the creek. Two corpsmen found me and patched up my leg. They rolled me into a stretcher and carried me to an amphibious tractor [amtrac]. An amtrac had tracks like a tank and a hull like a boat. It could drive on land or swim in the sea. They put me on board and took me back to the beach.

R. V. BURGIN

We had a hell of a fight. The Japs were all dug in along the other side of this creek, maybe twenty feet wide with steep banks, and anytime any of our men tried to cross the creek to flank them, they mowed us down. A lot of good men were lost there. The Japs were really dug in. Really hard to see them in the thick jungle.

T. I. MILLER

We held on to our position, close to the banks. A little later on, our platoons got all mingled up. I was the platoon sergeant of the third platoon at that time, but somehow the commander of Second Platoon, a man named Dykstra, he and I ended up behind the same log. While we were there, he got his elbow shot in two. I only had one compress left on my belt. So I put that on him there. I wrapped it up as best I could. I took two or three little pieces of timber, I took my mosquito net off my helmet, and tied that around the splint. The corpsman came and got him after that. He was in some pain, but he never did say anything.*

R. V. BURGIN

Someone had set up a five-gallon can of water with a canteen cup on it. In a lull during the fight, I stepped down there and poured me a canteen of water and drank it. Jim Burke decided he wanted a drink, too, but just as he reached for the cup, a Jap shot the cup out from under him. Jim took about three steps back, turned to me, grinned, and said, "I don't think I'm that damn thirsty."

Whoever had taken a shot at us was up somewhere in the trees. Jim and I fired several rounds into the trees, but we never hit anything, so I called for a machine gunner and told him to rake the trees over to get the sniper. He took that .30-caliber machine gun and raked the trees. Bits of leaves and branches showered down. Then the Jap fell about halfway out and jerked to a stop twenty feet aboveground. He had tied himself to the tree with a rope around his waist and the rope around his rifle. We left the body there swinging.

T. I. MILLER

There was one guy named Ray Newcolmb; he was a redheaded boy from Tennessee. The last time I saw him they were carrying him down through the jungle there. He had his kneecap shot off. He saw me and hollered, "So long, T.I., I'm headed for Tennessee!"†

---

* T. I. Miller would remember, "Later on, I ran into him down in Camp Lejeune, and I noticed that his elbow was still crooked. He never did get it straightened out."

† T. I. Miller would remember, "Never did see him again. Tried to find him and couldn't. If anyone knows where Ray is, let me know."

R. V. BURGIN

Finally three Sherman tanks showed up and stopped at the edge of the creek. But the banks were too high, so a bulldozer came forward to cut out the banks on both sides of the creek so the tanks could make it across. A sniper shot the bulldozer driver. Another Marine jumped in the driver's seat, and the sniper got him, too. A third Marine jumped on the bulldozer, ducked down behind the controls, and got the job done. The tanks crossed the creek and the Japs pulled back.

K Company settled in for the evening on the American side of the creek. K Company's commanding officer, Captain Andrew Haldane, dug in with them.

T. I. MILLER

Some people called Haldane "Ack Ack," but I called him "Close Crop" 'cause he had his hair cut real close! The way I would sum up Haldane was that he had a quality about him, a sort of calming effect on people. He didn't go off half-cocked. Haldane called me "T.I.," which stood for my name, "Thurman Irving Miller." Everybody called me T.I. We definitely did not call an officer or a noncom by their rank while we were in combat.

We were busy digging in on our side of Suicide Creek and thought we were relatively out of the line of fire. All of a sudden a group banzai charge of twenty Japs attacked Haldane and the guys around him at the company CP. When you're digging in, you don't always have your weapon at your disposal. It's laying on its side, nearby. The Japs just ran in and tried to overrun that position. I was on down the line a little further from them with my platoon.

They barely had time to reach their weapons. Haldane rushed into the Japs, shooting his pistol as he ran. The others grabbed some weapons—rifles with bayonets, shovels, anything—and wiped out the banzai charge in some close-quarter fighting.

R. V. BURGIN

Captain Haldane was a real leader. He was well built, about five-eleven, and weighed about 180 pounds. From Massachusetts. He played football for Bowdoin College in Maine. Never heard him raise his voice, not one time, to anybody. He was a compassionate man yet a disciplined man. Whenever he spoke, you listened. He treated you like he wanted to be treated and never threw his weight around. He had the respect of every man in the company.

Meanwhile, on the beach . . .

JIM ANDERSON

They carried me onto a LST ship [landing ship, tank]. By then, my stretcher was filling up with blood. I said, "Something's the matter here—I'm still bleeding!" A medic looked at me and said, "Oh my goodness, it's running out your stomach!" Well, they doctored me up more on that LST.

From there I was taken to New Guinea, where they put me in an Army hospital, made out of tents. All I owned was the clothes on my back, and there at the hospital they cut them off and threw them away. That first evening they operated on my stomach. They took a couple of bullets out of me. The next day they operated on my leg. Later, they told me that the bullets had hit my cartridge belt and glanced off into my side.

Meanwhile, K Company crossed Suicide Creek and continued inland . . .

R. V. BURGIN

We began to move again. It was all thick jungle. Too thick to even think about using the mortars. Wet. Muddy. Lots of rain. Impossible to see anything. We moved forward a bit and had a firefight. Then they'd withdraw, and we'd catch up to them again and have another fight. We could never see the Japs until they opened up on us. You never know when the enemy's right next to you. Everybody was nervous.

Night was no better. That small plane called "Washing Machine Charlie" or "Piss Call Charlie" would come over every night and drop a hundred-pound bomb on us, at about two o'clock. One night his bomb hit within our lines, and a piece of shrapnel hit the guy who shared a foxhole with Jim Burke that night. I remember Jim hollering for a corpsman. Just a second or two later he hollered "Corpsman!" again. A second or two later he hollered "Corpsman!" again. He knew that guy had been hit bad. Then he hollered it again. It only took the corpsman a minute to reach him, but Jim said it felt like ten minutes. That was the only time in my whole Marine Corps experience with Jim Burke that I ever saw him, the coolest Marine there ever was, really frustrated. The guy in his foxhole ended up dying later.

On January 8, K Company halted when the jungle began titling upward. They had hit a ridge, two hundred yards wide, with a gentle slope. K Company began climbing. Suddenly, a battalion of Japanese troops opened fire from fortifications above. "It was like all the seams of hell busted open," a Marine would remember.

T. I. MILLER

Aogiri Ridge. Nobody knew that thing existed because it didn't show up on the maps. In the final analysis, it proved one of the

Japanese main strongholds because it overlooked their supply trail. They had mortars on the reverse slope. They also had bunkers built at the top of that ridge that could fire straight down. We were going up and there was a terrible lot of fire coming down at us.

We knew getting up there would take something special.

R. V. BURGIN

Our tanks couldn't get near the ridge. We couldn't bring in our artillery either because the jungle was so thick the shells would hit a tree and explode before they hit the ground. So Gunnery Sergeant Elmo "Pop" Haney said, "I'm going to get something to help," and he ended up getting a 37mm cannon on two small wheels.

We called him "Pop" Haney, because he was forty-nine years old. Anyone in his forties in the Marine Corps was considered an old man. He had fought in WWI and then in WWII on Guadalcanal. He was about five foot eleven inches and skinny but tough.

A funny thing about Pop Haney was that he didn't have an assignment. He wasn't assigned to any platoon. He did not have a job. He was just there. That was it. They let him come in and stay. They'd send him to a base back home, and he'd go AWOL and catch a freighter, come back to the Pacific, and work his way back to us. So they just put up with him, I guess.

T. I. MILLER

I didn't see the cannon coming up the road, but I heard it coming. The pulled it by bulldozer on a corduroy road, which was nothing but a whole lot of logs laid across the mud. They did this for as far as they could get it. Then they pushed it by hand to the foot of the ridge.

The first time I laid eyes on Colonel Walt he was behind that 37mm gun. The day before our battalion commander had been shot, and his replacement was Lieutenant Colonel Lewis Walt. The cannon was his idea and he was behind it, pushing it up the hill with some other Marines. I was approximately ten feet away when a guy got hit, shot off the cannon. So I took his place. I joined them in pushing it a little ways then I got too far from my platoon so I rejoined them.

R. V. BURGIN

It had rained so much the ground was just oatmeal. We had to push that damn cannon up. Five or six of us would trade off, scraping and sliding up that hill. The Japs opened up on us every once in a while. The gun's got about a quarter-inch steel shield that goes into a V where the gunner can get behind it. That shield was a lifesaver. They were bouncing them bullets right off it. It sounded similar to hail on a tin roof. It wasn't a good sound. You knew that if it wasn't for that shield you would be a goner.

T. I. MILLER

Walt and the others went on pushing it. They came to this big log that had been blown down and needed a real extra shove to get over it. They managed to get some 37mm antipersonnel ammunition up there, shells full of nuts, bolts, glass, and whatever they could cram in it. Seeing what that 37mm could accomplish boosted our confidence. You knew you had something that could destroy the enemy if you caught him.

They would fire off a shot and it literally blasted the jungle away. The shells cut all the bushes down in front of the gun. Then they would push it up as far as they could and do it again. It sounded like a twelve-gauge shotgun, only magnified some. That's how we got it to the top. We were less than a hundred yards from the summit, and it took us three days to take it.

R. V. BURGIN

At the top of the ridgeline I fired the gun. That was the only reward. We knocked out a machine gun nest.

We were exhausted on top of that ridge. We could hear the Japanese in front of us as we were digging in. They were only about a dozen yards away. After it became dark, they started yelling. You could just see their silhouettes. "Raider, Raider," they called. "Why you no fire, Raider? Why you no shoot?" Raider was our machine gun sergeant. Evidently, they'd been close enough to us where they'd heard us saying his name. So they were just taunting him. We were that close. Raider told his gunner, "Give him a short burst of about two hundred rounds." He fired in the direction of the taunting. We didn't hear them call to Raider after that.

T. I. MILLER

Night came. We dug in where we were. They put some guys in front of the 37mm with three .50-caliber machine guns to protect it. Our guys camouflaged that gun as best as they could. We knew the Japanese would try their best to get through to that 37mm. They knew if they could get that gun they had the battle won.

We hadn't had any sleep for two or three nights. You would grab a few little winks here and there. You never knew what was in front of you. They would come any time, day or night. That was the night of all the banzai charges. We were down below the summit several yards. We could look up and see the silhouettes of them coming down.

R. V. BURGIN

About 4 A.M., they came screaming at us. I was in a foxhole with Jim Burke when the Japs charged. They were hollering, "Marine, you die! Marine, you die!"

One Jap charged right into my foxhole. I stuck my bayonet into his chest just as he was leaving his feet, heaved him right over my shoulder, and pulled the trigger, emptying my M1 into him. He was very dead when he hit the ground—I'll tell you that. It all didn't take but just a few seconds. I kicked him out of the way and didn't give him another thought. I just got ready for whatever might come next.

After that first charge, things died down and there was silence. It was raining slightly. Just enough to make things miserable.

Then they charged again.

And again.

They kept charging and charging that night. You're not think-ing. You just try to get your sites on a man and get him down. That was all that was going through my mind—*Kill that bastard! Don't miss! Make sure you get him!* I think most of us were wondering, *My God, how many times are we going to need to do this?! For crying out loud, how many of them are out there?*

T. I. MILLER

I had just picked up an M1 off some wounded man and was firing that. My Thompson was out of ammunition, but I kept it. Why I held on to it I don't know.

In between attacks I spent quite a bit of time crawling along and checking up on my men. I would crawl along and see who was missing. Our guys were about out of ammunition after the third banzai charge, so I made a trip down to the company CP. There a gunnery sergeant named Manihan loaded my shoulders with three or four bandoliers for my men. I made that trip down and back up, real quick.

I'll tell you one thing I saw that I'll never forget. I saw our pla-toon leader, Tully, a lieutenant, raise up a big rock. It was about eighteen inches in diameter. The kind you couldn't kick out of the way. He took his wedding ring off his finger. He looked at me and said, "T.I, I'm putting my wedding ring under here. I don't want those yellow bastards getting it off my finger if I get killed." And he hid that ring under that big flat rock. Tully was a good guy, real easygoing. He had just been married.

Dawn began to show on the horizon. The Marines on the summit had withstood four banzai charges. But at 6:15 A.M. they could hear the enemy preparing for a fifth charge.

T. I. MILLER

We were again almost out of ammunition. Out of gas and running on fumes. It was desperation. I told my men to hang in there. I told them to do their best, keep their heads down. I didn't bother telling them to kill the enemy because that was a given (laughs).

While this was happening, Gunnery Sergeant Pop Haney was in the company CP. They put him in charge of getting the ammunition up to us. I had known Pop Haney since he was in my platoon down in Guantánamo Bay. Back then he was a platoon sergeant and I was just a plain sergeant. He was about the most "GI" Marine around. A real Government Issue Marine. I don't think anybody ever called him that to his face though. Had I called him that to his face I would have probably got a lopsided grin from him.

He always kept his equipment up to par. He tried to do everything by the book. He never did talk about his time in the First World War, at Belleau Wood, besides saying that it was "pretty rough." When he addressed anybody in the platoon, he never ever used first name. He would say "Corporal Jones." I was "Sergeant Miller" to him, never T.I.

Haney came through that night. He and his men brought that ammo up to us right in time. They got it distributed about four minutes before that last banzai. The Japanese soldiers in the last banzai charge had been held on reserve on the opposite slope of that ridge. They were fresh troops, supposedly crack troops—Imperial Marines, who had captured our boys at Bataan. We were locked and loaded for them.

R. V. BURGIN

We defeated all five banzai charges that night. In the morning there were more than two hundred dead Japs in front of us. You could literally walk on them without stepping on the ground.

We found two of our men, Robert McCarthy and Lonnie Howard, had been killed that night when a short round of artillery hit a tree and exploded. It was our own artillery. Strangely enough, Lonnie had said to me that afternoon, "Burgin, if anything happens to me, I want you to have my watch."

"You're crazy," I told him. "Nothing will happen to you. You'll be okay."

"No, I'm serious," he said. "I want you to have my watch."

He got killed that night. The corpsmen came and got his body and moved him to the cemetery. I have no idea what came of his watch.

T. I. MILLER

The next morning our company clerk came running over to me and said, "Tully got it last night." Besides a wife, I believe he also had one child that he left behind. To this day, I've always wondered why I didn't get his ring out from under that rock. I would imagine that ring is still on top of that ridge today.

Having won the Battle of Aogiri Ridge, the Marines occupied the high ground.

R. V. BURGIN

The second night on the ridge, Jim Burke and I were moved down to the very end of the line, so there were no other Marines on our right. We were it. It's an unnerving feeling to not have any support next to you.

That was an eventful night, too. Jim and I set to work digging our new foxhole. One man stands guard while the other digs, then they trade off. Jim was digging, throwing the dirt in front of us to make a little mound, and I was on guard. Now, you're not supposed to get out of your foxhole for anything. We'd all been told this. But through the underbrush, I could just make out the shape of someone crawling toward us on his belly. Quietly I reached over, put my hand on Jim's helmet, pushed him down, and pointed toward the shape with my .45. The shape crawled up so close to me, I could nearly reach out and touch him. My pistol was within twenty-four inches of his forehead before I saw the silhouette of his helmet and recognized him as a Marine. He had to get that close.

It didn't scare me. But I guarantee you that if I'd shot him in the head with my .45, he wouldn't have moved ever again. It made me madder than hell that a man could be that stupid—or desperate maybe. I let the man speak first.

"Burgin," he said, "you got any water. I'm thirsty as hell."

It was Oswalt, another new guy.* "Yeah," I said, and gave him my canteen. He drank some, then I told him, "Oswalt, you keep your ass in that foxhole. If you get out again, I'll shoot you on general principles."

Later that same night on the ridge, in the hours of darkness, I could just make out another black shape sneaking through the trees.

---

* R. V. Burgin would remember, "Oswalt got killed later on Peleliu while going across the airfield. He was a fine Marine, but I was sure mad at him that night on the ridge."

The shape got close enough to where I saw a man's silhouette. This was no Marine. I figured he was a lone Japanese scout, trying to get behind our line. I shot and killed him with my M1.

T. I. MILLER

When that battle was over, they brought a platoon up to replace my platoon. I don't even know what unit they were from. At this point I was essentially the platoon commander. The lieutenant who was going to replace my platoon told me, "Well, I guess I better do this a squad at a time." He was thinking he would send twelve of his men up, then I would send twelve of mine down, and we'd do that three times.

I told him, "If you just bring one squad you can replace my whole platoon." Out of the forty-two or so men in my platoon we were down to thirteen men including myself. Some had died. Most of them had been wounded and taken off the line. Taking that ridge was about the worst fight I was ever in. We renamed the place "Walt's Ridge."

After we took Walt's Ridge, we were sent back to the beach and put in reserve. We were out of danger there and recovering the best we could. There was hardly anybody left in K Company. New Britain, in some ways, was worse than Guadalcanal. There were 242 enlisted men and 10 officers in our company when we went ashore. Ten days later, our ranks had been reduced to 88 enlisted men and 2 officers.

R. V. BURGIN

It's hard for people today to fully understand what exactly we were up against in the war in the Pacific. A sense of duty drives you more than anything else, sure. But anger factors in as well, and that anger grows. As the war progressed, I saw the brutality of what the Japanese soldiers did to some of our troops who they captured, and it makes a man angry, very angry. I saw our men with their testicles and penis cut out and stuffed in their mouth. I saw one of our men tied to a tree and used for bayonet practice. He had been stuck through thirty to forty times in the chest all the way up to his head. It was obvious that the Japs had not simply killed him, but had used his body that way. They were a brutal, sadistic enemy.

I believe I'll hate the Jap soldiers for as long as I live. In recent years I've been to Japan, and I don't hold any grudges against the Japanese people. But the Japanese soldier—I hate him. My wife talked to me a while back and said, "You think you should still be calling them Japs?" And I said, "I don't give a damn if it's proper or not. To me, he's a damn Jap then, and he's still a damn Jap. I'm talking about the soldier. And as long as I live I'll hate him."

CHAPTER SIX

MISERY

New Britain

On the coast, K Company rested and tried to recuperate in spite of the island's elements.

T. I. MILLER

Each morning while we were in reserve, when I got out of my hammock, I was covered with this strange pink stuff. This went on for a few days. I didn't know what the pink stuff was. I went all through my pack and hammock. Out crawled a huge jungle spider. The pink stuff was the spider's web.

R. V. BURGIN

During the monsoon season it rained and it rained, and if you weren't wet from the rain, you'd have your poncho on and be wet from sweat. It sometimes rained thirty-four inches in twenty-four hours.

A lot of guys went down with malaria, dysentery, and jungle rot. Jungle rot looked like little yellow pustules on your skin, each blister about the size of a match head. They'd show up under your arms, on your legs, your ankles, around your crotch, anywhere your skin came into close contact with your clothes. We all had it. That stuff ate us alive. Corpsmen would put a purple medication on them. It would clear up, but then be back again in a week.

T. I. MILLER

That Washing Machine Charlie would buzz around at night, and a lot of times we wouldn't even bother to get out of our hammocks. One night he dropped a bomb, and a piece of that bomb, a rivet, it hit the ground under my hammock and was still hot enough that it bounced and burned a hole through the hammock, through my jacket, and into my skin. So my buddy—Jack Windgate from Florida—I had him run his hand down the back of my jacket to see if he could find a hole in my back. He put his hand down there and jerked it right back out. He said, "Hellfire, T.I.! That thing burned my hand!"

The rivet fell out of my back when he done that. I should have kept that rivet (laughs). Jack always did think I got a Purple Heart from that, but I didn't even go to sick bay for it. He always kidded me, "Why didn't they give me a Purple Heart? I burnt my hand!"

JIM ANDERSON

I was in the hospital about a month and a half. Then they discharged me. They gave me all they had—Army clothes, which was a little of an insult to a Marine.

I hitchhiked by LST back to Cape Gloucester, to my outfit. They don't always send you back to your same company, but I was going to be certain I got back to my company. Everyone thought I was crazy for hurrying back.

Meanwhile, in early February, D Company and the 7th Marines prepared to move south through the center of New Britain to pursue
the retreating Japanese . . .

RICHARD GREER

New Britain wasn't a place fit for a fight. They had four hundred
inches of rainfall a year. Your shoes would rot off your feet in a
month. The sling would rot off your rifle in a month and a half. It
was the biggest damn mess I ever saw in my life. Mud up over your
knees. Water over your jeep's hood. It flooded all the time. Just
impossible conditions.

If you were with Chesty Puller, man, you sure got your share of
combat. That Louie Puller was something else. Puller volunteered
us for every damn mission there was. The biggest thing I was in on
was called the "Puller Patrol." Puller had recently been promoted to
executive officer (second in command) of the 7th Marines. He
gathered everybody and their brother, close to four hundred men.
He took everybody that wasn't on the line shooting and said, "Come
on, boy, get your rifle, we're going hunting." We went out in the
boondocks and went after the Japs wholesale.

He had been practicing for that moment for heaven knows how
long. He always talked about when he was growing up and everybody around him was some old man who had been in the Confed-
erate War. He lived for that stuff. Hell, I had been on many a damn
practice maneuver when he was practicing combat patrols. I can
hear him now, "A combat patrol is a patrol that goes out and kills
every damn thing in its way." Puller was bigger than life, I don't
think many people will argue with that.

There was two ways for the Japs to escape across New Britain to
Rabaul in the northeast: the north coastal road and the south road.
We went south, and on those trails we found them.

We just raised hell and killed everything in our path. It was a fearsome thing to be with hundreds of Marines being jacked up by Puller to slaughter everything in your path. He was always up front.

If someone got bogged down with the Japanese, they would call somebody in the weapons company to come up and bring a machine gun. Our first platoon would go off and assist A Company, the second would assist B Company, and so on. They would do some firing, we'd break through, and go on farther. We were so thick in the weeds they had to supply us by air, from Piper Cubs and B-17s.

I never knew whether Puller was being a wildcat or not in inventing that patrol. I always thought he had nothing to do so he grabbed all those Marines and took us out there. When we ran the Japs down and eliminated them, they were already starving to death. They were a sad-looking bunch. They weren't able to fight, but they were still fighting when they should just have surrendered. The jungle got as many of them as we did. It was the wettest, stinking-est place I ever saw. They were on the run from our patrol and damn few of them escaped.

Having returned to fighting strength, in March, K Company boarded a ship and sailed eastward along the coast of New Britain to the Talasea Peninsula. A strange terrain of volcanic mountains and vacant coconut plantations, Talasea lay along the northern trail to Rabaul. There, K Company landed to mop up stragglers left behind during the Japanese retreat.

T. I. MILLER

We took off from the beach area and marched on up toward Rabaul. I know one time they told us they were going to send some air support. One day a little Piper Cub spotter plane flew over and everybody was laughing about it and saying, "So much for our Air Force!" The Japs were retreating. We would find their supply depots more than anything. We destroyed many of their rifles, sometimes in the crates with Cosmoline grease.

R. V. BURGIN

The Japs had set up booby traps. You'd hike toward them and they'd ambush you. They'd get you when you walked into their sights. Then they'd retreat and set up further down the road in the jungle. Then you'd have to do the same thing again.

We got smart and went out on patrol with a war dog. We'd sneak up on those little lean-tos where the Jap soldiers were sleeping. The first time we went out on patrol, we figured we'd be nice and captured three of them and took them back to battalion headquarters. We checked on them the next day, and hell, the military had given them all new socks, shoes, underwear, caps, and dungarees—the works. We'd been wearing the same rotting clothes for over a month. We thought, *To hell with this*. After we saw that, we didn't take any more prisoners.

Sometimes we'd go out on patrols, and they'd be lying in there in those huts, and we'd go in both ends at the same time and bayonet or knife them. We didn't want to shoot them for fear the sound would alert other enemy soldiers in the vicinity. The war dogs could put us right on them, right where they were at.

JIM ANDERSON

At Talasea I was still on light duty because my wounds were not fully healed. I didn't see too much fighting up there. The others got in some firefights. It wasn't heavy fighting, but they ran into occasional snipers. Incidentally, I was in the company CP on light duty.

That's when I first met Captain Haldane. My job was, frankly, nothing (laughs). I spent most of my days in my bunk. One of my buddies would even go to the chow line and bring my food to me.

R. V. BURGIN

After you get into fighting, day after day, it's like a football player or basketball player or a boxer at the beginning of a game. You're nervous. The adrenaline is really flowing. But then you get going and get into the first round, and after the first few minutes you just buckle down. You control your fears and do your job. That's what we did, day after day after day.

Sure, there was still fear. Sure, I prayed. I'd pray to see Florence again. I grew up going to church and Sunday school and had all the faith in God in the world. But the way I figured it was that God had a lot of people to take care of, so I never wanted to bore him with any long prayers. I just always said, "God, my life is in your hands. Take care of me." I used that same prayer all the way through the war.

I certainly never had any pity parties, crying out to God about all the trouble that came our way. You just do your damn job and let things fall where they fall. That's what you've always got to remember. You've always got a job to do. You're there to fight a war, and you're there to get rid of the enemy. That was the business we were in.

T. I. MILLER

At Talasea I was still the platoon sergeant, in charge of K Company's Third Platoon. A platoon sergeant's job was to assist the platoon leader in keeping track of this, that, and the other thing. We got a new platoon leader to replace Tully, a lieutenant named Bill Bauerschmidt.

He was kind of green. It seemed that he had an attitude that he didn't want to be seen like the rest of us. He wanted to look like an officer. I took it on myself to warn him to take his lieutenant's bars off. If the Japanese would eye somebody with rank, he would automatically become a target. It wasn't very long until his bars disappeared.

We were on this patrol on Talasea, and we came to a place where there was a stream of water coming right off the mountain. You know, how they form a pool? Bauerschmidt told all the men to come up and fill their canteens, but they just stood there. We were all single file, and they all looked at me. All I did was hold my hand up with two fingers, and they knew I meant "two at a time." I explained to Bauerschmidt that if that whole platoon had congregated at that pool a grenade could have knocked them all out. After I did that, the men just came up two at a time and filled up their canteens until everybody had their canteens full and we went on about our business. Bauerschmidt was okay with it. He was learning.

R. V. BURGIN

New Britain never let up on us. Month after month it rained. The heels of my boots broke down. Both little toenails of mine rotted right off. We never got a change of clothes. The only time we ever got clean clothes was when we'd wade out in a stream or the ocean, wash them ourselves, and put our same clothes right back on again.

You'd get so exhausted you'd lie down in your foxhole to sleep at night and wake up the next morning in a coffin of water; the water would be up to damn near your chin. You'd be lying there in a puddle of deep mud and filthy water, but you'd be so damn tired it wouldn't wake you. It was like lying in a muddy bathtub with your head out of the water and your clothes on. Imagine doing that for a month or two.

T. I. MILLER

A boy in my platoon was named John Teskevich. He had a big mustache and was always cutting up and carrying on. We found out a general was going to patrol our front lines. We were set up on the edge of an extinct volcanic crater. Almost perpendicular ran a stream—it was only about two foot wide. Teskevich got himself a pole and put a string on it. He was sitting there fishing when the general came by. He thought it might have got him a Section 8 psycho discharge. But the general just walked by, looked at Teskevich, and said, "You catching any, son?" And went about his patrol. Teskevich threw his pole into the bushes and said, "The hell with this!"*

In May 1944, having driven the Japanese back to Rabaul, K Company and the 1st Marine Division prepared to leave New Britain.

R. V. BURGIN

While we waited to leave, we stayed at an abandoned mission on a hill overlooking a peaceful bay. We would swim and fish there. We ate hot food there for the first time—ham, potatoes, and cabbage.

We ran across some artesian wells. The water was warm. We all got in there and took hot baths. That was the first time we'd felt clean since Melbourne. We'd worn the same clothes the whole time. Everybody was in sorry shape. We all had red rashes from

---

* Jim Anderson was good friends with Teskevich and would remember, "Everybody in the company knew Teskevich. He was a very jolly fellow, with a mustache. We considered him an old-time Marine because he had been in before the war. On Peleliu, a sniper shot him as he was riding a tank up the west road. They took him off the tank, but he was gut shot and died in a ditch along the road."

jungle rot. A lot of men had "the shits." Others had severe fevers and chills from malaria. But we were alive.

In the Battle for Cape Gloucester, the division lost 1,347 men. In our company, 21 men got killed. We were there from January through the first part of May. That's four months of fighting in the jungle. I lost forty pounds in those four months. I'd say we stayed wet 80 percent of the time we were on that damn island.

T. I. MILLER

They put us in reserve again on the coast. I had a Japanese flag and I traded that for a .45 automatic pistol. Then I traded the .45 automatic for a .38 Colt revolver with a cutaway holster. Down there we didn't wear any clothes. All we had were shoes, what was left of them; most of the time we'd just run around in our skivvies. We would twirl them up and make them look sort of like a bikini. I put that belt carrying the .38 revolver around my waist, slung it down on the hip, and wore a big old pith helmet. Imagine the look of that.

ART PENDLETON

When we were on the beach, waiting to leave, the Japanese were lobbing some artillery on us, some pretty heavy shells. They must have still had a gun out in the jungle.

The shells were falling way too close for comfort when we were about to leave that place. One of the shells hit a DUKW amphibious vehicle and sank it. The guys all got killed.

We had some Japanese prisoners there on the beach. During this shelling, one of the guys who was standing guard told a Jap, "This is your chance, jump over that fence and get the hell out of here!" So the Jap did and the guard shot him dead.

Hell, that's nothing. When the Japs were in China, they were throwing babies in the air and catching them on bayonets, you know.

T. I. MILLER

In our last day on Gloucester, Captain Haldane came and told me my promotion had come through for gunny sergeant. Then he asked me, "T.I., would you care to keep your platoon for the rest of the campaign?" He didn't order me, he asked me. He knew I was familiar with the men in my platoon, and bringing a new guy in would create problems. That tells you a lot about the man, Haldane.

RICHARD GREER

We learned we weren't going after Rabaul. Instead, we left the Japs up there to rot. Cut them off with airpower and Navy. We never had to invade Rabaul. We felt pretty damn good about that. We knew how strongly fortified Rabaul was.

ART PENDLETON

The whole campaign was for nothing. We didn't accomplish a thing. We lost hundreds of men and it ended up being useless, as far as I know.

R. V. BURGIN

The rumor floating around was that we were heading back to Melbourne, Australia. That sounded good to me. More than anything else, I hoped to see Florence again.

Well, Melbourne didn't happen. I'll tell you that much.

CHAPTER SEVEN

THE HELLHOLE

★ ★ ★

Pavuvu

After three days of sailing, on May 5, 1944, the 1st Marine Division landed on Pavuvu, an eight-mile-wide island northwest of Guadalcanal. To sixteen thousand Marines, Pavuvu would be "home" for the next four months. The island would prove an unforgettable place.

SID PHILLIPS

I remember loading aboard a ship to leave New Britain. We had all figured we were going to go somewhere great, like back to Australia, and we kept that rumor going. Back to Melbourne! I don't remember anything about that trip, but I remember feeling intense disappointment about where we landed.

T. I. MILLER

Anybody who's been to Pavuvu will never forget it. A bunch of brass flew over the island, and all they did was look down and see how pretty it was, so they figured it would make a good place for the 1st Division to rest and recuperate. Boy, were they wrong.

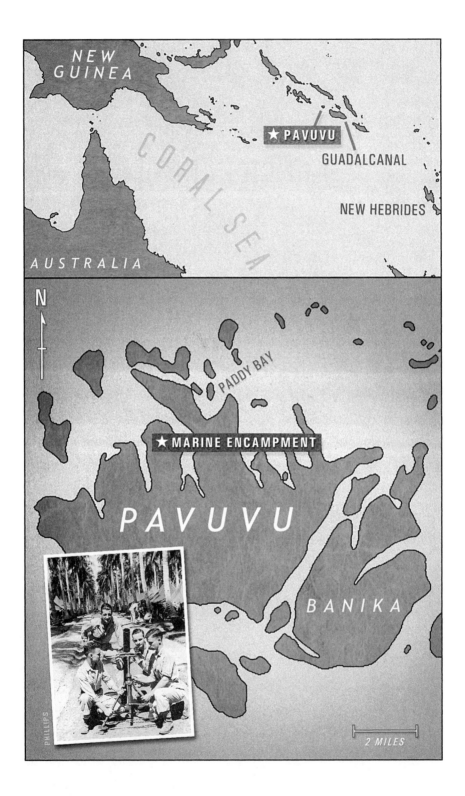

NEW
GUINEA

CORAL SEA

★ PAVUVU

GUADALCANAL

NEW HEBRIDES

AUSTRALIA

N

PADDY BAY

★ MARINE ENCAMPMENT

PAVUVU

BANIKA

PHILLIPS

2 MILES

RICHARD GREER

From up in the air, I'm sure Pavuvu looked perfect. It was a hell-hole. Pavuvu was the land of four million land crabs and six million rats. Rivers full of crocks. A real stink hole. We built streets and all that stuff, finally made an okay place out of it. But it was a bad, bad choice.

SID PHILLIPS

Pavuvu was an old coconut plantation, and it had been neglected for the whole war. Similar weather as New Britain. It hadn't been taken care of since before Pearl Harbor. There were millions and millions of sprouting coconuts. A coconut falls off a tree, and when it lays there during the rainy season, it sprouts. A big ole shoot comes out of the coconut, maybe a foot and a half long. They were all over the ground. They had a sour, stinking smell. They were just covering the ground. We had to collect these in order to do anything. We'd just pick them up all day long, and pile them up in huge piles. We spent days and days doing this, moving those damn coconuts around.

We had earthquakes on Pavuvu. If somebody was asleep, it would wake 'em up, and they thought you were shaking their cot just to be mean. They'd cuss you out. Then there were millions of land crabs everywhere. At night, they crawled into your tent, into everything you had. In the morning they'd be in your shoes, your clothes.

ART PENDLETON

There were millions of islands out there, millions. They selected Pavuvu probably because of its size and its location, but they picked a place that was in disarray. There were probably ten rats to every person. I thought, *Why would they ever put people in a place like this?* I wasn't there long enough to really understand why.

My appendix burst and I became completely ill. They decided to haul me away to the Navy hospital on Banika, an island just east of Pavuvu. I can remember lying on a stretcher on the dock waiting for a boat, and I'm talking to the guy on the stretcher beside me, and he wouldn't answer me. Finally I was turned over and was about to give him hell for not speaking when I saw he was dead.

I was in the hospital with Leckie when he was there. He said he was there for urinary problems. I had an appendectomy.

After they removed my appendix, the doctors said, "You can't heal fast enough in this climate," so they decided to send me home.

JIM YOUNG

They had rows of tents set up with lots of broken cots to sleep on. Who could sleep anyway? The tents were very old and leaked like sieves. Rats nested in the coconut trees during the day, and at night they came down to feed on the rotten coconuts on the ground. At night, they ran all over the place, leaping from one tent to another.

Instead of resting we worked our butts off. We got rid of all coconuts laying around and killed all the rats we could. This place also stunk. Mainly because it was the migrating season and thousands and thousands of land crabs were heading for the sea to do their thing. There were so many that you could hear them crawling along their way. Our roads were covered solid with them, and our trucks and tanks kept mashing them. The smell was awful.

T. I. MILLER

Right after we got our tents set up, a monsoon came up. The next morning I got up and hit water with my feet. The water was almost up to the sides of our cots. The water went down, but then the streets were a real muddy mess. The rats got in that mud and ran up and down your tent.*

SID PHILLIPS

The place was infested with rats. Big rats. Those Norwegian wharf rats. If it was a moonlit night, you could see them running up and down the tent lines. We would name 'em, and cuss 'em, but there wasn't any way of killing them. We didn't have any ammunition then, or poison. It would have been a disaster anyway, to poison them all at once. We would have been ankle deep in their carcasses. So we just lived with them. And named them. After a while you could distinguish which one was which. There was Oscar, and Tommy. They got to be pets: really, really gross pets.

ROY GERLACH

We had slit trenches to do our business in. A board went over it with some holes in it. Every so often, it got too full, so they poured gasoline over it and lit it, for sanitary reasons. One day a guy came along, opened the lid, and sat down. He went to light a cigarette and threw the match down between his legs. The methane fumes caught and exploded, burning his butt pretty bad. He spent the next couple weeks in sick bay lying on his belly.

T. I. MILLER

There were four gunnery sergeants in our tent, including me. We had been getting up to hold reveille each morning, so we made it so

---

* T. I. Miller would remember, "As to Pavuvu, about fifteen years ago I ordered an official certificate saying that I was an official citizen of Pavuvu. I found it in the *Leatherneck* magazine."

we could take turns. Monday morning was going to be my time to hold reveille with the company.

Well, the officers got in a shipment of liquor and wine. They gave the first sergeant, us gunnery sergeants, and the platoon sergeants each a fifth of wine.

It had been about nine months since any of us had any alcohol. Me and Gunnery Sergeant Malone had decided that we would open just one bottle of wine. We opened it at about ten o'clock on Sunday morning. We drunk a little of it, only a third of it, but in that tropical heat, combined with the fact that we hadn't any alcohol in our bodies, it just knocked us out.

Now, there is a certain time in the evening when you look out and it looks exactly like a certain time in the morning. Well, I woke up startled. It looked exactly like morning out there. I figured I was late to hold reveille so I ran out there and yelled, "K Company, outside!"

Here they come, straggling out. Some of them had just their pants on, some barefoot, no shirt, no hats. A motley-looking bunch. I got them all lined up. I got the reports from the platoon sergeants, and I done an about-face and was going to salute the company commander.

By the time I did the about-face, I felt the sand oozing up between my toes. I looked down and realized that not only had I called the company out that Sunday evening instead of Monday morning, but I was wearing nothing but my skivvies! I never have lived it down.*

---

* T. I. Miller would remember, "If I go to a reunion right now and some guy who was at Pavuvu is attending, too, he'll make me tell that story. I can't escape it (laughs)."

JIM ANDERSON

The food was quite bad on Pavuvu. There was no refrigeration. The eggs were so bad they smelled. I always covered mine with ketchup so I could get 'em down. This was the first part of the war yet, so it was hard to get fresh food over to where we were.

SID PHILLIPS

It seemed I was always stuck on KP, tending the fires we used to wash our mess gear in. Now, officers seldom talk to enlisted men, unless they're giving orders, but Colonel Chesty Puller always would. Almost every late afternoon, maybe thirty minutes before chow, the colonel came out of his tent, walked over to the galley, and talked to the cooks and the men like me tending the fires. He'd light this short little stubby pipe he always smoked and just talk to us.

I had always enjoyed reading about the Civil War, and somehow one day we got talking about that subject. We ended up having several long conversations about Stonewall Jackson and the campaigns in the Valley of the Shenandoah and all. He was from Virginia, but I think his interest as a Marine officer was probably more in Jackson's tactics than North versus South. You could tell he really knew what he was talking about.

This happened several afternoons, these conversations with the colonel. I always spoke to him in formal tones, of course, always "Yes, sir," "No, sir." But what I experienced was certainly a different picture than the Colonel Puller you read about.

He's often portrayed as a tough guy, or shown as the general he later became. He would become one of the most decorated Marines of all time. He wasn't any of those things those afternoons on Pavuvu when I was tending those fires. Sometimes we would talk for hours. To me, I'd say we became as much friends as a colonel and a private could ever be.

T. I. MILLER

At Pavavu I was still in charge of a platoon. I had a new Marine who was a good old boy from Oklahoma, and he was always sounding off in ranks, being disobedient. One day during a platoon assembly, I dismissed the platoon, but I called out his name and had him stand in place. I told the rest of the platoon, "Go back to your bunks and lay facedown and don't look until you hear me whistling, coming up the company street."

I didn't have nothing on but my T-shirt and slacks. I told that boy, "You've been sounding off in ranks and causing trouble. Now, I'm just going to be a plain old Marine like you are—not a gunny. Down there are a clump of bushes, let's go down there and we'll have it out, and one of us will walk back up here."

So I went on down toward the bushes. I didn't hear him following, so I turned around and looked, and that boy was sitting on a log with his head down between his knees, balling like a little young'un. I walked up to him. He told me, "Sergeant, I hate this outfit. When I left Oklahoma, I had never been out of my county. I've just been scared to death and homesick and just plain miserable." I just sat there with him until he cried it out. I told him, "Now, anytime you want to talk, you come down to my tent. All right?" He nodded, sniffling. So I said, "We'll go back there and sit down and talk, and you can tell me about your troubles."

He seemed to be all right after that. I don't know what happened to him when I left, where he went, but I never had any more trouble with him while I was on Pavuvu. I had several boys who had come in as replacements, and I had to ride them a little bit. One thing you learned after you become a noncom was when you inspected their rifles and all that, it was a good time to sort of look 'em over. I had to be a self-appointed psychologist at that point. It was a natural thing that had come to me without me realizing it.

R. V. BURGIN

The "old salts" were my mentors. The old sergeants. Whatever they did I thought, *I want to be like them.* T. I. Miller, Harry Raider, John Marmet—those were some of my favorite people. All solid as the day is long.

Now, Captain Haldane and Lieutenant Hillbilly Jones were the two best officers I ever encountered in the Marine Corps, bar none. They were the best two. Neither one of them put up with any bullshit either. Hillbilly Jones was Haldane's second in command. He was the most GI, strict guy I ever served under. He had served as a seagoing Marine for five years and was sharp—you'd never even see him sweat. When you fell out for inspection in the morning, your cuffs better be buttoned, same with the top button on your jacket, and you stood straight. "You are a Marine and you're going to act like a Marine and look like a Marine"—that was his whole thing. Just because you are out here in the boonies doesn't mean you're going to slouch off.

Hillybilly wasn't just all business. After hours, he'd come toting his guitar and we'd have a sing-along, songs like "Danny Boy" and the Australian ballad "Waltzing Matilda." Hillbilly wasn't from West Virginia or Kentucky—he was actually from the hills of southern Pennsylvania. In battle, you'd want Hillybilly close. He had a calm voice, a relaxing manner, and he wasn't afraid of anything.

One day a few of us caught a real break. Captain Haldane gave about ten of us guard duty on Banika, the main base on the Russell Islands, where all of our main supplies came in. I tell you, he was a real fine officer. Firm but always kind. He'd been with us the night we fought off those five banzai charges, and they'd awarded him the Silver Star for that. We were handpicked, I know, for this duty.

Everybody who went was an outstanding Marine from K Company. I didn't include myself in this bunch, but I went along anyway. Lieutenant Hillbilly Jones, Sergeant John Teskevich, and a couple others. All the men there were real solid Marines.

Truly, this guard duty was meant to be R&R for us. I thank the captain for that. It was just guarding a big outdoor storage area and it was only four hours on duty every four days. We guarded soft drinks and beer. Real tough duty there. And we helped ourselves to the beer, even though it wasn't cold. Banika was where the ships came in, and we'd go aboard the ships and eat lunch with the Navy. The first day I went into one of those ships, I was never so surprised in my life. They had white tablecloths and brought me a menu—I was from Texas so I ordered a streak and potatoes. They cooked it just right.

JIM YOUNG

After a while we got the place in good shape. We also got decent tents. Then all we did was play volleyball and basketball and look for shells at the beach. We got a big surprise. Bob Hope and his party flew in to put on a show for us. With him were Jerry Colonna, Lena Horne, Eddie Peabody, and dancer Patty Thomas. Some of the boys got to dance with Patty. We all really enjoyed the show.

SID PHILLIPS

Leckie was our unofficial company librarian. He had about four boxes full of paperback books. He had joined the company intelligence section by then, and they let him haul these books around, where the rest of us could have never done that. You had to carry everything on your back. I don't know where he got all these books, but he must have had 150 of them. He had quite a little library—*Ben-Hur*, and joke books. He had one, I remember, Merriam Webster's *How to Improve Your Vocabulary*. It was a yellow-and-blue cover. I'd take that thing over and read it, because I wanted to get some education. I wanted to get to college. So I'd go over to Leckie's tent and borrow a book from his library. He'd make you sign it out, just like you were at a public library. You would have to give him your name and that you were in the mortar platoon or such and such squad. He would tell you when the book had to be back then he would write it down.

If you didn't bring it back, he'd come to your tent and take it.

Hanging in his tent, Leckie had a picture of a girl. She was dressed in a white dress with lace, all set to go to church. But she had no underpants on and you could see everything. It was hilarious. The guys would go in there and look at it and laugh and come out beating one another on the back and all.

RICHARD GREER

By that time we were on Pavuvu, we knew Basilone had returned to the fleet with a new outfit. That didn't surprise Morgan and me at all. I don't think John enjoyed the war bond tour, because as soon as he could he got himself transferred back into the fleet. By then he had been promoted twice, earning a stripe as platoon sergeant and then another as a gunnery sergeant. I wrote him a letter or two and got a response back. John wasn't much of a writer. He would always get someone else to write for him. Morgan and me, we wrote his letters when we were with him. We even wrote his love letters!

R. V. BURGIN

I didn't really reflect much during this time. You try not to think about what you've been through. Course, you can't help but thinking about it from time to time. But you don't need to have a pity party, thinking about what happened and who it happened to. I always figured if you sit around and dwell on it, well you'd go nuts. So I never did.

There's a phrase, "going Asiatic," it means to go off your rocker a bit. After you've been in a few battles, it can put you in a certain frame of mind. Sergeant Pop Haney was the most Asiatic man I knew. Whenever he took a shower, he scrubbed his whole body head to toe with that hard-bristled Marine brush we'd all been given. Even his testicles. I tell you, that Pop Haney was as tough as nails. He had skin like a rhinoceros hide.

We'd see him many, many times with a full transport pack on, coming down the street, and do physical drill under arms, muttering to himself. I think he'd done something that he felt he needed extra duty for. Pop Haney was okay in his head, just a bit off.

Around July 1944, the division began rotating home its "old-timers," the veterans of Guadalcanal and New Britain.

RICHARD GREER

Some of our guys started to do pretty strange things, going "Asiatic." Then some people came from Washington and saw this. In little or no time the military came up with a rotation plan to send us home. You got a point for each month overseas, five points for each campaign, five points if you had a Purple Heart. I qualified in the first go around.

SID PHILLIPS

When you first went overseas, you just figured you would be over there until the war ended. After two years went by, they had lots of replacements coming through training, and word got around that we were eligible to go home after twenty-four months overseas.

T. I. MILLER

If I remember correctly, the requirement to go home was 92 points. I had already chalked up 138. Captain Haldane called me to his tent to offer me the job of company first sergeant if I stayed on with him. He had at least two other gunnery sergeants he could have asked, so this was an honor. I had the utmost respect for him, but I wasn't interested in the job. I'd had enough war the day we landed on Pavuvu. My response was "No, Close Crop, I think I'll go home." So that was the end of my combat. I was to be sent home.

The night before we shoved off from Pavuvu, Lieutenant Bauerschmidt come right up to my tent. He told me to come out in the company street because he wanted to talk with me for a few minutes. He thanked me and said, "I learned a lot from you. You helped me out a whole lot. I want to thank you for that." I told him, "Well, that's just part of my job. I would take care of a green lieutenant the same I would a green private." I shook hands with him. He turned out to be a good officer.*

JIM YOUNG

All the platoons were called together for important news. We were going back to the States. We were so excited that the sarge had to quiet us down. He had at least two years overseas at that point. He said that was the good news, now for the bad. "Most of you are going home," he said, "but not all of you."

---

* T. I. Miller would remember, "I never saw him again after that but heard he got shot in the stomach on Peleliu and bled out and died before they could get him to an aid station."

SID PHILLIPS

Just because you had enough points didn't mean you were going to go home. It just meant that you were eligible. You can be sure that if they really needed you, you stayed. They couldn't afford to send the whole division home.

So they did something strange. The regiment organized a lottery to see who got to go home. Literally life-and-death. Some would go home and some would stay for the next battle.

We understood they were doing this for morale purposes. After a guy had been there for twenty-four months, he knew how to goof off, he knew how to get out of doing anything, he knew how to hide and not work; the old-timers became almost worthless. They needed some fresh blood in there.

ROY GERLACH

The company held the lottery to go home. There were sixteen of us in the same category I was. You had to have two campaigns and a clean record to be eligible. So the sixteen of us lined up. The officer put sixteen slips of paper in a hat. If you drew a paper with a number on it, you were going home. If the paper was blank, well, you were devastated. I was the second one to draw a slip. It had a number. I still have that piece of paper.

SID PHILLIPS

When I pulled a number, I thought, "Hot dog, I may get to go home!" In the back of your mind you didn't trust the Marine Corps. They were always telling you lies, giving you rumors that were not true. You didn't believe anything in the Marine Corps until it happened.

JIM YOUNG

The sergeant told the rest of us a bunch of bull, that we had been handpicked by the captain because of our experience on 81mm mortars. "We want you guys to train the new replacements that are coming in," he said. When the replacements arrived, the lottery winners would go aboard the same ships for deployment back to the USA.

SID PHILLIPS

By some stroke of luck for me and misfortune for him, my best friend from Mobile, Eugene Sledge, came to Pavuvu. Eugene, of course, didn't sign up immediately for the war due to a minor heart condition that his father, a doctor, had detected. But he felt that he didn't want to miss out, so eventually he convinced his parents and joined up.

Eugene and I exchanged letters every month or two. I knew that he had gone to boot camp in San Diego, on the West Coast, which was different than most Marines. There was an epidemic of meningitis at Parris Island just then, that's why he didn't go there instead.

He was put into an infantry training unit and sent out to the Pacific, and came out with a shipload of replacements to us in the 1st Marine Division on Pavuvu. They sent out two shiploads of replacements, and Eugene was in the first.

He came in one morning, and my buddy W. O. Brown went out on the same ship that Eugene came in on. But there were thousands of men, and they didn't see each other. W.O. knew Eugene really well, but there was no way of knowing they were in such close proximity to each other.

So Eugene got permission to come over and find me in the camp. The second morning after he landed on Pavuvu, I saw him coming down the company street. He was my best friend. He was fifty yards away, but immediately I knew it was him. I jumped up and ran out of my tent, hollering his name. He ran to meet me. We hugged each other, and beat on each other. Actually, we were rolling around, wrestling on the ground. People thought we were fighting, and a big circle of guys formed. We stood up, and I introduced him around to all my friends.

We were with each other about two weeks before I shipped out. We would see each other every afternoon. They had training during the day, but late in the afternoon he could get off and come over to see me. He'd help me with my galley work. I had to empty the wash water out of those cans and put fresh water in. It would take me several hours to do it myself. But when I had him there, I could do it in half the time.

We'd go to my tent, or else sit under the trees. Twice a week they'd have a movie. They didn't have any theater. It was just a clearing with coconut logs you could sit on. We'd just enjoy each other's company.

R. V. BURGIN

Pavuvu was where I first met PFC Eugene Sledge. He was a replacement assigned to my squad as an assistant gunner. Sledge was just like any other raw recruit who stepped in, no different than anybody else. We knew pretty shortly that he had been in OCS and had a year or two of college behind him, but that didn't impress anybody. He was just an ordinary green kid like I was whenever I first got there. His dad was a medical doctor, and they were pretty well off. They had a yard boy and a nanny and a cook, and Sledge's only responsibility growing up was to feed his dog. For a kid coming out of an environment like that and coming into the Marine Corps, with all the physical and mental training we went through, he did pretty well. I always admired him for sticking it out like he did.

JIM ANDERSON

Pop Haney, some of us were kinda wondering about him. He could have gone home when they rotated out the guys with lots of time under their belts, but he chose to stay on Pavuvu. That alone should have got him sent home.

Every day he would jump around doing these exercises I'd never seen. He didn't have many close friends; I guess because some of them figured he was just a little too long in the Corps.

JIM YOUNG

The sarge had a list and called off the names of guys who were going home. The reading took a while. I've never felt so low. Every one of my close friends was leaving, guys like Dick Carr. We had been together since boot camp. I would say this was the saddest day of my life.

Saying good-bye to my friends was very hard. I stood down at the dock and watched the ships until they were out of sight.

SID PHILLIPS

The next ship of replacements came in, and I went out. When I left Pavuvu, I couldn't believe it. Nor could anyone else on the ship. We wouldn't have been surprised if they had turned the ship around and taken us all back. Maybe two days after we got under way, we said, "Maybe this is really going to happen!"

When we actually touched the docks in San Diego and went ashore, it was unreal. I saw guys get down and kiss the docks. I think all of us had decided that none of us were going to survive the war.

We returning veterans were a curiosity. The recruits there in San Diego would come over in groups and stare at us. We were all orange from all that Atabrine, the anti-malarial drug. All thin. They'd actually stare at you, ask you what it was like. We'd make light of combat and say, "Well, if you can keep from going crazy, you'll be all right."

RICHARD GREER

We were on a fast Army transport without escort, and we were in San Diego in late July. I was sure glad to be home. We were quarantined and vaccinated. By then Basilone was just down the road at Camp Pendleton, but it wasn't the sort of thing you could just up and leave to visit your friend.

J. P. Morgan was on the same ship coming home that I was. He was in front of me when we got to the telephones to call our loved ones. He got his chance, hung up, and was kind of funny-looking. I said, "What's the matter, Mo?" He said, "That damn wife of mine took that four thousand dollars that I made playing poker and took off with a damn 4-F'er." A 4-F'er was someone who didn't have to go to war due to medical issues. "Oh hell" was all I could think to say. We traveled across the country on the same train to Atlanta. I never saw Morgan again after that.*

I was assigned to Naval Air Station Norfolk. I'd been a first sergeant overseas, and they made me acting first sergeant in Norfolk. I was there through the end of the war.

T. I. MILLER

On Cape Gloucester I had lost all my weight again. When I got back to civilization, San Diego, I didn't weigh more than 120 pounds.

---

* Richard Greer would remember, "I heard Morgan died in 1980, when he was sixty years old."

On a bus going back to New River, I knew I'd come down with malaria. I got on that bus, and I don't remember anything after that. When I came to, I was in the hospital. After I finally got well enough to report in, I'd been listed AWOL for fourteen days.

When I went home, I got married right away. I'd known Recie since she was four and I was eight. She lived down in a coal mining town, and I lived out on a farm about half a mile outside of her town. We were childhood sweethearts. I used to deliver milk to Recie and her baby sisters.

She was a very pretty woman. Beautiful. We'd always known we were going to get married. All the time we were overseas she wrote me letters. She asked me why we didn't get married before I went overseas. I said, "Well, I didn't know if I was coming back, and I didn't want to saddle you with that."

After we were married, Recie came down to New River (Camp Lejeune) with me. One night we went out for dinner in Winston-Salem. I was in my uniform complete with my Guadalcanal patch. We were in the restaurant, waiting on our order, when I noticed a middle-aged guy sitting four or five tables away. He was staring at me. Most of us who had come back, we were yellow-looking from taking all that Atabrine. *I guess maybe I look obnoxious to him*, I thought. I told my wife, "That guy over there has got something on his mind. If he starts over here towards us, you get up and leave and get away from the table." About that time, I looked up, and there he stood, looking right down at me. I was thinking to myself, *Uh-oh! This guy is going to do something!*

He stuck his hand out and said, "Thank you, son." His eyes were misty like he was starting to cry. I shook his hand. He turned around and walked out. I remember how humble I felt. I turned to my wife and told her, "That meant more to me than if they gave me a Silver Star. That citizen gave me all the awards he had available." That really happened.

ROY GERLACH

There weren't many units coming back yet from overseas. We were one of the first ones. I was down at Camp Lejeune and was a butcher in their kitchen for the next year and a half.

SID PHILLIPS

When I got home to Mobile, I was a bigger curiosity than in San Diego. The streets were not full of veterans yet. People would look at you and say, "Have you been overseas?" And I'd say, "Yeah I have."

Coming back to my house, back to my parents and my sister Katharine—I just figured it would never happen. And now that it was actually happening, I couldn't believe it. You'd just figure you'd wake up and find out you were in your hammock in Pavuvu. For a long time, I had that feeling—that I'm imagining all this, that it's not really happening.

In the midst of this all, I met Mary Houston, the prettiest girl who ever lived. She was a teller at the local bank. I knew her in high school when I worked in the cafeteria and punched the cash register in the girls' food line. I was an expert girl watcher back then. But I never imagined she would stay single and unmarried in time for me to grow up and make something of myself. There's not much to tell except that she was perfect. I knew this was the girl I needed. We started dating, and for a moment I was glad there was a war on because it kept all the other boys away from Mary Houston.

It was summer 1944 when I came home. There was still another year of the war to go.

CHAPTER EIGHT

NEW ISLANDS, NEW BLOOD

★ ★ ★

Stateside

As some Marines lingered on Pavuvu and others returned home, during the spring and summer of 1944 the Corps replenished its ranks with boys eager to fight island battles. One such Marine hopeful was teenager Chuck Tatum.

CHUCK TATUM

When Pearl Harbor hit, me and the buddies in the neighborhood were out rabbit hunting. We didn't catch any. Rabbits run pretty fast. It was Sunday afternoon, and as we went home I pulled up in the driveway with my bicycle, and my younger brother said, "Guess what, the Japs have bombed Pearl Harbor."

I said, "Where's Pearl Harbor?"

"Mom said it's in the Hawaiian Islands. She also said this means war."

I was fifteen at the time, too young for the service, but I wanted to enlist right away the next day. My biggest worry was that the war would be over before I got in. My father had been a corporal in WWI. He'd died of pneumonia in 1934 when I was only eight years old, but I remember seeing a picture of him in uniform. So I thought *If I get to be old enough, I'll be a soldier, too.* I'd always looked up to soldiers.

It was a sense of duty, too. That's universal throughout manhood. You go to the oldest tribe in Africa, and if someone attacks them, they want to fight to defend themselves. It's inevitable. What could be more dastardly than what the Japanese did at Pearl Harbor? Two days after Pearl Harbor, I remember walking by the post office, and there was a long line of guys out the door waiting to sign up and enlist.

I saw Marine Corps films. They always had the best-looking uniforms, and I thought, *I'm not going to give my business to the Army or Navy. I'm gonna get one of those Marine uniforms,* which would certainly be an attraction to girls.

But my mother didn't want me to join up. I pestered that poor woman. One of my neighbor's older brothers had joined, and we heard that he got killed on Guadalcanal. That really brought the war home. Still, I wanted to enlist. I kept pestering my mother. The next year she agreed that I could join up. I think she finally just gave in. Finally, after my seventeenth birthday, on July 23, 1943, I joined the United States Marine Corps.

Years later, I thought for the first time about how brave my mother had been as a parent. She was only thirty-seven when she signed the papers that allowed me to join up, and already she'd lost two husbands—one, a state trooper, was killed in a shoot-out, and her second, my father, had died of pneumonia.

I was the first one from my age group of friends who joined. When they found out, two more of them went down right away and joined the Marine Corps the next day.

I never liked boot camp. I needed to do it twice. It was eight weeks long then. The first time I went through, things went pretty good overall, but I came down with a form of pneumonia called "Cat Fever," which is pretty common, I guess, whenever you get a lot of people together for the first time. I spent six days in the hospital in San Diego. When I got well enough, I went to a reassignment depot and tried to tell the sergeant in charge that I already had six weeks in and to please put me in a platoon that was almost finished. All he said was, "Okay, see those people over there. Stand over with them." I went over there, and these guys were fresh off the bus. So I had to repeat boot camp from the very beginning. Sure, it was easier the second time I went through (laughs). I was kinda the authority on what was going to happen next.

Actually, I don't remember ever being troubled by boot camp. I was never troubled by any of the physical exercise. I *wanted* to do this, see? What did we sign up for?! I wanted to be a Marine! There was no other place I wanted to be. We got to go shoot rifles and cannons and aim bayonets. It was the greatest adventure a seventeen-year-old boy could have.

Our drill instructor's name was O'Leary. He'd just returned from Guadalcanal, where he'd been wounded. He was the first guy I ever saw with a Purple Heart. He was a good-looking Irishman, and his uniform was always perfect. Everything he did was always perfect. I thought, well, I'd like to emulate that guy.

I didn't see any of the guys I went through boot camp with ever again, but we all had a good time when we were there. You get a bunch of seventeen-, eighteen-, nineteen-year-old guys together with no radio, no TV, no newspapers, and they make their own fun. There's this term, "grab ass," that basically means to goof off when you're supposed to be working. There are a lot of ways you can be a grab ass. For instance, you can be in line and poke the guy in front of you so he jumps—that's a grab-ass thing.

One time we were at the rifle range, and we had these pith helmets. We were in a long line and it got boring. One guy took off his pith helmet and hit his buddy over the head with it, just sort of lightly. It drove the helmet down so the inner band hit the guy's ears. Well, the other guy turned around, took his helmet off, and smacked the guy back. The DI saw it. So he brought the two guys out, stood them an arm's length apart, and ordered them to take turns hitting each other over the head. This was extremely funny as long as it didn't happen to you. They smashed their helmets over each other to the point where the helmets were wrecked. Not to mention how sore their heads were. They had to go buy new helmets.

Another time there was this guy there from Tennessee or somewhere, and he always had this sort of smile on his face. It was just the way he normally looked. Well, the DI didn't like it. So he went over to him, grabbed his collar, and pulled him out. "What the hell do you think is so funny?" he yelled.

"Sir, I'm not laughing," the guy said. "I always look this way."

"Goddamn you!" said the DI. "You get in front of a mirror and get a new expression. You practice looking different!"

In January 1944, Tatum reported to Camp Pendleton near San Diego. There, the Marines were forming a new division—the 5th Marine Division. Tatum would soon find himself in the company of hardened Marine veterans assigned to shore up the new unit, men like John Basilone.

CHUCK TATUM

Boot camp was over. I went to Camp Pendleton. Pendleton was brand spanking new and very vast—it seemed to stretch up and down the California coast. Any military base is an austere place, but Pendleton had nature's beauty working for it. On one side was the sea, which produced an eerie coastal fog most mornings. Behind the base, the coastal mountain range provided a scenic backdrop. Between the mountains and the sea were rolling hills—the perfect place to train.

I was the first guy in the new barracks except for another guy who was just lying there asleep in his bunk. The next day John Basilone came in and right away took charge. He started us cleaning the barracks. It was intimidating meeting him. I knew his name and his reputation. I'd read about him. He said he was going to be in charge of B Company, machine guns, and I thought that's exactly what I'm going to do—work a machine gun. So Basilone came in and told us to relax, and that was the first time I met him. The other guy left, because he was in the wrong place. So it was just me and Basilone in that platoon at first. Someone asked me if Basilone and I had ever gone on liberty together. I said, "Hey, privates don't go on liberty with platoon sergeants."

In the next few days they shipped more people in.

That spring, the 5th Division gained additional veterans when the Marine Corps disbanded the Raiders and Paratroops—the Marines' Special Forces—and sent their personnel to bolster the new units. One such ex-Raider was Clinton Watters. He had recently survived the island battle of Bougainville.

CLINTON WATTERS

After Bougainville they shipped me home. I'd had my two years over there by then, so they sent me to Camp Pendleton in California, where they assigned me to a rifle platoon. I didn't have much choice. I'd been in machine guns all the time before that, but that's where they put me, in some rifle platoon.

One day at Pendleton I was out with a group on a field maneuver and somebody hollered, "Hey, Watters, what in the world are you doing here?" I looked, and it was John Basilone. I said, "I'm back in duty again." Then he says, "What are you doing in a rifle company?" I said, "Well, that's where they assigned me." We had a good time catching up because we'd known each other back in the 1st Marine Division.

I first met John back in February 1942 when I joined the 1st Marine Division after Pearl Harbor. Originally I was in D Company, a machine gun platoon. I carried the tripod and ammo and then became a gunner. The guys in the machine gun platoon were all older than me. I was nineteen years old, almost twenty. John Basilone was my sergeant and he taught me machine guns. He was really good with them, and he even taught us to strip down the machine guns blindfolded and put them together again. I have a feeling that Greer and I probably knew each other back then, too.

I didn't really get to be friends with Basilone at that point. I was just a "boot" [rookie] and he was an old-time soldier who hung around with all the other sergeants. The 1st Division had a lot of old, salty Marines who had been in for a long time. Before he was in the Marines, for instance, Basilone had already been in the Army.

It was a good outfit. Our battalion commander in the 7th Marines was Colonel Chesty Puller. He was quite an amazing guy. I helped him pitch his pup tent once. We were out into the woods on a field problem, and it was just a miserable day. Raining. Windy. Most of us had half a shelter, then whoever we bunked with had another half, so we'd put it together and have a full shelter. But Chesty had a whole pup tent to himself, and you needed someone to pitch it with you, because you can't hold it down alone. So I heard, "Hey, Marine! Come over here and help me." I happened to be near to where he was, so I went over and helped him pitch his tent. He just was as friendly with everybody and never took advantage of his rank. He would get in the chow line and he wouldn't get up front. He would get right in the chow line and go through the line with you.

We went to the island of British Samoa and trained to go to Guadalcanal, although we didn't know yet where we were going. Chesty signed my promotion from private to PFC on board ship on the way overseas. Training involved a lot of hikes, a lot of exercise, just getting us used to the tropics. Chesty Puller was a remarkable leader. He used to go on twenty-mile hikes with us. A lot of the guys would pass out from the heat, and he would go and talk to them. He wasn't yelling at them, but talked to them like they were kids. He would say, "What happened, son?" He was not rough as far as talking to them. He would hike back and forth along our column and travel double the distance by the time we got through a hike. He was old but he could do it. John Basilone thought Chesty was really special and always did. He was John's hero, no question about it. He wanted to be like him. I am feeling that he was cut from the same material.

In August 1942 I ended up with infected tonsils and yellow jaundice, so they put me in the hospital. While I was in the hospital, my unit shoved off for Guadalcanal. So I missed out on all the fighting there with Basilone.

When I got out of the hospital, they put me in a new unit, the 22nd Marines. I was very unhappy about that. I'd been ready to go into combat and was disappointed that I'd missed Guadalcanal. In my new outfit, there were a lot of young recruits. They hadn't done much training, and I figured I'd have to go back with them and redo a lot of training I'd already done. Then the 3rd Raider Battalion was being formed on Samoa, and I volunteered for that and got in.

The Raiders had a reputation as a tough unit. They were good to me, and I made some great friends. We were in the initial wave to land on Bougainville, November 1, 1943. Bougainville is one of those battles you don't hear much about, and that's a shame. It was a rugged battle. Very difficult landscape. Swamps. Heat. Very messy.

This was my first landing under fire. I was a sergeant by then, a section leader in charge of twelve men and maybe three air-cooled machine guns. We were very unprepared. We landed on Bougainville in those old Higgins boats. They weren't the ones where the front end drops and you go out. With these, you had to go over the side. The boats were wooden back then, and some guys got hit even while we were still going in. The shells just came right through the side. We discovered that there were tons of Japanese on the island. Some were tied into the trees even, shooting at us from above. We had some tanks that came in behind us. If you can picture it, they had, like, an open body on them, and the Japanese were dropping grenades on our tanks from up in the trees, right into the body. It was a real mess.

Now, what follows takes a bit of telling, but I vowed to tell this story wherever I could. I'd never been the religious sort. My father was not a Christian at all. He was an alcoholic. My mother was French-Canadian and Catholic, but Dad didn't approve of being Catholic. So we'd never been active in church as children, although I'd go to churches with my friends sometimes. I had an aunt who was a nun, and she gave me a rosary before I went off to war. I took the cross off of it and wore that cross on the chain of my dog tags.

Anyhow, heavy fire was all around us. We were still on the beach and hadn't gone very far inland. Suddenly I found I couldn't move. This wave of fear swept over me and completely immobilized me. I think every man who ever goes into action is worried he's going to get into that condition. But that was me. I didn't know what to do. I literally couldn't move. I ended up stopping my advance, right in the middle of the invasion.

In the middle of that battle, I did the only thing I could think of. I dropped to my knees and asked God for help. There was nobody around me, but I'd swear somebody touched me. There was an actual physical presence, just like somebody put his hand on my shoulder. He told me to get up, stand up, go forward, and that he was going to take care of me.

Well, that was all I needed. I stood up and led my men in. We went into Bougainville and cleaned up there and went on with the battle. That incident I had with God at Bougainville changed my life. I committed myself to serving God for the rest of my days, and I never felt fear in battle ever again.

CHUCK TATUM

We had Basilone for just a short time in our company. We already had a gunnery sergeant named Stanley Kavato. But another company, C Company, didn't have a gunnery sergeant, so when John Basilone got promoted to gunny, that meant we now had two. So they gave Basilone to C Company, a few blocks up the street. Kavato stayed to be our gunnery sergeant. I was a little irritated that we lost Basilone. I thought, *This guy's our personal hero, what's he going over there for?* I never told anybody that, but that's how I felt. Sergeant Kavato didn't like me at first, but eventually we became friends. Our loss was C Company's gain.

CLINTON WATTERS

Soon after my arrival at Pendleton, the company commander called me in and said, "You're being transferred to Basilone's platoon." I know Basilone arranged this. So I became a section leader there. Basilone and I were the only ones, to my knowledge, that had combat experience in that unit. I was still a sergeant and kind of served as his assistant. John wasn't a great leader. He never delegated anything as far as I was concerned (laughs). He always ended up doing it himself. He was leading by example more than delegating tasks.

John was into boxing and I boxed with him once. We had a ring, and you know, one day he said, "How about putting on the gloves with me?" and I did. I always thought, *Golly, people are always talking about how he was a great boxer, and I'm no boxer.* I boxed with my brother as a kid. But when I fought John, he didn't do much, he didn't seem to have a lot of science in his boxing. Didn't knock me out or anything. I wasn't impressed. Supposedly when he was in the Army, he was some kind of a champ. He was a little larger than I was, a little taller. He kept in pretty good shape. When I went back, I told the guys at the parade grounds, "He must have taken it easy on me!"

CHUCK TATUM

One day it was raining and we were indoors in the barracks. Like all guys, I was bored with it. I was looking out the window at the rain. Our platoon leader, Lieutenant Dreger, was getting testy. Finally he snapped and singled me out. "Tatum," he said. "Explain to the group the theory of flat trajectory fire with a machine gun."

I remembered what Basilone had told me. I said, "Sir, that's where the bullets don't rise over the height of a man at six hundred yards," which was pretty correct. I know he was surprised that I knew that.

Another time, we were out on a field maneuver at Pendleton, wandering around in the boondocks. This one kid was staring off, not paying attention. Finally Sergeant George Lutchkus called him out. And the kid says, "Well, I'll tell ya, I'm sick and tired of all this training. I want to get over there and slap me a Jap." Oh, the sergeant just blew up. He'd been wounded at Guadalcanal. He called that guy out in front of everybody. Here's some of what he said:

"Hold on, sonny! Let me tell all of you a thing or two about the Japanese soldier! Number one, he is not the caricature you see in newspapers with bombsight glasses and buck teeth. The average Japanese soldier has five or more years of combat experience. Their army doesn't have a 'boot division' like ours . . . Japs are the world's best snipers, experts at the art of camouflage, and get by on a diet of fish heads and rice. They will never surrender and will commit hari-kari rather than be taken prisoner. Heck, they don't have corpsmen; if they are wounded, they are considered damaged goods.

So, sonny, mull all that over, and don't ever let me hear you complain about your training again."*

I'd say we all wised up real quick. That's what our enemy was like. They weren't afraid of anybody. We were going up against hardened soldiers. They were well trained, no doubt about it. Plus, they thought that if they got killed fighting for the emperor, they'd get their tickets punched straight to heaven. So they were fearless.

CLINTON WATTERS

I never felt anger toward the enemy. But I never remember being uptight or upset about needing to kill them either. The Japanese did awful things, which I first saw on Bougainville. You'd find a Marine staked to the ground somewhere and they had done horrendous things to him. We would see mutilated bodies, too. It was awfully rough. After you've seen stuff against your own people, it makes it easier to do something when you're fighting the other guy. We never considered being captured. You would have fought right to the end rather than let them have their way with you.

We didn't take a lot of prisoners. We didn't have any compound to store them, or a stockade, so we seldom took them. Where would you take them? What would you do with them? There wasn't much choice sometimes. Lots of times when we were going through areas, we found wounded enemy soldiers, and we either shot them or bayoneted them. You didn't know if he was dead or not, but you wanted to make sure. The Japanese often faked death then would shoot you from behind.

Sometimes you didn't want to make noise or announce to the enemy where you were, so that's why bayonets were used. And that bothered me. I didn't like doing that. I could shoot the enemy, sure.

---

* The full description of Lutchkus's advice to the rookie Marines can be found in Tatum's book, *Red Blood, Black Sand*.

But there's a whole lot of difference between shooting someone and bayoneting him. I'd say that sticking a knife in someone is more difficult than shooting him. Sometimes if you bayoneted one who was still alive, they would grab on, you know, and all that. But you wanted to make sure they weren't alive whenever you went by them.

CHUCK TATUM

We had an NCO named Raymond Windle, who was excellent on the machine gun. Windle was really the hero in my book. By the time he got to us, he'd already been a Paratrooper and been in two battles. Of course, these paratroopers thought their shit didn't stink. They were real elite and hated going from the Paratroopers to regular Marines. Plus, they lost $50 a month, because they got that other fifty for jumping. They had jump wings and polished boots and kept their trousers tucked in their boots. But Windle was great.

Another ex-Paratrooper who reported to Pendleton was an "Old Breed" Marine named Clarence Rea. He was assigned to C Company with Basilone and Watters.

CLARENCE REA

You've heard of the term "Old Breed." If anybody's an Old Breed, I guess I would be—one of the guys still around today who was in the service before Pearl Harbor.

I joined the Marine Corps in August 1940, straight out of high school. It was going to be my career. At the time, Hitler was over-running the low countries of Europe and people were still saying, "We're never going to get involved over there," but I got to thinking, *Y'know, they're bombing the hell out of England. We're going to be in this for sure.* I'd gotten out of high school by then and worked as a dispatcher for a trucking company. I was just a country kid who hadn't been around much, and I always wanted to travel, see the world. America wasn't at war yet, so I thought that by enlisting early, it would give me the chance to see some stuff before war broke out.

I lived in Bakersfield, California, so they sent me to San Diego to go to boot camp. When I finished boot camp, I went to sea school. My DI at boot camp had recommended that I try to get on a light cruiser, which he considered the best sea duty for a Marine. So I volunteered for a light cruiser, sailed to Hawaii, and went aboard.

In the latter part of September 1940 we sailed the South Pacific and Pacific on goodwill cruises. This was before the attacks on Pearl Harbor. It was considered duty at peacetime, and it was really nice. We had parades and went ashore and marched out to cemeteries and placed flowers at graves, then we'd be free for the rest of the day on liberty. About the middle of 1941, we took a replacement group of Marines out to Wake Island and dropped them off. That was their garrison out there when Wake was bombed.

In October 1941, our cruiser division left Pearl Harbor and sailed to the East Coast to escort convoys to England and other destinations.

On November 10, 1942, we made the first assault on North Africa and landed at a small town named Safi, south of Casablanca. Our mission was to take an airstrip because the planes in the armada coming to make their initial raids were Army planes on carriers, and once they took off they couldn't land on a carrier again—they needed an airstrip. So we secured this airstrip.

My two years of sea duty were up, so I came back to the States. I still had two years left in my enlistment, and I didn't want to get out of the service. They were asking for volunteers for the newly formed U.S. Marine Corps Paratroops. I volunteered and was accepted and went to Camp Lejeune, North Carolina, and went through parachute training, then stayed there as an instructor. It was a great school. The first and second battalions from the school landed at Tulagi. I think we were the first ones to ever parachute in the military. The Army sent a lot of their boys to us. I enjoyed jumping—it's the most exhilarating thing there is. I made about two hundred jumps, mostly as an instructor. I lost only one kid in my classes—his chute wrapped around him, and he panicked and forgot to pull his reserve. In those days every man had to pack his own chute.

Toward the end of 1943, they formed a new 5th Marine Division out of Camp Pendleton, so the Marine Paratroops were disbanded, and the Marine Raiders were disbanded, and we were all sent to Pendleton to start this new division.

I was assigned as a platoon sergeant to C Company, 27th Marines. I had a platoon of my own—three rifle squads, an attached machine gun squad, one of Basilone's, and a mortar squad. By that time I'd been around a little bit, and many of the guys were coming in new. Most of them were seventeen to nineteen. I was twenty-two, a few years older than a lot of them. My men called me "the Old Man."

Camp Pendleton is where I met John Basilone and Clint Watters, two very good friends of mine. We were together all the time we trained these new guys at Pendleton.

CLINTON WATTERS

Basilone was a really fun guy to go with on liberty. He used to put his hat on sideways once in a while, just to be goofy. People knew who he was. Everywhere we went, you would go to a bar some place and sit down, and the drinks would just come to the table—you couldn't drink them all. We left a lot of times with drinks on the table. People today always talk about how much Basilone drank, but I never saw him overdo it. He liked to goof around, but he was never wild or totally out of hand. I don't care what's been said—I never saw him dishonor that medal. Sure, he drank. We all did. But I never saw him go overboard. I think the medal quieted him down from what he might have been before I got to know him up close.

We used to hang around the Biltmore Hotel in Los Angeles; it was a pretty fancy place. They always had a room for us and took it awfully easy on us as far as cost went. We would split the room cost. They had a rendezvous room, a little dance hall and dining area that we used to go in, a lot of times in the afternoon, and they used to have a little orchestra there and dancers. The women went for John. He was a pretty handsome guy dressed up and everything. And of course him being a big hero—they were all interested.

They also had a bar on the entrance floor. On Saturday mornings after being out on Friday night we would all gather there and guys would come who weren't even staying there, and they had a little breakfast area and we used to have breakfast together. John and I dated girls from that breakfast room. We took them all kinds of places, including dive bars down on Main Street. Some of those gals had never gone down there and they wanted to see what it was like.

CLARENCE REA

That Biltmore Hotel accepted Marines all through '43, '44, until we left, like we were adopted. We couldn't do anything wrong. The guys would get in fights in there, tear the place up, and hell, they would be back the next night and the hotel would be buying drinks for them.* It was crazy. It was a lot different in World War II than it is today or in Vietnam. They really did treat the service guys great.

---

* Clarence Rea would remember, "If you stop by the Biltmore these days, ask them about the 5th Division Marines who used to hang out there—they'll remember us."

Marines could go into high-end clubs like Coconut Grove and Romanoff's and were welcomed, high-end places that today you would never see a serviceman in. One night we were in there and Charlie Chaplin was there with his wife. Every time somebody in the house would buy you a drink because they saw you in uniform.

One night John and I were in a bar in LA, I think it was Romanoff's, and we met this guy standing at the bar, he was an attorney. So we got to talking with him, and John had received the Congressional [Medal of Honor] you see; every place he went everybody recognized him from his war bond tours. So this attorney says, "How long are you going to be in town?" John says, "We come up every weekend." The attorney said, "When you come, call me and I'm going to give you a car for the weekend." So this attorney did. Every weekend we would come up there, John would call him, and we would have this Chrysler sedan, a beautiful new car. We drove that thing every weekend that we were in Los Angeles. It was just amazing how people treated us.

CLINTON WATTERS

We used to go to the Jungle Room at the Clark Hotel. It wasn't a great hotel, not a classy place. They had a lounge in there with palm trees and a little band. We had a young Marine, his last name was Phillips as I remember, and he had a really great voice. They used to let him get up there and sing to us, a Marine on stage.

CLARENCE REA

John and I were both dating Marine women. He dated Lena, of course, the girl he eventually married, and I dated another girl who worked with Lena in the camp's kitchen. We used to go to shows on base with them, or we took hikes out in the hills, stuff like that. If we took them to the city we'd end up at the Biltmore.

CLINTON WATTERS

After John started going with Lena Riggi, he never dated any other gals. He knew who he wanted. Lena was a real nice lady, very strict, quiet, conservative. She was a sergeant in the Marine Corps Women's Reserve. We would sometimes double-date. In fact, I had a Marine girlfriend that was also a cook. Lena was probably the one that got us together, originally.

After a while he and Lena decided to get married, and John asked me to be his best man. I was happy to do it for him. It felt good to know he felt that way about me.

CLARENCE REA

Lena was a great lady. She reminded me a little of Martha Raye, not that she had a big mouth. But just her actions, the way she talked. Lena was funny. Just a nice lady. She really fell in love with John.

I missed John Basilone's wedding down at Oceanside because my grandmother had just died and I'd gone home that weekend for the funeral.

In July 1944, John Basilone and Lena Riggi married.

CLINTON WATTERS

The Basilones' wedding was in held in a Catholic church in Oceanside, California. It was quiet, not that big of an event really. All the guys in his wedding party were Marine sergeants. There were four of us, and the girls were in uniform, too; they were some of Lena's cook friends who worked with her. Father Bradley was the priest that married them. He was really a nice guy, a young priest at the time. We were wearing our green drab for the wedding. John wore just the little blue Medal of Honor ribbon on his chest, not the medal around his neck. He never made a big deal out of it. We didn't have the sword thing.

After the ceremony we went to a hotel near the base and had a reception. A lot of Marines attended, of course. There was a lot of champagne, and the people buying it weren't part of the wedding. It was a really nice party and social time.

CLARENCE REA

On weekends, John used to come home with me because I lived in Bakersfield, California, which was a couple hundred miles from Camp Pendleton. My sister had a ranch where we always had these great Western barbecues. Well, John was from New Jersey, where they didn't enjoy too many western barbecues and he loved them. He was like one of us. My family loved him. I had two young nieces, maybe ten, eleven years old then, and they thought the world of him.

John wasn't like what people think he is. He wasn't a rough, tough Marine like everybody thinks. He was never a braggart or loudmouth. In my days with him, I never saw anything like that. He was the softest kid I ever knew. He wasn't too big. I called him "the little wop." He wanted to be a singer, but everybody would tell him to shut up when he started to sing (laughs). He was always trying to sing something. He would try everything. He was kind and generous and a very good instructor. Everybody loved him.

CLINTON WATTERS

After John got married, he never went off without Lena, anywhere. I think he felt he had a good Italian gal and things were going to be great. He never mentioned having a family or getting out of the

Marines. He was just happy. I don't know of anything else that John knew to do, really. He didn't have the education to get into college or anything. The military was his life.

The Basilones weren't married very long before we shipped out. He didn't need to ship out with us, but I think that's where he felt he belonged. He was respected for this ability, for what he did. He was considered a specialist. He was in his element, being among the guys, the warriors. I think Lena accepted that that was his position.

Here's a sad fact. All the sergeants in Basilone's platoon were in his wedding party—me and three others made up the four grooms-men, so with John that made five men total. Out of the five men total in Basilone's wedding party, three were killed on Iwo, one man lost an arm, and I was wounded, too. So all five of us in the wedding party ended up getting hit.

On August 11, 1944, the 5th Division Marines were told to prepare to ship out to Hawaii the following day. There, they would train for a future island invasion.

CLARENCE REA

On the last night we were in San Diego, we were already on the ship at the dock, but Basilone and I decided that evening we needed to get off that ship one last time and have one last beer. There was no liberty. They had guards at the gates at the docks. We couldn't just get permission to go, but we saw some garbage trucks going in and out. So Basilone and I climbed in the back of a garbage truck and drove out the gates. It was just a big open truck. A few blocks away, the truck stopped and we hopped out of it.

We partied till about two in the morning, then came back to the ship about two-thirty. The officer of the deck couldn't say anything when he saw us except "Welcome aboard." So we got back on board.

CHUCK TATUM

We shipped out and went to a place on Hawaii called Camp Tarawa. We were on this so-called cattle ranch. Camp Tarawa was a great place to train a division because it had a lot of room. It was named such because the 2nd Marine Division had stayed there; heck, they built the camp, after fighting the bloody battle for Tarawa atoll. But it was a horrible place. Nothing like what you imagine Hawaii is like. It was actually a desert. Maybe six thousand feet in elevation. We had rain, snow, hail, everything.

One day we were out in the field cooking, maybe half a mile from camp. We didn't have any salt or pepper, so Sergeant Windle got ahold of me and said, "Tatum, go see the mess sergeant, and get some salt and pepper for these guys." So I went to the mess sergeant, but nobody was around. Instead, I saw all these fresh chickens already plucked and just sitting there. I realized the birds were for the officer's mess, not ours. So I grabbed the salt and pepper and some butter, stuck two of those chickens under my dungarees, and returned to the field camp. I wasn't wearing a T-shirt, and those chickens were colder then hell. We cut the chicken up and put it in the pot. All was going fine, but all of a sudden there stood a lieutenant with a rifle and an MP. The lieutenant said, "Go with him, you're under arrest."

This MP marched me back to the camp. I was put in my tent and told not to leave. Apparently this was a real crime punishable by court-martial: theft from an officer's mess. I stayed there for a while, until all the guys came back. The corporal said, "Chuck, you really f-ed up this time; the lieutenant wants to see you over at his tent." So I went over there. I envisioned myself going to the Marine prison. The lieutenant came out and said to me, "Dammit, Tatum, your chicken was just okay. Too much salt, but we ate it all anyway. Now, see those pots and pans over there. Go wash them out, and don't ever do anything like that ever again." He laughed.

So that was my punishment.

CLINTON WATTERS

The time was coming to ship out, and we knew it, so John had made arrangements to meet his brother, George, in Hawaii. George was over there already. On our last leave we went to Honolulu and saw him. Even though we were going into battle, I don't think John went to Mass very often, although it was known that he was religious and wore a rosary, as I recall. We had the chaplains around all the time—I remember they used to even come to our tents sometimes.

We were practicing landings for Iwo. I ended up on an amphibious tractor. We went out and did exercises all day. We came back, and they wanted to refuel the tractors before they were put back in the belly of the LSTs. That LST had barrels of high octane fuel on top, and all kinds of ammo and shells aboard.

They drove us alongside the ship, and the ship dropped down a hose so we could refuel the tractor. This rope got caught on the trigger of the hose and sprayed gasoline all over the tractor's hull, which was hot from running all day. It caught fire, all over, and fire went up the side of the ship where the gas had also spilled.

Right away, the whole crew deserted that tractor, except me and a couple of my men. The others just dove in the water. I grabbed a fire extinguisher and we fought the fire. When we got it out, I dove in the water where one of the guys was struggling to swim and ended up bringing him back over to the ship so they could get him up.

I've always felt that God gave me another opportunity to prove myself then. There would be more chances where we were going.

CHAPTER NINE

HERE WE GO AGAIN

★ ★ ★

Pavuvu

Meanwhile on Pavuvu, the 1st Marine Division prepared for its next battle . . .

R. V. BURGIN

We trained quite a bit on Pavuvu. Marches. Drills. Inspections. Rifle range. Maneuvers. Forced runs at night. I was promoted to corporal.

JIM ANDERSON

I still couldn't walk very good, so, in the military's wisdom, they reassigned me to be a runner for Captain Haldane. I had more contact with him when I was a runner. He was very well liked by all the men. He always treated everyone—from a private on up—as a man, rather than a servant to be ordered around. He wasn't afraid to get right up on the front lines either. Some officers would stay back, but Captain Haldane never would.

Replacements came in to take the place of the old-timers and lottery winners. Among these new Marines were Dan Lawler and Sterling Mace.

DAN LAWLER

Pearl Harbor was a Sunday afternoon. Just a light snow on the ground, I remember. I was at the Paramount Theater in my hometown—Glens Falls, New York. The manager turned the lights on and said, "The Japs have just bombed Pearl Harbor." Somebody said, "Where the hell's Pearl Harbor?" Nobody knew.

I ran home to see if my mother had it on the radio. She did. At that time my older brother, Jack, was in school in Canada. He came right down to Albany the next day and enlisted in the Marine Corps.

I wanted to enlist but had a problem. When I was a baby in the hospital, a nurse was powdering her face. She dropped the can of powder, and some got in my right eye. She wiped it out but didn't say anything. When I got home, my eye got infected and it left me cross-eyed. So I wore thick glasses as a boy. High school was really rough. Everybody used to call me "Igor" because I was six-foot-two and cross-eyed. I couldn't study too well. I couldn't play any sports or anything. I loved the outdoors though. I did a lot of deer hunting and fishing since we had a camp on a lake. They had ponds in the city that I ice skated on. I went to the movies a lot, too, and read a lot of comic books. On Sundays I was an altar boy at church.

Even with my bad eyes, I wanted to be a Marine. My older brother was in the service, and I wanted to do whatever he did.* So

---

* Dan Lawler would remember, "My brother went all the way through boot camp, then they gave him an examination before he went into the elite Marine Raiders. They found out he had a leaky heart, so they discharged him right then and he came home. Later, while I was overseas, my older brother was studying medicine when he died from heart failure. He was only twenty-five."

I went down to the recruiting office. They took a look at me and said, "You couldn't get into the Salvation Army with those eyes!" I went home, my mother said, "How'd you make out?" I told her, so she said, "Well, let's get those eyes operated on."

So we did and my eyes got fixed. That's how I got in. I've still got a 4-F card with my name on it. I didn't have to go in the service if I didn't want to. I was only in my second year of high school. But I wanted to enlist. Nobody wanted to be left behind.

On the first day of boot camp, I remember this kid from New York had just signed up and he was wearing this big overcoat. They told you to wear just a sweater, but he had a big coat on. He was from a gang or something, because he had these two young henchmen with him, and all three of them had pistols. I thought, "Holy shit, this will be good."

When the drill instructor came to the kid with the overcoat, he reached down, grabbed the kid's pistol, and held it to the kid's head.

"You wouldn't dare," said the kid.

"You want to try me?" said the DI.

"If you weren't holding my pistol right now, I'd kick the shit out of you," said the kid.

The DI threw the pistol to one side. "Come on and try," he said.

The kid took a poke at the DI, but the kid swung wide. When the DI got through with him, the kid bled for two days.

That's what the Marine Corps did. They broke you down so they could build you back up. They knew what it was going to be like once you got into combat.

When I left the States, they put us all in different outfits. On Pavuvu they assigned me to K Company, K-3-5.

STERLING MACE

I was born and raised in Queens, a borough just miles away from Manhattan. Back then it was a blue collar neighborhood near the

Italian district. My dad had medical problems, so financially we had it tough. I worked at Philip Morris, in the mail room.

When Pearl Harbor happened, we were getting ready to play a county league football game. We were out on the field, and cars are starting to pull up and park along the sideline. There was a lot of commotion. They all had the radios on, and the fans were starting to gather around the cars.

So I tossed the ball to this guy and said, "I am gonna see what's going on over there." I went over, and we were listening to the news report. I mentioned it: "Where the hell is this Pearl Harbor?" That was it. As far as I was concerned I was too young to get involved.

The kid across the street, Sunny Campbell, he went and joined the Navy. He sent me a picture of himself in his Navy uniform, holding a rifle. That looked pretty good to me. He later got killed on the carrier *Hornet* off the Solomon Islands.

Anyway, I went down to Wall Street to enlist in the Navy. I was rejected because of my right eye. I didn't realize it, but they said I had no depth perception. The reason I could play football and all was because one eye compensated for the other so I never had a problem—until I took an eye test.

I went down to the Marine Corps. This time I was clever. As we stood in line I studied the chart and watched how the guys ahead of me did it. That's how I got into the Marines.

Boot camp to me was depressing. When I got to the riflery range, everybody had to shoot right-handed. But I was left-handed— always a lefty. They could care less. I barely qualified shooting right-handed with my weak right eye. I think you needed 267 to pass, and I got 268.* At Pavuvu I ended up in K Company, Third Platoon. I don't know when the civilians left, but we knew it had been a coco-

---

* Sterling Mace would remember, "I may have been a miserable shot stateside, but I shot expert overseas where it really counted (laughs)."

nut plantation. There were signs like PALMOLIVE PETE'S PLANTA-TION, 1903.

The first thing we did was go to our tent. As we're passing the tents, one of my best friends, a Jewish kid named Seymour Levy, was looking at all the other tents and saw how the guys were using Coke bottles with gasoline in them for light, since there was no electricity. So Levy made one, but he did something wrong with his cocktail. It exploded and set our tent on fire and it burnt down. This gunny Malone, he was a veteran, he said, "Boy, we got some good recruits here, in five minutes they're burning the tents down!" Then he put us in a working party.

DAN LAWLER

I met Eugene Sledge as soon as I got to Pavuvu, and we became friends. Sledge was a mortar man, a Rebel from Alabama, and I used to raise hell with him because I was a Yankee. We had a lot of fun teasing each other. He would say in his deep drawl, "Hey, Lawler!" And I would say, "You talk just like you've got marbles in your mouth!" He would get madder than hell. He chased me down the goddamn road. He was a good egg and took it.

STERLING MACE

When the company would fall out in the street in the morning, someone would come along handing out the anti-malaria Atabrine pills. When the company went back to their tents, you could see the pills all over the ground. The guys weren't taking them. The ones who did turned sorta yellow in their faces, like yellow jaundice.

I didn't have a weapon or assignment yet but wanted to be a company runner. I heard about Jimmy Anderson, so I went down and I spoke with Captain Haldane, and we couldn't come to an agreement. I was kidding around saying I would run in the other direction. He just looked at me and said, "I've got a better job for you, Mace. Try the BAR."

One day I spotted George McDevin, a kid I went to high school with, on a work party on Pavuvu. He was a Marine, too. He used to live across the ball field from me in Queens. He was in a base regiment, and he came over one night to visit me. He brought me a slice of cake. There was a big difference between his cook and our cook. I mean, they had cake four times a week. We got it every two weeks. So I found two cigars somewhere and we went out to the movie. He had a BAR and got cut in the face on New Britain by a Jap with a knife— not bad, but enough to get the hell out of there. He told me the BAR was the closest thing to a left-handed weapon.

So I asked for the BAR. They gave me one, and I went down to the rifle range just to shoot it, just to feel what the hell it was like, and I was very happy with it. So I became a BAR man.

They had little tents set up where we could hang out, not too far off the beach. Like a sideshow, the veterans from different outfits would come down and look for friends and tell us their bullshit stories. This one guy, I can still remember him, he had blond hair, and me and Levy went over to talk to him, and he had this little sack around his neck, like a little string sack for tobacco if you rolled your own cigarettes. He says, "You want to see something?" So we says, "Yeah." He opened it up, and it had gold caps removed from teeth. Not the teeth themselves. People think all the guys were taking pliers and pulling teeth from dead Japs, but they were just taking the gold caps. Levy said, "You probably got about a hundred dollars' worth of stuff there!" The guy said, "Are you kidding? There's gonna be a thousand dollars in it!" After he left, Levy said, "Why, don't we associate with a f--king bunch of cannibals."

JIM YOUNG

Brownie, my ammo corporal, had to stay behind with me, and we got to know the replacements. We didn't end up training the new guys. They had already been trained.

The new guys asked us all the time to tell them about our combat experience. They thought we were heroes and listened to every word we had to say. I hoped they would do well when the shooting started.

One of H Company's replacements was an eighteen-year-old Texan named Wayburn Hall.

WAYBURN HALL

I came into Pavuvu as a replacement, along with about fifteen hundred other guys, and was assigned as an 81mm mortar man to H-2-1. A lot of the old guys had already been on two campaigns, so they sent some of those older guys back home. Sid Phillips was a mortar man in H-2-1 just like me, but I never met him. He was on the way out while I was coming in. I could have been his replacement.

I was from Sugar Land, Texas. There were just thirteen boys and twelve girls in my senior class in high school if that tells you anything. I still didn't do too well. I wasn't too good at studying. I was small, just five foot seven inches and just over one hundred pounds. I broke my leg and ankle playing football, so I became a manager. Got nowhere with the girls. Being short didn't help. But we had some nice girls—I loved them all.

As a young person I was mischievous, I guess you'd say. I always wound up in trouble, but not real bad trouble. I lost a lot of fistfights to bullies. I was quick to jump on somebody bigger than me. We'd shoot marbles, and if somebody tried to push me around, I'd be quick to go to fist city! They'd pull us apart of course. Just part of growing up back then.

When the Japanese hit Pearl Harbor, I was living in what was called a Humble camp outside of Sugar Land. It was a small community, just a dozen small houses and a company store owned by the Humble Oil and Refining Company. My daddy worked in the hardware department of the store.

We had a little battery-powered radio, where we got the news. I was still in high school, just fifteen years old, but Pearl Harbor hit me hard. I looked forward to getting involved.

In February '43 I joined the Marine Corps at age seventeen, just a youngster. In boot camp, when a Marine platoon is lined up, the tallest man is in the front and that line tapers back to the shortest guy. Well I was one of the ones that brought up the back end of the platoon. We short guys took a lot of grief from some guys who were six-foot-two or -three. I had a tangle with one or two of the big guys in boot camp, much larger than I was, but we had a guy in our platoon who could box who really saved me from this one guy who would have beaten me up badly. This guy stepped in and took the big guy on. I will never forget that incident. The guy who saved me was named Bayling.

On Pavuvu, when I got integrated into the platoon, I found all the guys were all pretty friendly. We had a good platoon sergeant, John "Deacon" Tatum from Alabama—he's one of the best guys I ever knew. Tatum was one of the most friendly, experienced sergeants you'd ever want. He never treated a guy badly.

If you've ever been in a hellhole, you'd know what Pavuvu is like. It rained three days out of every five. In places, the mud came to your knees. We had no running water, no lights, no electricity. To get a shower, you waited until it started raining, shucked off your clothes, and got a helmet full of water. If it stopped raining before you were finished, well, you dumped the helmet full of water on you.

Anyhow, we got into our training for the next big fight.

STERLING MACE

We shipped out to Guadalcanal for maneuvers. We landed on a beach near one of those Jap freighters that had run aground. Beforehand I found a machete. I got this gung-ho idea: *We're going to hit the beach, and I'm going to go smashing through the jungle like Zorba the Greek.* And, I tell you, when I ran up the beach with that heavy BAR and that machete in the other hand, that machete got tossed within ten yards. *The hell with this.* I was back to being just a BAR man.

WAYBURN HALL

The scuttlebutt was flying that they were getting ready for another push, as they called it. We didn't know where we were going, but all kinds of names were being talked about. We wound up going to a place called Peleliu.

On September 4, 1944, the Marines boarded ships at Guadalcanal for the 2,100-mile cruise to Peleliu.

JIM YOUNG

The transport ships and LSTs arrived and we got ready to leave. Our ship was an LST and was loaded with anything and everything needed for combat.

One bit of cargo caught my eye and gave me an odd feeling. It was pallets of grave markers, hundreds and hundreds of them.

CHAPTER TEN

BLACK SMOKE, WHITE SAND

★ ★ ★

Peleliu

By summer 1944, the brass authorized Army General MacArthur's plan to retake the Philippines. MacArthur, however, wanted to see Peleliu neutralized first, because the fortified island contained two airfields and 11,000 troops that threatened his flank. Some generals argued that Peleliu could be bypassed and cut off using airpower, at minimal loss of life. Instead, MacArthur ordered the 1st Marine Division to invade.

WAYBURN HALL

We were in a convoy with all the other ships headed for the invasion. We must have been ten days at sea. To go to Peleliu we were assigned aboard an LST with all our gear and equipment. Ours had bay doors that opened on the front end. On the lower deck, they loaded it with those amphibious tractors, amtracs or LVTs [landing vehicles, tracked], twelve or fifteen of them.

On our ship, we had an LCT [landing craft, tank] on the top deck. An LCT is a flat-bottom smaller boat that's used for transporting supplies, like tanks, from a ship to a dock. I slept on the top

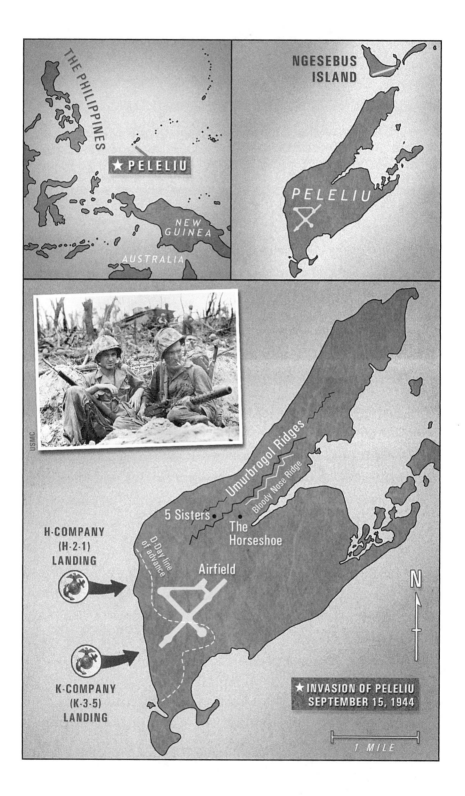

THE PHILIPPINES

★ PELELIU

NEW GUINEA

AUSTRALIA

NGESEBUS ISLAND

PELELIU

PELELIU

USMC

Umurbrogol Ridges

Bloody Nose Ridge

5 Sisters

The Horseshoe

H-COMPANY
(H-2-1)
LANDING

D-Day line of advance

Airfield

K-COMPANY
(K-3-5)
LANDING

N

★ INVASION OF PELELIU
SEPTEMBER 15, 1944

1 MILE

deck, up on this LCT they had up there. No cover, just a poncho, and it was always raining and miserable. And it was close confinement on board. All you could do was eat your chow and look over the rail and play cards and smoke cigarettes.

R. V. BURGIN

I remember First Sergeant Paul Bailey telling us about where we were headed to. He was a helluva good Marine. He said the fighting wouldn't be easy, and that a lot of us wouldn't be coming back. But we were going to take it as quick as possible with as few casualties as possible. The faster we killed those Japs, the faster we'd get off the island. General Rupertus [the 1st Marine Division's commander] told us it would be a real quickie, that we'd be in and out in two days, three days at the most. We ended up fighting on Peleliu for thirty days.

We didn't have any intelligence on that island beforehand. Nobody knew that Peleliu was a coral island with over five hundred man-made caves. Nobody knew there were swamps up to your armpits. Nobody knew it was going to be 100 to 120 degrees hot, every damn day we were on it. Nobody knew we were going to hell.

JIM ANDERSON

The night before we were to land, they issued us six K rations—small packets covered in wax paper, to make them waterproof. You could also start fires with the wax paper. I think those K rations were left over from WWI. They also issued us two canteens of fresh water that you hooked onto your belt.

Predawn, September 15, 1944 . . .

STERLING MACE

You could tell when our ship stopped because all the motors went silent. It was four in the morning. We crawled out to see what was happening, but we couldn't see the island yet. All I saw was the flash from one of the ships firing onto the island. We're taking in the firing as we were all waiting to be called down to the mess hall. Then it started getting lighter, and we could just see the island's shape. Everything was dark blue. Then we started seeing all the battleships and cruisers and whatnot. They started blasting away.

We watched a Navy Hellcat fighter being shot down. When that thing got shot down, everybody's attitude was a little more serious. We went down, got the farewell breakfast, which is always steak and eggs.

WAYBURN HALL

The Navy always tries to feed you well before you go ashore. That steak and eggs was a delicacy after being on Pavuvu.

The bell rang. You grabbed your gear and followed your instructions. They got us all lined up and we went down into this steel cavern in the belly of the ship.

STERLING MACE

It's like a big steel garage down there. The deck, the walls, the ceiling—it's vast, and all these amtracs were in there, and the motors were running, getting warmed up. The deck was steel and the tractors were made of steel, so it's nothing but squeaking and screeching.

JIM YOUNG

We were ordered to board. The amtracs were ready to launch although the doors in the mouth of the ship were still closed. All these small landing craft had their engines running. There was so much exhaust it was like we were in a blue fog. Some of the guys got sick. There were big fans that were supposed to clear the air, but they didn't do very well. The noise drove us nuts. Even though we were nervous about what lay ahead, we just wanted to get the hell out of there.

WAYBURN HALL

The amtrac we were in didn't have a ramp on the rear. You had to crawl up on the track and get up in it that way, and then when you got to the beach, you had to jump over the side of the darn thing, which was about six or eight feet out of the water.

JIM YOUNG

The big doors opened and bright light poured in. The first thing that hit us was the horrendous noise of the pre-invasion bombardment. In addition to battleships, a new weapon was being used— "rocket ships." The rockets were in racks, each holding about a hundred. There were four racks of these on the bow of the rocket ships. They fired two racks at a time and the noise was awesome. We could see Peleliu. It was completely covered by smoke and fire.

STERLING MACE

Someone had the audacity to roll a 37mm cannon into our amtrac. We could hardly get in with that damn cannon in there. But finally we got squared away.

The tractors revved up their motors, making all this smoke and shit. We start forward and move up towards the doors. The tractor is grinding away. We're going up very slow. And then we get to the peak of the ramp and she drops down, like you're going to go straight into the waves. But once we were out in the ocean it was okay. We could look back to the ship. Sailors were standing on the deck, in white T-shirts with towels around their necks and coffee in their hands. They were waving good-bye and giving us this "give them hell" shit. Hoo boy, you're almost saying then that you joined the wrong outfit.

WAYBURN HALL

It was a relief to get out of the hole of that LST. I wound up in the back left hand corner of the amtrac. My back was against the end of the amtrac, and my arm was lying on the gunwale. I could lean out and put my arm on it. Once we were in the water, I could drag my hand in the water. We were running that low in the water. I think those amtracs go about four to five miles an hour in the water. We stopped and formed a circle. Did that for a little while. Started toward the beach again, then circled again. The Higgins boats were directing the amtracs, directing us to the proper area.

R. V. BURGIN

We hit the water in our LVTs and wallowed around like a buffalo until we got the word to go in. While we were heading to the beach, the Navy was bombing and strafing, sixteen-inch guns; all the big guns were working it over. It looked like the island was on fire.

STERLING MACE

Everybody's looking over the side because we've got plenty of time. We've still got a half hour yet. Ahead of us in the water was a whole line of ships loaded with rockets. Just as we got even with them, they let loose with those rockets. Twelve thousand of them were supposed to hit the beach just as we got there. That was a good sight to see.

I heard the destroyers and battleships grinding away. Putting shells on shore. Those shells couldn't fly in fast enough for me. Then all I saw ahead was black smoke. I couldn't see the island at all. Then the smoke cleared a bit, and I could just make out the beach. The water looked black then, and the contrast made the beach look even whiter.

JIM YOUNG

We were about three miles out and started to form long, straight rows which we called waves. These waves were numbered, and my boat was in the second wave. Some of the new Marines yelled that there wouldn't be any Japs left because of the heavy naval gunfire passing over us. I yelled at my men to keep their heads down because the shells were from Japanese shore batteries. All throttles on the landing crafts were now wide open.

K Company (K-3-5) would land in the first wave, in the center of the two-thousand-yard-wide beach. H Company (H-2-1) would land in the second wave, on the left side of the beach.

JIM YOUNG

We passed close to one of our gunships and could see they were fighting a fire on board. A Jap shell had made a direct hit on the starboard gun. The turret was mangled and we saw our first casualty of this invasion. A sailor was all entangled and crushed in the wreckage of the gun mount.

We approached the reef that surrounded Peleliu, at least a hundred yards out. We hit the reef and almost upset. After crossing the reef, all hell broke loose. We received all kinds of fire—small arms, machine gun, mortars, and some real heavy stuff. Some of it landed very close and we got wet from the near misses.

JIM ANDERSON

We thought nothing could possibly live through the bombardment. But even when we were several hundred yards away from the island we started receiving machine gun fire.

DAN LAWLER

I was a front-line machine gunner, .30-caliber, in the first assault wave. We could hear the machine guns ricochet off the side of the tracks as we were going in. *Ding, ding, ding, ding.* As a Catholic, I wore a scapula medal around my neck. Man, was I reaching for that.

STERLING MACE

Halfway to the beach our amtrac got hung up on a corral outcropping. Everybody in the amtrac started getting excited, hollering, wanting to get unstuck. It's dangerous, sure—we're sitting ducks there on that reef. The driver was getting nervous, everybody yelling at him like that. But you gotta figure he's never done this before either. He kept his cool and did a good job backing off and getting us off the reef.

R. V. BURGIN

We got hung up on a reef. You could hear the track spinning and grinding. We were sitting targets. It seemed like we were hung up there for minutes. But it might have been only seconds. The Jap gun was already zeroing in on us. He hit to the left of us, to the right of us. Just as we broke free and pulled out, a shell landed right in front of us. I mean splattered water on us. In hindsight, I think getting hung up on the reef was a God thing—if we hadn't gotten hung up, we'd have run right into that shell and never made it into shore.

WAYBURN HALL

We climbed up onto this coral reef, and our amtrac almost stood up on its nose. Man, that was scary. I didn't know if we were going to fall over backward. But it righted itself. We were maybe in no more than three feet of water then, and we headed—*chug, chug, chug*—straight toward the beach.

JIM YOUNG

We were still out from the beach about a hundred yards when we took a bad hit in the front of the amtrac and it stopped. I saw one of the drivers was hurt and slumped over. The other driver made signs that the amtrac was out of action. Some of the new Marines were very scared and looked pale. Our lieutenant seemed to be in a daze. He didn't give any orders at all. We began to take hits on our starboard side. Some of our boys were hit. Some were screaming, "I'm hit! I'm hit!" The officer in charge seemed out of it. He was just sitting there.

Sergeant Miller and I knew we had to get the men off the am-trac as fast as we could because we were receiving more and more fire from machine guns. Miller was one of the old gang that had been picked to stay with the unit to help the new Marines in their first invasion. So was Brownie, my buddy who was on the beach with me the night the battleships shelled us. We decided to leave the amtrac regardless of what the lieutenant thought. He wasn't talking anyway.

We told the young guys to follow us. Miller and Brownie started over the amtrac's right side. As I went over the left side I noticed Sergeant Miller fall back in the amtrac like he was pushed real hard. I found out later that he was hit badly in the right shoulder. I didn't see it but heard that when Brownie got out of the amtrac he had his entire head blown off. I'm glad I didn't witness that.

I hit the water on the left side. The water came up to my chest. I started for the beach as fast as I could. It was very hard going. Small arms fire zipped all around me.

STERLING MACE

Luckily our tractor had a back ramp that dropped out. Our sergeant was right by the door, and as soon as he went out, I went out, too. Right on the beach was this little dog, running around, yapping. How the hell that dog made it through all that shelling, I don't know. He ran away from us down the beach. That was the last we saw of him.

R. V. BURGIN

It was about eight o'clock in the morning by the time we landed on the beaches. The motto was to "Get the hell off the beach." You're a sitting target there. The Japs had the place zeroed in.

DAN LAWLER

They put someone with us who had been on Guadalcanal, to keep us all cool. He said, "Just put your head down and keep going." We got on the beach and moved as fast as we could inland. It was hell. If you stood up, those Japs were all too glad to kill you.

When you stepped on the beach at Peleliu, you knew it was kill or be killed. The Japs didn't take prisoners so we didn't take prisoners either. The Army took prisoners, but we didn't. When you went in, you knew that rule, in place ever since Guadalcanal.

JIM YOUNG

As I was making my way toward the beach, I saw another Marine about a hundred feet ahead of me. Just as I saw him, a huge shell hit between us. A huge geyser of water rose up about fifty feet in the air and I thought my eardrums were broken. When the water fell back, I could not see the other Marine. All of a sudden he rose up, took a few steps, and fell again. He must have been up and down about five times. I finally caught up to him, and he was screaming, "Please help me!" He put his arm over my shoulder and we started for the beach. We both fell about three more times. We finally made it to the beach. It had a five-foot-high bank where the waves had eroded the coastline. This offered us some safety from the Jap machine guns. I had no idea who this Marine was or what outfit he was from. We were both exhausted. I lay back against the bank to catch my breath and looked out to sea. From the reef onto the beach the water was littered with wreckage. Many of the amtracs were on fire. While looking, I saw one boat take a direct hit. Marines flew twenty feet in the air. It seemed to all be in slow motion. Body parts, legs, and arms splashed everywhere.

I turned my attention to the wounded Marine. He had been hit in the rear end. The right side of his rear was barely hanging to his body. I told him to stay put and to stay on his stomach. He was in terrible pain and thrashing around so much I was afraid he would tear his whole ass cheek off. I pulled him up as close to the bank as I could. I took a quick look back toward the boat that I was on, and I saw nothing of my men. What men I did see were from other units. I told him I had to go forward and try to locate my outfit. He was begging me not to leave him. Then I left. I never saw him again.

WAYBURN HALL

Our amtrac stopped right on the edge of the beach. Of course, when our driver stopped, we were immediately supposed to jump out over the side, get our gear, and get off the beach.

Mortar rounds began landing around us. Somewhere off to our left was a Japanese gun emplacement, and it seemed to me they had a straight trajectory of fire right to us. Boy, those rounds were coming fast and furious. I was scared to death.

Each guy worked in tandem with a buddy. A guy from South Carolina was my partner that day. As we jumped over the side of our tractor, a mortar round exploded, right on the end of our tractor. In the blast, I lost my helmet and my rifle. We landed in the water, both belly-up. The water was about knee-deep when the waves came in, about ankle deep when they went out. My partner looked at me.

"You're hit," he said.

"Where?" I said.

"Your face."

I put my hand up. Sure enough, my upper lip was hanging down bloody all over my lower lip. I guess I'd caught a piece of shrapnel right across my face. It cut a gash about 3 inches long just under my nose, straight across my lip. Luckily it didn't damage my teeth. But it went on through to my gums and took the upper part of my gums.

Other guys were jumping out, all around us.

"Let's get out of here!" my partner said.

"Let's go," I answered back.

Quickly we crawled around to the front side of the tractor, where it was snub-nosed, and took cover there. We thought we were being safe, I guess. The amtrac backed up from under us. There was no way I could get back on that amtrac and go to the ship. That guy was backing out as soon as he unloaded, to go get another load.

I never found my helmet or saw my rifle again.

We crawled up on the beach a little ways. There was a bomb crater there, a pretty good size in diameter, and maybe three feet deep. I climbed in the shell hole. My buddy needed to keep going. He wasn't wounded. So he kept crawling up there with the rest of the platoon.

It wasn't long before a corpsman came by and saw me in this hole. He put some sulfa drug in my wound. It was all bloody and hanging down. He put a bandage around my lower face and tied it around the back of my neck.

"Just stay in this hole," he said. "Don't move." We'd been trained to get off the beach, but he thought I was safe there, and I probably was. It would have taken a direct hit inside the hole to get me.

So I just stayed there. I had a ringside seat to the waves of am-tracs coming in behind us. They were going and coming, and the Jap gun over there to the left was knocking them out something terrible. You could see bodies flying in the air, and equipment burn-ing on the tractors, and all that bad stuff.

STERLING MACE

I turned and started heading up the beach toward the mangroves. Right away a machine gun opened up. I ducked behind an amtrac to find out where the fire was coming from. But the amtrac drove off, so I quickly ran and dropped in a hole. There were seven other guys already in there. I can still hear our battalion commander, Lieutenant Colonel Shifty Shofner. He was up on a knoll ahead of us, yelling, "C'mon! There's not a Jap alive on the island!" And everybody believed him. We got up and heard all kinds of shots. Somebody said he saw a dead Jap. We kept moving. I heard "Corpsman!" And then I knew for sure the enemy was out there. Then all I heard was "Corpsman!" here and "Corpsman!" there.

JIM ANDERSON

In all the experiences I ever had on the front lines, that day on the beach at Peleliu was the heaviest fire I ever seen or experienced. The noise was deafening. You couldn't hardly talk to the man next to you. I legged it just as fast as I could, ran up to the first shell hole I saw, and jumped in. As soon as I got my breath again, I ran farther inland. That's what a man did. You just kept moving farther and farther in from the beach. I didn't think I'd live another hour if I had to stay under that heavy fire.

The farther I moved inland, at first I didn't see anything to fire at, so I didn't shoot at all. I came up to a pile of sand and looked over the top. Here was some Japanese running along a trench on the other side. By the time I got my rifle around, they were gone. Lesson number one: always be ready. In combat, if you're not quick, you'll be dead.

I went another fifty yards inland and crawled up on another little hummock of sand. I pushed my rifle ahead of me, and sure enough a few yards over there was another Japanese soldier. I pulled the trigger on my M1 without even aiming. Quick, about four times. It was *bang, bang, bang*, then I didn't even look anymore. I ran to get away from there. When you're that scared, you don't take time to see what happened. I would swear that I killed that man. I presume that because he never shot back and because I'm here and he ain't.

JIM YOUNG

I jumped over the bank, crouched down, and started to run for another spot of safety. An explosion knocked me to the ground. I said to myself, *I'm hit, but I must be in shock.* I could feel what I thought was blood running down my right hip and leg. I put my hand on my leg and there was no blood on it. I realized that a big piece of shrapnel had ripped through my canteen. What I thought was blood was just water.

The noise was deafening. As I looked around a big tree stump, I felt as if someone had pinned me to the ground. When I twisted around, I almost passed out. A Sherman tank had come in and stopped with one of his tracks resting right on my pack. The tank had come in from the sea blind. All openings were taped shut to keep water out. The driver saw me when he came out to take the tape off. He yelled, "Are you okay?!" and got back in and moved off of me. My toothpaste and some of my rations were squashed. I thought to myself, *Someone must be watching over me.*

WAYBURN HALL

Near the shell hole I was in, there was a big two-by-two concrete block buried in the sand. It was an obstacle that the Japs had placed there. There was another one just like it about twenty feet down. Between them was a shiny thing sticking out of the sand. It dawned on me, that's a darn land mine or a bomb set in there. A vehicle came along, maybe a jeep that they'd already got ashore—I didn't see it closely, but it ran over that mine. It exploded and blew sand everywhere. Man, you couldn't imagine the sand that blew up. I was just covered with sand in that shell hole. I didn't get a scratch, but it blew my bandage right off my face. It was completely gone.

So I was still just hunkering down. There's fire all over the beach, but it was all going over my head.

Another medic came along, dumped some more sulfa on me, and put another bandage on.

"Stay in this hole," he said. "Don't move." So I didn't.

JIM YOUNG

I couldn't find any of my squad. While helping the wounded Marine, I had veered to the left while my squad went straight. I came to what we called a Jap tank trap. I leaped in and there were about fifteen other Marines in there. As I looked around, I didn't see anyone that I knew.

Private Bender, from my outfit, jumped in the tank trap and said, "Where in the hell is everyone?" About that time one of our sergeants dropped in and said, "Follow me." We crawled about a hundred yards to the right, and there was Private Dignan, also from our outfit. The sergeant told us to stay put while he looked for more of our men.

The shit was really hitting the fan, the enemy fire was so intense. I saw a Jap run out of one of the caves. He was in flames from head to toe. He was cut down by gunfire before he had gone two feet. Private Dignan screamed, "I'm hit! I'm hit"! Shrapnel had broken his right hand in half. I asked him if he could crawl back to the beach, and he said he thought he could if he didn't have to carry his rifle. I told him to forget the rifle and just go.

R. V. BURGIN

We got off the beaches and got inland a bit. I remember Sledge didn't smoke. But it wasn't twenty minutes after we got off the beach that Sledge said to me, "Burgin, you got a smoke?"

"Yeah, but you don't smoke," I said.

"Yeah, but I do now," he said.

I gave him a cigarette. He was really nervous. Rightfully so.

DAN LAWLER

We moved up the beach and moved as far as the airstrip. There was a blown-up Japanese tank there, next to us. It had taken a direct hit from some kind of shell. I looked inside, and what I saw couldn't be put on paper. Severed heads. Two heads on the floor. One guy's arm is off. All blood, everywhere. Everybody dead. The shell had blown the tank to hell. It was real rough, I tell you. I thought, *Well, this is a hell of a good start.*

WAYBURN HALL

You lose track of time. I think we hit the beach about 8:30 A.M. Maybe about an hour later, maybe two, the firing started to let up. Somebody came along and said, "If you'll crawl up the beach, there's an aid station set up in a ditch on the other side of that mound there."

So I got up and crawled, with my lip dragging in all that sand up the side of that mound. It might have been a hundred yards. The Japs had dug an anti-tank trench running parallel to the beach, and our side had set up an aid station in it. It was pretty well protected. I was sort of out of it by then, maybe from blood loss, but I just rolled down to the bottom of that ditch. About the time I stopped, somebody got a hold of me. They put a shot of morphine in my arm, pumped me up real good, and laid me up on the other side of that ditch with my feet toward the bottom alongside—oh, I don't know how many other guys they had laid out like that—and I was gone then. That's all I knew.

JIM YOUNG

We moved inland from the beach about three hundred yards, to the edge of the airstrip, and could see Japs scurrying around on the

other side. We needed our mortars bad. Most of the new men had dropped them on the beach because of the ferocious gunfire. We sent men down there looking for them. The men got back and no one was hit. They located the parts of two of our mortars and we quickly put them into action. We fired across the airstrip. There were some large buildings there and the Japs were running all around. We figured they were planning an attack in an attempt to drive us into the sea.

We got word from our spotters that at least eleven Jap tanks were preparing to attack across the airstrip. We increased our volume of fire and had to keep pouring water on the guns to cool them down.

Above all this noise we could hear their tanks getting ready. The tanks came from in back of the buildings and headed at our lines full-blast. The tanks were covered with Japs. Some were even tied and chained to them. We opened up with everything we had in an effort to stop them: mortars, machine guns, bazookas, and hand grenades. Airplanes flew over.

We got lucky and destroyed all but one tank. That one tank jumped over our lines and got stuck in an old bomb crater, pinning a Marine under it. The tank swung its turret gun toward the back of our defense line and started to rake our lines. A captain yelled, "Blow that damned tank!" Other Marines yelled that there was a Marine trapped underneath it, but the captain yelled back, "Blow that tank right now!" It was hit with several rounds of bazooka shells. That was a tough thing to do, but I'm sure it saved many other lives.

Things slowed after the tank attack, and we prepared for nightfall.

WAYBURN HALL

It might have been late afternoon when I felt somebody kicking me on the bottom of my boots. I woke up. "Can you get up?" he said. I said, "Yes."

He talked to all of us stretched along there. "All you guys who can walk, get up and go down to the beach, and an amtrac will be sitting down there, and he'll take you out to a hospital ship."

About four or five of us could stand up. Another guy, we helped him hobble down.

This amtrac had a ramp on back of it, and we were able to get up on the tractor. He turned around and headed to the edge of the coral reef where a Higgins boat was sitting. We transferred into that, and it took us out to the hospital ship. It was flying a flag, to let them know where to go to.

I don't know how long it took us to get out to the ship. But when we got there, they dropped a line down with a hook to put on each end of that Higgins boat. The water was pretty rough. We bounced up against the side of the ship. The guys were trying to corral that hook, and one guy got hit with the hook and got knocked cuckoo. Anyway, they finally got us up to the main deck.

This one doctor took a look at me and washed out my wound. Then took a needle and stitched it up right there. He didn't give me no shot or nothing. Then they moved me out of there to a lower deck and put me in a bunk.

STERLING MACE

We ran around until ten o'clock that night, until we finally dug in. You wanted to laugh. You couldn't dig in even if you had a drill. That coral was hard as rock. So guys would wake up, two in the morning, and you'd hear somebody still trying to dig. He's not satisfied with the hollow he's scooped out of the coral. That's how we spent the night there. You didn't sleep.

R. V. BURGIN

Picture an island completely made out of coral rock. That was Peleliu. I tell you, all that rock was tough on your skin. It bloodied your knees. Your elbows. It just shredded your clothes apart. There was no place to sleep at night. You couldn't make a decent foxhole because you couldn't dig. If there was any loose coral around, you'd kind of pile it up around you. That was your foxhole.

Every place we made a beach landing we had gas masks. I think every single guy on Peleliu was rid of them by the day's end. I know I was and my men were. If they didn't gas us when we hit the beach, we figured they weren't going to.

JIM YOUNG

When night fell, the naval guns fired flares over us. It helped in case of a mass attack by the Japs. The flares made the landscape look like scenes out of hell. They hung from small parachutes, which swung and swayed. This caused creepy dancing shadows that looked like Japs.

Word came from the general that everyone was to stay put where they were and that after dark to shoot anyone, standing up or crawling, on sight. This meant if you had to take leak or crap, you did it right where you were.

For about an hour some wounded man out in front of our lines kept screaming, "Oh God! Someone please help me!" We didn't know if the cries really came from a Marine or a Jap. He kept begging for help and it was about to drive us crazy. One Marine yelled, "For Christ sake, will somebody shoot that S.O.B.!" Nobody did.

DAN LAWLER

I was in light and heavy machine guns. We used the heavy ones at night mostly. The air-cooled we used during the day. That first night the sergeant sent me back to the beach for more ammunition. When I came back, there was no one to share a foxhole with. You've always got two guys in a foxhole. One sleeps while the other keeps guard. Finally I found a rifleman, and we shared a foxhole. I had a carbine, and he had a rifle. He put his bayonet on his rifle and stood it against the corner against the dirt. He took the first watch while I slept. Sometime in the night, he shook me.

"My rifle's gone," he said.

"What do you mean, it's gone?" I said.

"It's gone," he assured me. "Give me your carbine."

"Bullshit," I said. "You lost one. You ain't gonna lose this one. It's all we got."

At daybreak the sergeant walked by our foxhole, motioned behind us, and said, "Hey, you two did a great job." I wondered what the hell he was talking about. My foxhole buddy just shrugged.

Well, we sat up and looked behind us. "Holy shit," I said. My buddy's rifle and bayonet were behind us. Impaled right on top of the bayonet was a Jap. He must have tried to jump into our foxhole in the middle of the night. But he landed right on the bayonet without a sound.

WAYBURN HALL

I woke up in the middle of the night on the hospital ship and there was a guy on the bunk next to me. He had a rubber sheet under him, and it was full of blood. I'm afraid that sometime after that he died, because when I woke up the next morning, he wasn't there. The hospital ship pulled anchor and got under way.

So that was my experience at Peleliu.

CHAPTER ELEVEN

THE DAYS OF HEAT AND FURY

★ ★ ★

Peleliu

The second day on Peleliu, September 16, 1944 . . .

STERLING MACE

The next morning you see shapes of guys walking around. You hear "Corpsman! Corpsman!" and think, "Geez, the Japs are already up and around at the crack of dawn."

There was sort of a mist in the morning between the heat and the ground. A foggy mist. That added to the spookiness.

That's how it was that next day. Then somebody would say, "Okay, K Company, we're moving up!"

JIM ANDERSON

Captain Haldane treated a private just like a lieutenant. He would call us by first name if he knew us. He always called me "Andy."

As a runner, sometimes Captain Haldane would give me a message, like "Andy, go over there and tell the Third Platoon to move up." So I'd go over there and tell the Third Platoon commander that

Captain Haldane wanted such and such a thing. Then I'd go back to company headquarters, to where the captain was. And he'd say, "Good work, now go back and tell the mortars to go over here." So I would. I was only a PFC and he treated me like a gentleman. Captain Haldane was 100 percent professional.* He was there to defeat the Japanese, and he did it in the most efficient manner he could.

R. V. BURGIN

I had a guy named Sam who was a screwup in our outfit. He was a slacker. He was our bazooka man. We were marching in single file, then stopped for a little bit. When we moved out again, I looked down and there was a bazooka laying there. Hell, I knew whose bazooka it was. I picked the bazooka up and gave it to Sam. I had a few choice words for him. Being a bazooka man was a dangerous job, but so was carrying a rifle or a mortar.

The Marines prepared to launch a sweeping attack across the airfield with H Company on the far left of the attack and K Company on the far right.

JIM YOUNG

We had some boys killed by Jap infiltrators during that first night, so we woke up on edge. Then our orders came. We were to attack

---

* K Company veteran Jesse Googe was the company's youngest Marine and one of Haldane's runners. He passed away just before this book began. He once told the author, "Ack Ack would come to the front and talk to us, trying to spot any guy on the edge. One day, a guy that he was trying to help just snapped. He started flailing and screaming. Ack Ack reached out to grab his shoulders and calm him down, and the guy kicked the Skipper in the groin—hard. Ack Ack fell, rolling in agony. He didn't scream or curse. He just took it. But you bet someone 'secured' the offender and dragged him away. When Ack Ack returned to his senses, he told me: 'It can happen to any man, at any time.' Then he limped away."

across the airstrip at 0800 (8 A.M.). We tried to eat our rations. We hadn't had a thing for twenty-four hours. The temperature was already ninety-five degrees. We needed lots of water. I took salt tablets to replenish the salt your body sweats, but they made me sick and I threw up.

R. V. BURGIN

You wouldn't believe how hot it was. Peleliu was just north of the equator. Hot and dry. During the days, it would be 120 degrees. It never did get below 100 degrees, not even at night. It never cooled off. Of course you had your pack on most of the time. You're carrying your rifle, your pistol, and ammunition, your canteen. Besides the guys who were carrying the mortar plates and all. Your cuts would fester in the heat. The temperature never ceased to be unbearable.

We were always thirsty. Almost right from the start, there was never enough water. It seemed like your canteen was always empty. If there was water in it, it came from the water supply brought up from the beach in old fuel drums. It was the color of rust and always tasted like oil. Some of the men who drunk it got sick. I've been hungry, and I've been thirsty—and I'll take hungry any day of the week. When a man's thirsty, he can get panicky.

STERLING MACE

We came across a Hellcat that had been shot down, right on the edge of the airstrip. The pilot was dead, still in his seat, but the Japs had wired his body with hand grenades—booby-trapped. Corporal Van Trump reached in and got a pistol. From then on, every spare moment he had, he was trying to clean that thing, because it was all burned.

Scenes from boot camp, where the USMC turned boys into Marines

USMC via Eric Hammel

USMC via Eric Hammel

USMC via Eric Hammel

Scenes from New River, early 1942
Right: Sid Phillips holds a BAR.
Below: Art Pendleton (L) sets up a machine gun.

Art Pendleton

Sid Phillips

Right: W.O. Brown (L) and Phillips in a photo booth. **Far Right:** Roy Gerlach. **Below:** H Company's Number 4 gun squad: Tatum, Phillips, Lucas, Ransom, and Doyle.

Sid Phillips

Roy Gerlach

Sid Phillips

USMC via Eric Hammel

**Scenes from Guadalcanal,
August to December 1942**

USMC via Eric Hammel

USMC via Eric Hammel

Left: The aftermath of the Tenaru battle.

Below: An H Company 81mm mortar crew. Pictured (L–R): Tatum, Lucas, Doyle, Phillips, and Ransom.

Sid Phillips

Vera Leckie via Joan Leckie Salvas

USMC via Eric Hammel

USMC via Eric Hammel

*More scenes from Guadalcanal,
August to December 1942*
Top: Robert Leckie with his
.30 caliber machine gun.

USMC via Eric Hammel

Richard Greer

USMC via Richard Greer

R.V. Burgin

Art Pendleton

Scenes from Australia, January to September 1943 **Above:** John Basilone (L) and Richard Greer. **Right:** R.V. Burgin. **Far Right:** Art Pendleton (L) and "Stretch" Campbell. **Below:** Pendleton aims his gun during training.

Art Pendleton

Scenes from the "Green Inferno," New Britain, December 1943 to May 1944

Below (L–R): Andrew Haldane, T.I. Miller, and Jim Anderson.

USMC via Eric Hammel

Steve Moore

T.I. Miller

Jim Anderson

USMC via Eric Hammel

***More scenes from
New Britain***

Right: A memorial
service for the
fallen.

USMC via Eric Hammel

Scenes from Pavuvu, May to August 1944, and new arrivals

Above: Carbine training. **Right:** Eugene Sledge. **Far Right:** Robert Leckie (R) and his friend Russ Davis.

Below: H Company machine gunners in the company street. **Below Right:** Sterling Mace.

Henry Sledge via Auburn University

Vera Leckie via Joan Leckie Salvas

Sid Phillips

Sterling Mace

*Scenes from Peleliu,
September 15, 1944*

Right: An amtrac
motors for the beach.

USMC via Eric Hammel

Jim Anderson

Above: Marines stay low to avoid Japanese gunfire. **Below:** H Company on White Beach.
Jim Young is visible in the lower right corner, third from the right.

USMC via Jim Young

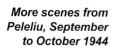

USMC via Eric Hammel

USMC via Eric Hammel

More scenes from Peleliu, September to October 1944

Right: Chesty Puller's 1st Marines depart the front lines with H Company among them.
Below: The survivors of K Company just before leaving Peleliu.

USMC

USMC via Jim Anderson

Scenes of John Basilone between battles, Stateside, 1944

Above: Basilone and Clarence Rea's nieces. **Right:** Basilone and his sergeants in Hawaii before shipping out to Iwo (top, L–R) Jack Wheeler, Clarence Rea, Clinton Watters (bottom, L–R) Basilone and Ed Johnston.

The Basilone wedding party. The women worked with Lena, whereas the men were sergeants under John. Three of these men would be killed on Iwo Jima and two wounded. (L–R) Jack Wheeler, Rinaldo Martini, John Basilone, Ed Johnston, and Clinton Watters.

Scenes from Iwo Jima, February to March 1945

Left: Chuck Tatum and the B Company Marines study a map of Iwo Jima prior to the invasion. Tatum is in the center, above the map, with his hat tipped back.

USMC

USMC

USMC via Clinton Watters

USMC via Clinton Watters

*More scenes
from Iwo Jima*

USMC via Clinton Watters

Above: A wrecked
Japanese bomber
alongside one of
the island's two
completed airfields.

USMC

USMC via Clinton Watters

Scenes from the battle for Okinawa, April to June 1945

Below: These pictures were taken during the fighting on Wana Ridge.

USMC via Eric Hammel

USMC via Eric Hammel

USMC via Jim Anderson

More scenes from Okinawa

Above: A small road doubles as an airstrip for an American observation aircraft.

USMC via Jim Anderson

Scenes from the aftermath of World War II in the Pacific

Right: Sgt. Earl Dobrinsho at a baseball field named for Andrew Haldane on Pavuvu. **Below:** Tired K Company survivors including Burgin (back row, second from left) and Sledge (front row, right).

Above: A Marine interpreter hands candy to a Japanese child.

K Company Marines display their souvenirs. Dan Lawler holds a bugle on the far left, while Eugene Sledge smokes a pipe in the center.

JIM YOUNG

At 0800 waves of Marines started crossing the airfield. This was it. We could see our guys getting hit by Jap machine gunners and riflemen. Then it was our turn. There was no cover, so we ran as fast as we could. It reminded me of a dream I once had about being chased where my legs were only moving in slow motion.

STERLING MACE

We started heading across the airstrip. It was a big thing—a three-hundred to four-hundred-yard run at a stop-and-go. Japs were shelling us. There were explosions all around. We started out. Marines were running, heading right into that misery.

JIM ANDERSON

I started across, dodged and darted and so forth. There was practically no one ahead of me. I thought, *Well here goes a fellow, and there goes a fellow. If they can make it, I'll give it a whirl, too.* The machine gun fire was extremely heavy. Part of the way over, I ran into a man from K Company named Guy Farrar. He'd been shot through the arm. I kept going, and here was a fellow named Frank Bachelor. He'd been shot in the leg. As we ran across the airport, I shot back. I didn't see any Japanese soldiers to shoot at, but I shot at something that was firing at me to pin them down a bit. At times like these I was more mad than anything, mad at the Japanese for making us come all that way to fight them.

DAN LAWLER

Machine gun fire was always on us, but as we ran we'd count a random number between one and five, then hit the dirt on that number. It might be one. It might be three. The next time four. Always different. So the Japs could never zero in their sites on us.

Halfway across the airstrip, a big artillery shell landed by me. I said, "Geez, that was close." All I remember was the pavement coming up to meet me. When I woke up, I put my hand down. It was all bloody. I said, "Shit, I've been hit." The corpsman came along and said, "Well, you got some broken fingers here." So he wrapped them up. I'd broken three fingers and a thumb. I started to get up, but he said, "Wait a minute; you got something sticking out of your back, too." He reached over and pulled this piece of shrapnel out of the middle of my back. I never felt any of it. That stuff is red-hot. It's just like a poker when it goes in. Everything freezes up. All I remember about the whole experience was going down. I don't remember getting hit. You're looking out for every-body. Your friends—did they make it? Did they get across? It's tough, because a lot of guys didn't.

Anyway, I could still walk, so I got up and hiked back to the beach and was transported to a hospital ship.

STERLING MACE

I was running, running. Finally I came to a hole. This hole had to have been dug with some kind of machine because it was perfectly round, about four and a half feet deep. Inside at the bottom was a dead Jap. He must have been put out there to knock some of us off before he got it. He was huddled up in the fetal position. We made it across the airstrip, got to the other side, and everybody sort of asked, "What now? Where we going?" I think we had six or seven killed, running across that damn airstrip.

JIM ANDERSON

By the grace of God, I made it to the brush on the east side of the airstrip. We moved along the edge of the airport. There were some buildings there, and I shot around those buildings, although I did not ever see any live Japanese soldiers. There were some dead ones lying around. Somebody had knocked out a Japanese short-barreled howitzer, and it was lying beside the trail with a couple of dead Japanese soldiers lying beside it. But you tried to move fast and not pay too much attention to them. I understand that they had quite a fight over at the main buildings at the airport.

JIM YOUNG

We crossed but lost eight men from H Company on our run. I was sure glad the guys talked me into becoming a mortar man and not a machine gunner or rifleman. Those boys went first and were slaughtered. Our losses in the 2nd Battalion were tremendous. At least half of them were dead or wounded. We had very few officers left. However, our lieutenant from our landing craft rejoined us and had completely recovered from his combat fear.

We were exhausted from the crossing and all very thirsty. The temperature was now around 120 degrees, and our clothes looked like we were caught in a rain shower, because they were drenched with sweat.

They brought water to us, but we could hardly drink it. What they had done was try to wash our fifty-five-gallon drums of gasoline and then put drinking water in. We had to drink it anyway, and a lot of us got sick.

After the crossing, H Company settled in at the foot of the ridges north of the airfield while K Company swung east to clear the swamps on the airfield's flank. That night, K Company dug in "with our backs to the sea," as one Marine remembered, along the island's eastern cliffs.

R. V. BURGIN

We fought both day and night on that island. During the day we fought the Japs. Then at night, they came out of caves and tried to infiltrate our lines. You just couldn't sleep, hardly even a nap at night—if you did, you were a dead man. They'd sneak up on you and try to get within range to throw a grenade. If you slept, you knew you could be dead within a minute. The Japs wore those split-toed shoes with rubber soles like sneakers. You could barely hear them coming. You could look to the left, then look to the right, then by the time you looked straight ahead he'd be there. You just couldn't see them. It wears you down physically, but it also wears you down mentally.

At night, we'd try to get close enough where you could reach out and touch the next guy. One guy would stay awake for an hour, one guy would sleep, then you'd switch off. Once, during the night I heard scuffling from down the line. It was the fourth man down from me. I couldn't see what was going on, but I knew there was a Jap involved. And then a long, bloodcurdling scream. The guy told me the story later.

He was sleeping flat on his back when he felt this weight on his chest. He woke up with fingers around his throat. The Jap had snuck in, sat on the Marine's stomach, and started to choke him. The Marine could feel himself going under, losing consciousness. He knew he was choking to death.

Like lightning, everything that he had ever been taught about self-defense ran through his mind. He reached behind the Jap's head, grabbed him by the hair, and gouged his fingers in the Jap's eyes. The Jap released his choke hold, and the Marine broke loose. He got up, grabbed the Jap by the nape of the neck and seat of his pants, and threw him over the cliff.

So the bloodcurdling scream I heard had been from the Jap,

screaming all the way down until he hit the ground. I'd never heard anybody scream like that before and haven't since.

The next day, the Marines attacked northward. As K Company cleared the eastern shoreline, H Company attacked Peleliu's most formidable landmark in the island's center—the Umurbrogol ridges. There, the Japanese had built countless interconnecting gun positions into the coral ridges.

JIM YOUNG

We set up our four mortar emplacements at the base of the Umurbrogol. We couldn't dig regular pits because the soil was all coral, so we used chunks of bombed buildings for protection from shrapnel. We were lucky we placed our mortars in this spot because we started to receive very heavy enemy big gun fire. Every barrage flew about 20 feet over our heads and hit about 150 yards in back of us. We couldn't figure out what kind of guns they were. The shells were shaped like ash cans, and the explosions were deafening. Only one guy was hit.

We received word from our OP [observation post] that the Japs were also setting up mortar batteries. The OP gave us the range and we opened up on them. They were trying to get us before we got them. It turned into a battle royal. We fired fast and furious. Our gun tubes grew so hot that our loaders were getting their hands burned. We wrapped the tubes with burlap bags and kept pouring water on them to keep them as cool as possible. The Japs got a mortar round close to our number four gun and wounded three guys. But they were able to go back to the beach without help. We must have fired three or four hundred rounds. The OP said to cease fire because we put the Jap battery out of action.

We took a break and tried to find some shade. Our lips were

cracked and bleeding from the heat and dehydration. By then we had not had sleep for three days. When we sat for a catnap, the sweat ran down our faces, hit our eyelids, and coagulated. You couldn't open your eyes until you soaked them in water. This was scary the first time it happened.

I had just picked a spot in the shade when a bullet hit the coral about two inches from my head. I got out of there quick! Private Bender was close by, and the sniper took a shot at him and missed. The lieutenant then sent a runner to the command post and requested them to send up a Marine with a war dog. Shortly after they arrived, the dog located the sniper and that ended that.

Meanwhile, hospital ships whisked Wayburn Hall and Dan Lawler toward a Navy base in the Admiralty Islands . . .

DAN LAWLER

The ship was a tough place. Wounded soldiers everywhere. I was considered "walking wounded," so I went to work right away, helping out wherever I could. It was all volunteer, but these were your friends, you know, so you pitched in wherever you could. I could still use one of my hands, and my back wasn't hurting too bad. Lots of guys were dead when they were brought in. Others died on the operating table. One doctor I know of operated around the clock for so long he finally dropped dead from exhaustion. Anyway, the bodies piled up. We had to have room. More were coming. The worst thing I ever had to do was burial at sea—to slide Marines' bodies off the back of that ship.

During training at Camp Lejeune, I had made three friends all from upstate New York, like me. Harold Chapman from Gansevoort. Jim Butterfield from Glens Falls. John Murray from Hudson Falls. We stayed together as good friends and all went to Camp Pendleton for further training, although later we all went to different units. Harold got killed on Peleliu. He got outnumbered in a bayonet fight. Course I never told his folks that. John got his kneecap blown off. And Jimmy got both eyes blown out by a mortar blast. So we all got hit.

After I was patched up, I went back to Pavuvu and rejoined the 1st Marine Division.

WAYBURN HALL

We sailed for the Admiralty Islands, where there was a Navy hospital. They put a bunch of us up in a Seabee camp. Those guys were great, the best friends we ever had during the war. They brought everything they could think of to us—cigarettes and candy and beer.

I couldn't keep up with time, but another ship came by and they put us on that. They took us back to Pavuvu, where we had come from. I went right back to our camp and went straight to my cot, which was still set up. The idea was that we weren't supposed to be fighting too long on Peleliu. So, I just healed up on Pavuvu.

Back on Peleliu, on September 19, K Company conducted a combat patrol of the island's eastern swamps.

R. V. BURGIN

About forty of us were sent out on an extended patrol down to the tip of a long, narrow peninsula that ran along the southeast coast of the island. Hillbilly Jones was in charge of a group. A dog handler came with us, an army man with a big Doberman that could smell Japs.

We went out and got set up out in the jungle before dark. Pop Haney was with us on that one, and he began to get nervous, almost panicky, telling us to come around and lock and load, check out bayonets, stuff we had already done. It grew dark. We were close enough to the Japs that you could hear them talking every once in a while.

All of a sudden, the dog handler began to talk, to call out, and talk pretty loud. "Help me, help me, help me, dog. They're going to kill me. Help me, dog." We didn't want that, because it gave away our position. He just got worse and worse, louder and louder. He was cracking up. Everybody was whispering, "Shut that man up. Every damn Jap on the island will know where we are." The doc gave him morphine, but that didn't seem to faze him at all. The doc gave him another shot. Still no effect. Another. I think he gave enough morphine to him to kill a horse, but he kept getting louder and louder. I was right in the middle of it. Holding him down, trying to keep him quiet. Finally one of our men hit him in the head with his entrenching tool.

It was just one of those things that had to be done. You're damned if you do, damned if you don't. It was either him or all of our lives. It killed him. The action actually saved the lives of others. I hated it, but at the same time I never regretted it. If the Japs had come across us, we'd have been in a hell of a shape. There's never been anyone that I know of that told who used the shovel. I know who it was. He wasn't proud of it. Even though that guy's already dead, I'll carry that secret to my grave without telling anyone who did it.

As K Company fought northward along the coast, they heard the fury of battle as H Company and the 1st Marines fought in the Umurbrogol ridges. "We pitied the 1st Marines attacking the ridges," Eugene Sledge would write.

JIM YOUNG

We got word that our riflemen were having a terrible time climbing these jagged mountains and were being shot at from all sides. We'd had about two hundred riflemen in the company, and they said there were only about forty-five left. A wounded Marine came through our line without a helmet on. His head was wrapped with a bloody bandage. One ear hung by a small piece of skin, and his head bled through the bandage in spurts with every heartbeat. Our lieutenant sent a Marine to help him get back to the beach. I don't think he would have made it without help.

Casualties were extremely high. It grew so bad they couldn't get the wounded out. They pushed some of the wounded off the ledges in the hope that they survived the fall and the stretcher bearers could get to them. The luckiest thing about this battle so far was that the Japanese had not attacked us from the air or sea.

After a week, our colonel, Chesty Puller (who had been promoted to lead our regiment) was ordered by the general to withdraw the entire 1st Marines from action because of our severe losses. We were worn out physically and mentally. It didn't help that Puller's style was to keep going even if it was just about impossible.

On our way out, the column was stopped by the MPs. We were told that there were some Jap machine gun nests on both sides of a pass we had to go through. We were ordered to run through the pass in groups of ten and as fast as we could. The MPs would give us cover fire from their machine guns. Most of us made it through the pass. But we had about ten guys hit who needed to be rescued by stretcher bearers.

On our way we passed several stacks of dead Marines. They were piled five one way and five the other way. The stacks were about five feet high. Seeing this gave me an awful feeling. It's a sight I'll never forget.

The near destruction of Puller's regiment convinced the operation's commander, Marine General Geiger, to send in reinforcements. On September 23, the Army's 81st Infantry Division relieved Puller's regiment and H Company.

JIM YOUNG

We finally arrived at the other end of the island and were fed our first hot meal in over a week. While in the chow line, a Jap sniper started firing and we had to scatter. It wasn't long before they had the war dogs on the Jap's ass, then it was back to that hot meal.

Word came in. We were leaving. The regiment was no longer deemed capable for combat and we were returning to Pavuvu. The official word is that our regiment suffered 60 percent casualties.

CHAPTER TWELVE

ASSAULT ACROSS THE BAY

* ★ ★ ★ *

Peleliu

While the Army troops and 7th Marines assaulted the ridges, on September 28, 1944, K Company and the 5th Marines staged an amphibious assault on tiny Ngesebus Island, north of Peleliu.

JIM ANDERSON

When we got to the north end of Peleliu, we was put on amphibian tractors again, and we had to cross a short spit of water to get over to a small island, Ngesebus. It was an island with a fighter strip on it and, guarding this fighter strip, a battalion of Japanese.

R. V. BURGIN

On Peleliu we had all the enemy's artillery knocked out within three days' time. We did have one section of Jap guns on Ngesebus that they were firing over to the mainland of Peleliu. Ngesebus was a small island about five hundred yards away from the northern end of Peleliu. We were thinking that at low tide they'd come across to the mainland. So we were sent out there to make sure they didn't come across.

STERLING MACE

Ngesebus was shaped like a boomerang, with a beach and an airstrip at the bottom of the boomerang. There was a causeway between Peleliu and Ngesbus, about fourteen hundred yards long. We were all lined up on the Peleliu side, ready to go across. Cruisers shelled the beach. Corsairs flew up and down the beach, strafing and bombing. It was like watching a beautiful show, seeing those guys in the Corsairs go back and forth. Finally we got the signal to go across. We were on the left flank.

R. V. BURGIN

We got in amtracs and went across the bay. The Corsairs bombed and strafed for us. Those Marine pilots were the best ever. Absolutely fantastic. You'd see them in a steep dive, bombing and strafing, and they'd disappear in smoke. You'd think, *My God, they crashed!* But then you'd see them pull out the other end. They did a hell of a job, I tell ya.

It was about eight-thirty in the morning when we hit the beach. We moved forward. The airstrip was pretty small. There wasn't any real resistance. Just some sniper fire.

JIM ANDERSON

Captain Haldane and all of K Company moved along the fighter strip. We ran into some pillboxes along the north end of Ngesebus. We could hear soldiers talking in there. An interpreter went and talked to the Japanese. I suppose he told them to come on out. But they never did. We threw in hand grenades. But they never would give up. In all the front-line duty I ever had, I never ever seen one Japanese soldier surrender.

Captain Haldane wanted me to go back and bring up two tanks to knock out a pillbox. Instead of giving a direct order, he said to me, "Andy, would you go back to battalion and bring up a couple of tanks?" In a nice manner. So I put my rifle on my shoulder and headed back. We was then ahead of the lines, and I had to walk along the airport to get to the tanks.

I was walking along, I had my M1 in my hands, and here, fifty yards away, a Japanese soldier stepped out. All I did was pull my rifle up a little bit and fire from the hip. I missed. He put his rifle up to his shoulder and shot at me at that distance, and I seen the flames come right out of the muzzle. But he missed me, too. By that time I had my rifle to my shoulder. I sited right down the barrel, and I shot him, two quick shots, and saw him fall. That's the closest call I ever had with a Japanese soldier. Even today if I close my eyes, I can see that flame shoot out the end of the muzzle of his rifle.

I saw other figures firing in my direction from a cave. Then I did a smart thing: I ran—maybe fifty to sixty yards—and jumped into a shell hole. Some other Marines jumped in with me. All of a sudden, *bang*, one of the guys was shot in the shoulder. Nobody knew where the shot had come from. I put my hands over his wounds on the front and back of his shoulder. The blood was coming out, gushing. In a few minutes he was dead.

I got back to where the tanks were and brought them up to K Company. I rode on the back of a tank. The tanks went up there and did their job on the front lines. When the tanks went back, the Japanese soldier I'd shot wasn't there anymore. I don't know what happened to him. Maybe his friends came and got him.

STERLING MACE

On the left side of the beach toward the end of the island was a ridge, probably fifteen feet high. It ran the whole length of the island. The left side of that ridge sloped down to the shoreline, then the beach itself there was only three feet wide. My platoon covered that ridge the whole time going. Just moved out slow, catching a Jap here and there.

Finally this guy, Nippo Baxter (they called him "Nippo" because he was always looking for Japs), spotted two Japs down by a sinkhole. The sidewall of the sinkhole had a cave. So he fired down, killed two, and then spotted me because I've got the BAR. He pointed down, meaning he wanted me to take care of things. I studied the situation and thought maybe I could come around and go over top of them. So I climbed the ridge. In hindsight it was stupid because the Japs could have been down there looking at me climb. But I've got a machine gun squad ten yards back watching my every move.

As I am going up there, I hear a voice on top of the ridge. *Who the hell is talking?* When I got up a little higher, this guy from headquarters company was spotting for the 81 mortars. He was looking at his map and then calling in his coordinates. So I told him, in a whisper tone, "There's Japs right below you." He looks at me like "So what, f—k you." Whatever. I had no qualms about putting my head over the ridge.

I peeked over and looked down. Three Japs. I can still see the first one—this moon face, yellowish skin, dark-shaded hair, helmet on, he's in uniform. He had his rifle and was trying to line up Baxter. The Jap looked up and saw me. Real quick, he stared straight at me, then swung his rifle around. But I already had my BAR on him and let about eight shots go. I got him and the two Japs lying in front of him—the three of them were trying to get Baxter.

We figured there might be more Japs near the cave in that same position. So I ducked back and hollered to the machine gunners to throw me up two hand grenades. They did. I pulled the pins and dropped the grenades in. We had to wait. Somebody said, "Get a flamethrower." A sergeant brought up a bazooka guy, which won't do any good in that situation. We needed a flamethrower to blast into that cave—even if you don't kill them with the flame, you suck all the oxygen out and get them that way. So they brought up a flamethrower, but his flamethrower doesn't work. So he's got to go back, and we got to wait for another flamethrower. Then another flamethrower came, and he did a nice job. He squirted just enough in so in case there were any Japs in there, they'd come running out. And then he gave it the full blast.

We moved up the line. About ten minutes later we heard, "Fire in the hole!" That was the composition man behind us. He put this stuff like putty around the entrance of the cave, then wired it up, and it exploded to seal the cave.

JIM ANDERSON

Most of us were carrying Composition C. It's an explosive that looks and feels like stiff putty. To blow down a pillbox door, you break it in half, put the Composition C against the door with a detonator, and set it off. *Bam!* There you have it. Or if you wanted, you could also use it to heat your coffee. You put water and coffee in a tin cup, tear off a piece of Comp C about as big as the tip of your thumb, put it up against the side of your cup, and light it with a match. When the explosive is out in the open like that, it doesn't explode. Instant hot coffee!

STERLING MACE

Nippo Baxter was the greatest Marine I ever saw. When we would take a ten-minute break or something, he would be out running around looking for Japs and souvenirs! I'm certain he would go out at night into the Japanese area, because the souvenirs he had, you couldn't pick up just running around. He picked up a saber. He picked up a Japanese record player with records. He picked up a Japanese officer pack, which was covered with fur. When we moved out, Nippo had the saber on, the fur Jap pack, and then on top of this pack was the freaking Japanese record player. When we stopped and he would play a record, we couldn't tell if they were singing kids or singing goats. They were awful.

But anyway Nippo got it later on, killed in a mortar barrage.

R. V. BURGIN

The mortar section moved in about two hundred yards across the airstrip, to where there was an empty Jap bunker with a few shell holes around it. The bunker faced the channel. Our orders were to set up our guns on the far side of the bunker, so we started to dig in. Our gunny sergeant, W. R. Saunders, confirmed that the bunker was clear. Two of our men began laying a phone line.

But Sledge wasn't convinced. "Burgin," he said, "there's Japs in that bunker."

"Hell, Gene," I said. "You must be cracking up. Saunders said there wasn't any Japs in there."

"I don't give a damn what Saunders said. I hear 'em jabbering. I know damn well there are Japs in that bunker!"

So I eased up against the side of the bunker and looked down in a vent. Sure enough, a Jap had his face stuck right up inside the vent. I shot him right in the face. Then I stuck the barrel of my rifle further down the vent and emptied the clip while wiggling it around. I put another clip in and did the same thing again.

Then all hell broke loose. Well, that was kind of like walking up and kicking a beehive. It swarmed. I didn't have a clue how many Japs were in that bunker, but from all the commotion, I knew it was a bunch. They started shooting their machine guns and rifles, and throwing grenades out at us. Everything got real tense. We messed around there with those rascals for a while, maybe twenty minutes or so, and two of my men got hit by grenades. They weren't evacuated, but the doc had to patch them up. I was the only NCO there, so I needed to do something. All the rest of the men were private first class. I started thinking, "Hell, this could go on for a damn week. Some of my men are going to get killed unless I wrap this thing up."

I knew that an amtrac was down on the beach. I ran down there, about two hundred yards, and got the driver. All I said was, "I need your help for a few minutes. Follow me." On the way back I ran into Corporal Charles Womack, who carried a flamethrower on his back. So I brought him up, too.

When we got up there, about thirty-five yards out, I stopped the driver and told him what I wanted him to do: blow a hole in the side of that bunker. It was about a foot of steel-reinforced concrete. I said, "Knock me a hole in there. It's full of Japs."

So he did. He had a 75 howitzer, and it took three shells to knock a twenty-four-inch hole in the side of the bunker. As soon as he was through, Womack came up and scorched them with his flamethrower.

Some of the Japs ran out and we shot them. Some stayed in there. I don't know how in the world any of them could live, but I wanted to make damn sure everything was secure, so I went down in the bunker to find out myself. John Redifer followed me in. One of the Japs was moving. So I stuck my foot in his ribs under his right arm, and sure enough he wasn't dead. I shot him in the head with my .45 at point-blank range. That was the only alive one in there. We killed seventeen Japs there—ten inside and seven outside. We didn't lose a man, and I was proud of that, so I thought that was a job well done. We secured that bunker.

JIM ANDERSON

On Ngesebus, Don Shwance, another friend of mine, got wounded. He gave me one of his most prized possessions, a pair of dry socks. I hadn't picked up any souvenirs at all. But off of one soldier, I picked up a Gospel of St. John, written in Japanese. Their religion is Shintoism, so how he ever got this, I don't know.

R. V. BURGIN

We were only on Ngesebus overnight. I was in a shell hole that night with our bazooka man, Sam. As always, one guy was supposed to stand guard while the other slept. One hour each. I woke up early, when it was still Sam's time to stand guard, and saw that he was asleep. That kind of negligence could have got our throats slit.

I straddled him on his stomach and put him in a chokehold. He thought the Japs had him and fought like crazy. I got him choked down until he was about to black out and then I turned him loose. I told him, "You son of a bitch, if I ever catch you asleep when you're supposed to be standing guard, you'll never wake up!"

Then I told Captain Haldane about it, about the two instances, including the time Sam left his bazooka behind. I said, "Captain, if I can't trust this man, I don't want him in the unit." Haldane was always fair and reasonable. When we got back, Sam got transferred out of K Company, to an MP outfit some place.

The battle for Ngesebus raged throughout the following morning, September 29, and into the afternoon.

STERLING MACE

We kept moving up. Suddenly our fire team leader, Corporal Van Trump, called me. "Mace. I want you to take your assistant. Go forward and take a position up twenty yards ahead. If you see any Japs—maybe they're trying to surround us—you come back and tell us." I looked at this guy like he's got two heads—*Are you kidding?* I know we didn't have more than thirty yards left to the end of the island! But he was a corporal and I was a PFC and you've got to follow orders. The only reason Van Trump was working with our lieutenant was because our sergeant was walking around with his thumb up his ass.

So Charlie Allman, my assistant gunner, and I moved up without the rest of our unit. We sneak up and find a nice spot, I mean it looked nice. Our position looked like a miniature dormant volcano. We got into that recess in the top, and you couldn't see us, but we could see if anybody was passing by. I knew it wasn't a perfect spot though—if we got into a firefight we couldn't have gotten out. We both got in there and took a look around into the jungle.

We sat there awhile. Pretty soon between the sounds of gunfire, we heard twigs snapping to our left and right. The Japs were walking around out there—we knew it. I said to Charlie, "Don't open your freaking mouth, don't say a word, don't sneeze, don't do anything, because these suckers are walking all around us." I caught a glimpse. We were surrounded by Japs. When we were sneaking up the ridge, they were sneaking the other direction toward our lines. All they had to know was that we were in there, and it would have been just "hands up." They kept walking. We kept waiting.

Something else was wrong. I whispered to Charlie, "I can't hear any gunfire. We got to get out of here." But we couldn't make a run for it until we knew the goddamn Japs were gone. Finally, I said to Charlie, "I think they're gone—I don't hear any snapping of leaves." He didn't hear anything either, so we start back slowly. When I felt we were clear enough, we made a run for it to the place where our unit had been.

None of our guys were there. There was a poncho lying on the ground with a slew of unspent bullets and a pool of blood. So we're wondering, *What the hell happened here?* Everybody in our unit was gone.

There was nobody around; I mean no Van Trump, no Levy—they were all gone. We started running through the jungle. We were getting stabbed with freaking branches all over, but who gives a shit? When we get out of the jungle, we reach the beach and see the whole battalion getting on the amtracs, ready to leave Ngesebus. Now I'm furious because I figured the guys just up and left us. I am really pissed, so I start looking for Van Trump because he knew we were out there.

I spotted him sitting on a stretcher. His whole head was just wrapped with bloody bandages. He had taken a bullet on the left side of the chin, and the bottom of his jaw was blown away. So that's why they had to pull him out. Charlie and I didn't know this until we saw him. So I didn't say anything to him.* Instead, I went over to the sergeant and had some words with him. I was still pissed off that they left without telling us, but I got over it.

R. V. BURGIN

We left Ngesebus that afternoon. We'd knocked out their artillery and killed about five hundred Japs. We had a few wounded and about fifteen men killed, but they didn't butcher us up like they did when we came into Peleliu. We came back to the regular island to pick up where we'd left off.

---

* Sterling Mace would remember, "You should have seen Van Trump when he come back up from the hospital on New Caledonia. He was gonna make the trip back to the States, and they stopped in Pavuvu. He looked like that cartoon Andy Gump. No chin. He couldn't even talk. He was really pissed because they weren't moving fast enough. He spent eight years at a VA hospital. For some reason, after the war he never saw me. Maybe he thought I was pissed off at him, but I wasn't. I would have been just as nice to him as to anybody."

STERLING MACE

They told us we were going to leave Peleliu. We were so happy to leave, that Levy and I started trucking—you know that jitterbug dance from the 1940s where you've got one finger up and all.*

But the next morning when we got up, they said, "The Japs have got the high ground. We're going to head up to take a ridge." So we weren't leaving Peleliu after all. You talk about being disgusted.

---

* Mace would remember, "There was a film crew right on the beach filming us . . . when Levy and I saw the film crew, we broke rank for about a minute and started cutting up for the camera. It was probably the last "fun" moment we had. I think the film still exists because someone claims to have seen it a long time ago. At any rate, the film would be worth a lot to me, to see myself again at twenty years old with a very good pal of mine." If any reader has seen this film, please contact Mace or the author.

CHAPTER THIRTEEN

INTO THE HILLS OF HELL

★ ★ ★

Peleliu

In early October 1944, K Company and the 5th Marines attacked the coral ridges in the island's center. All of Peleliu was in American hands except this, the Umurbrogol Pocket. There, in a series of rugged peaks and jagged valleys just four hundred yards wide by twelve hundred yards long, the enemy had concentrated a complex of caves and bunkers. These ridges had chewed up H Company before. Now K Company moved to take their place.

STERLING MACE

We were headed alongside this long ridge, about sixty feet high, toward an area called the Five Sisters (due to the ridge's five sharp peaks). We were in an open area with rough ground, no trees. On our left was the ridge. On our extreme right you could see the airport and the ocean. The airport was like a busy little city—people were walking around like nothing was going on. They didn't realize that just a few hundred yards away guys were getting killed.

Throughout the ridge were little caves here and there. We got to one, a bit larger. With us was a tank with a flamethrower on it. We fired up into the cave entrance and waited awhile. After we thought the place was sealed up, along came a guy, Raymond Grawet—real macho, open jacket, bare chest exposed, a .45 in his hand—and he went right up dead center to the entrance of the cave, thinking it's secured. He promptly got shot in the chest and killed.

JIM ANDERSON

The fighting in those ridges was tough. The heat we had to put up with during the days, it got up to over 110 degrees, and we had steel helmets on, packs on our backs, and we had to climb, which caused us to sweat.

Sometimes you didn't see a pillbox until you walked right up to it, they were so camouflaged with rocks. Captain Haldane would sometimes get an interpreter up there and try to talk to them inside the pillbox to get them to surrender. In three campaigns, I never saw one Japanese soldier surrender. Not one.

When they wouldn't surrender, we would call for a guy with a flamethrower. When he arrived, two or three of us would fire into the pillbox slit to keep them back. This guy with the flamethrower would come up, and he would shoot the flame into that pillbox and incinerate anyone inside. I always admired the courage of the Marines who operated the flamethrowers. We wouldn't go into the pillbox after that.

STERLING MACE

We walked up the trail, headed for the ridges. A pretty good shell dropped in and hit a couple of guys, including my platoon sergeant. I spotted him sitting by himself with blood dripping from the side of his head and went over, trying to help comfort him.

"Mace," he said. "What does it look like? Is it bad?"

"I don't know what kind of neighborhood you come from,

Harry," I said. "But it looks like some kind of wise-ass kid threw a rock and hit you in the head. That's all it is." So he felt better about it then.

We kept going, knocked out a couple of other caves, got up to the Five Sisters, and spread out.

R. V. BURGIN

We were setting up there on top of one of those ridges, trying to dig in. The cliff we were on was about sixty feet to the ground, almost straight up and down. A guy was setting up to my left. From across the valley, a Jap shot him right between the eyes.

The names of the ridges on Peleliu all run together anymore. I didn't put myself in a position back then where I cared to remember their names. A ridge was just another damn ridge to me, one damn ridge after another.

STERLING MACE

At the top of this ridge there were these swaths of white everywhere. I thought it had snowed up there. You know what it was? Used toilet paper. There was a lump of crap on each piece of toilet paper.

Then there were all these dead Jap bodies up there, decomposing. That's where we had to stay. The stink—forget about it.

We got set there and got into position. After about ten minutes you heard the crack of a rifle. Nobody said, "Corpsman," so I figured it was probably a miss. We sat there awhile longer. Finally I said to Charlie, "Hold the fort. I'm going down to see Levy. He's got my cigarettes." Because he could put them in his pack and keep them dry.

So I got down to where Levy was, but I didn't see him. I said, "Frank. Where's Levy?"

"I didn't want to tell you, Mace," Frank said. "But Levy took one in the head."

"Christ Almighty," I said.

"Yeah," Frank said. "Levy was sitting there shooting the breeze with the lieutenant. He turned around and said, 'I'm tired of this shit.' He looked up and *bing*. Wasn't two seconds later, and they got him."

JIM ANDERSON

At night you settled into a foxhole with a good friend. You're not supposed to fire at all, unless you're in heavy action. You see something out there in the dark, and it grows arms and legs, but then it turns out to be a stump. So your imagination gets you a lot of times. I tell ya—I was more afraid at night than I was in the daylight.

R. V. BURGIN

The Japs weren't *on* the island. They were *in* the island. All over the islands were these caves. The Japs had been on the island since WWI, and they'd brought in hundreds of Korean tunnel diggers in the years that followed. One cave was big enough to house about fifteen hundred Jap soldiers. This big cave started on one side of a ridge, went all the way under, and came out the other side. They had a dispensary set up in there, a hospital. All kinds of stuff. We had to close three or four entrances to those caves. If you used a charge to close one entrance, you didn't do much damage. They'd come out of another entrance and take another shot at you. So we did that, one cave by one cave.

K Company lost eight men in the Five Sisters before pulling out to rest.

R. V. BURGIN

You get so worn down, so exhausted. We fought them during the days, then at night they'd come out of their rat holes and infiltrate the lines. You get to the point where you don't give a damn whether you live or die.

We had come off the ridges and were down below the Five Sisters there. I'd been up and spent two straight nights with the men on the line. Not a wink of sleep. The third afternoon I found I couldn't focus my eyes anymore, so I called my sergeant, Johnny Marmet, and told him I need to come off the front line. So John said, "Yeah, come on in."

We had two mortars, each firing mostly harassment rounds. There was a shell hole right in front of one of the guns, and I crawled right into that hole. They fired those guns every two to three minutes. I went straight to sleep at eight that night. John woke me up the next morning at 8 A.M. Those guns had fired the whole time I'd been asleep, right over my head. But I'd slept all night in that racket, a full twelve hours, and I'd never once heard those guns.

STERLING MACE

We pulled back about fifty yards and set up lines that extended from the ridge toward the direction of the airport. The front was a U shape, and the back was open, because there wasn't supposed to be anybody behind us. Okay. You talk about a jury-rigged hunk of junk. A piece of wood here, a rock there. That was our security.

Everybody was all set up and keeping an eye on the Five Sisters. The password was Bull Run, because you gotta have everything with L's in it. The Japs can't say L's. Just as it got dark, we heard, "Corpsman!" When you hear this, you know there are problems. I looked and saw these two guys running toward me. I wasn't putting things together at first. I said to my assistant gunner, "Charlie, you see these guys coming? Are they stretcher bearers or what?" I held off shooting because I'm looking for a word of assurance from him, but Charlie didn't say a word. They peeled off to the right. They were two Japs. Evidently we passed a cave, went right by it, and they spent the whole day in the cave watching us set up our lines. So they knew where to run.

The Japs kept running and came to the machine gun squad. A guy named Gilbert Amdur saw them and challenged them. He hesitated and challenged them a second time instead of opening fire. That was inexperience on his part. After he hesitated, the grenade that killed him was already on its way.

I thought to myself, *I bet there are more Japs in the caves.* It got darker. Soon enough I saw silhouettes coming right at me. Four or five. We're watching. I took my BAR and just let the whole BAR go. I could hear them tumbling down. Charlie said to me, "What are you shooting at?"

"I'll show you in the morning," I said.

It grew quiet. Next thing you knew, the same thing. Another four or five silhouettes. I mowed them down again.

I had a magazine of tracers. I got those out of there and stuck another magazine on. Out came the Japs again—three or four. I got them again. Again, I heard more coming. Without thinking, I grabbed the tracers, shoved the magazine up, and pulled the trigger. It lit the place up. I could tell that the Jap on the end of the line could see the flash from my BAR. He peeled off to his right and hid.

I couldn't tell exactly where he was, but figured he was no more than five feet away from me. I turned around to Charlie and held my finger to my mouth and pointed. Charlie didn't say a word. I changed my position and got down on my right knee with the BAR resting on my left knee. I aimed right where I thought this Jap was. He was waiting for me to make a noise. I was waiting for him to make a noise. It might have been five, ten minutes, whatever. The Jap flipped something. I let twenty rounds go.

Charlie said, "What are you shooting at?"

"I'll show you in the morning," I said again.

The next morning there was this dead Jap. He took twenty rounds right dead center of his stomach. Half of his face was blue. That was the first time I'd ever seen a blue face on a dead Nip, so I asked a corpsman about it. "We all have blue blood inside our body," he said. "When it comes out, it comes out red. The reason it looks blue now is that you hit him so fast, the blood in his body didn't have a chance to flow."

All those Japs I shot were night fighters. They wore black pajamas. Sneakers. No uniforms except for the guy with blue blood. None wore helmets. They were armed with hand grenades, but that was it. They'd plopped on top of each other.

One guy had this wristwatch on. I tell ya, I'm not in for souvenirs. People ask, "What souvenirs did you bring back from the war?" and I say, "I'm sitting on it." You know what I mean. But stupidly I took a piece of twine, all I could find, and put it around his wrist. I didn't want to touch his hand. Finally it shook loose. So that wrist watch was one souvenir I had. I took the watch home to my mother. She went to a jeweler and had a new band put on it. But when I told her where I got it from, that was the end of that watch.

R. V. BURGIN

Pretty soon, dead corpses were all around. There was no dirt to cover the corpses on Peleliu. Just coral. If there was dirt, we would've covered them. They'd bloat up larger than they really were. You couldn't bury them. The sour stench of those corpses was everywhere. You'd often be in a certain place and you'd have to stay there all day and night, three days sometimes, and a corpse would be right by you, within stepping distance. There was no way to get away from the corpses.

The flies were unbelievably thick. Big ole green blowflies would be everywhere on those corpses. I've seen flies so thick on a corpse, something would disturb the corpse and they'd form up like a bunch of blackbirds—flies so thick they cast a shadow. When you were trying to eat, you couldn't shoo the flies off. You had to knock them off with your thumb. They'd come up from the body of a dead Jap, fly right out of his mouth or butt, and land on your food.

JIM ANDERSON

There was approximately eleven thousand Japanese soldiers on Peleliu. We killed the vast majority. Only half of them ever got buried. So you can imagine in the heat what it smelled like. Every day a plane came over and sprayed Peleliu with DDT to try and kill the flies and all the diseases. We didn't see a difference.

After a brief rest, on October 7, K Company returned to the Umurbrogol Pocket. This time they avoided the ridges by staying in the valleys.

STERLING MACE

They told us we were going to do one more big push. But they always said that.

R. V. BURGIN

We were going in to clear out the pocket in a horseshoe-shaped valley. We were down low, with ridges in front of us and on both sides. The Japs had those caves set up in those ridges, higher in elevation than us. From three sides, they were looking down on us, and we were looking up at them. To me, that was a death trap. We were sitting ducks, going in there. But it had to be done.

JIM ANDERSON

At the Horseshoe Valley they assigned at least two Army Sherman tanks with their 75mm guns to K Company. Unlike the ridges, where the tanks couldn't help us, this terrain was perfect for them.

When the tanks came up to our front line, a squad or platoon was assigned to each. We infantrymen would have to accompany them because the Japanese soldiers would often come running out of their caves in suicide attacks with sticky bombs or mines to knock them out.

At the Horseshoe we got about two hundred yards in, as far as the tanks could go, and got into a real battle. When we would run up against a pillbox where an enemy machine gun was firing from, we would get ahold of the telephone on the back end of the tank and say, "There's a pillbox seventy-five yards to the right, give him a couple of rounds, would ya?" Eventually the tanks used up all their ammo, so we had to pull out with them. There would have been too many casualties otherwise.

K Company returned to the ridges. On October 12, the company found itself on a ridge named "Bloody Nose."

R. V. BURGIN

We were heading up a ridge and taking fire from three sides. Someone needed to see what was beyond the hill, in order to direct the battalion's counterfire. The captain's runner, Jim Anderson, and his right-hand man, Dick Higgins, were with him. Someone had to look over the ridge to see what we were up against.

JIM ANDERSON

We were going through Bloody Nose Ridge when we moved up with Captain Haldane to an observation point on the ridge. We were all sick and tired of fighting. Captain Haldane was just as fatigued as the rest of us fellows.

Captain Haldane went to look over this coral ridge, down into the valley where K Company was going to advance. Dick Higgins and I were next to him, just below the ridge so the Japs couldn't see us. When Captain Haldane peeked over the top of this ridge—bang—one shot was fired. He was shot right through the forehead. It killed him immediately. I was standing not more than a foot away, and he slumped right beside me. We don't know where the shot came from. I'm guessing that some Jap rifleman had seen the activity there and had it all sighted in and ready to fire at whoever appeared over that ridge.

It just hit us—our leader had been killed.

R. V. BURGIN

We were about three-quarters of the way up the ridge. It was Johnny Marmet who came back and told us about Ack Ack's death. The best I remember, he said, very simply, "We've lost our captain."

JIM ANDERSON

A couple of us carried the captain's body back down the hill from the front lines. The men of K Company took Captain Haldane's death extremely hard. After all the fighting and suffering and misery we had already put up with, having our commander die seemed too much to bear. I seen some good hard fighting men just turn around and walk away because they didn't want to be seen crying.

I seen the gunny sergeant in our company, he just took a rock and threw it down on the ground and said a bunch of swear words.

R. V. BURGIN

Some of the men took it very deeply. It affected different ones differently ways. Some said, "Oh shit," "Oh my God." Some of us never said anything. But it was a real blow. Captain Haldane was as good a captain as ever led a company in the Marine Corps. Everybody liked the captain. He was an extraordinary man. A great leader. Whenever we marched into battle, he was the first to lead us in. It cost him his life.

The future Senator Paul Douglas was a Marine who served with our regiment. He was a politician who joined up at age fifty as a PFC, then became an officer to get overseas. He went to the same alma mater as Ack Ack, and this is how he remembered him: "His company always suffered fewer casualties than any other company, but in every engagement Andy was always wounded—always wounded and always wound up each engagement twenty or thirty pounds less than when he began because he would give his rations away. He would give his blankets away, he would give his shirts away; and we always had to protect him at Peleliu to see that he got enough food."

JIM ANDERSON

After the captain got killed, we were still on the front lines for a while. We all felt really bad, all of us did. But you had to keep going. You had to do your job. The company's executive officer, Thomas "Stumpy" Stanley, took over. It was near the end of the fighting, and the fighting was still going real hard. The Japanese that were left were real dug into their caves. They was very good soldiers. They put up with a lot. But to utterly throw their lives away seemed very foolish to me when they could have surrendered. When they stayed in those caves and pillboxes and we went in with flamethrowers, they could have surrendered first and still been alive today.

R. V. BURGIN

Did the Japanese soldier have a sense of surrender? Oh, hell no. On Peleliu, I believe there was ten or eleven thousand Japs on the island. We captured nineteen. And I wouldn't have been surprised to learn that some of them captured were Koreans or Okinawans that they had forced to come into their army. When it came to the Japanese soldier, you were going to have to kill them all.

They were brainwashed. The head of their government, their emperor, was divine in their eyes—literally a god that they could pray to. So the fighting became a religious thing for them. They were taught that it was an honor to commit suicide for their god. I've never actually seen a Japanese soldier commit *hari-kari* up close, but I've found plenty of their bodies after they did it, with a sword stuck through their gut. And I've seen plenty of them after they'd blown themselves up with hand grenades. I always thought, *Well more power to them*. I wish more of them would have done it. In their minds, it was an honor to kill themselves for the emperor. But I always thought the other way around—that it was an honor to live for Uncle Sam. I always wanted to live. I never wanted to die.

JIM ANDERSON

We was ordered back to this real tough, last-ditch fighting on Peleliu. The Japanese soldiers were fighting an effective defensive battle. They were very well disciplined. The Japanese were so dug into the caves that the artillery couldn't touch them. So we would call in air support, Marine Corsair fighter planes, loaded with napalm. We laid out orange panels, "air panels" they were called, to mark the front lines so the pilots would know to not drop the bombs where we were.

The Corsairs would take off from the airstrip we had captured earlier in the campaign. They would not even retract their wheels—they would swing around and drop this jellied gasoline on the ridges, then they'd strafe the area and set it on fire to burn the Japs out. After that they would land, all within five minutes. We were told it was the shortest bombing run of WWII. They were a real help. That napalm did more damage to the Japanese than our artillery. It didn't necessarily burn the Japs—it would burn the oxygen out of the cave and suffocate them. Napalm is terrible stuff.

On October 15, the Army relieved K Company and the 5th Marines and inherited the Umurbrogol Pocket, still four hundred yards wide by five hundred yards long. K Company moved to a secure area on the island's north shore for evacuation to Pavuvu. Six weeks later the island would be declared "secure," although the last thirty-four Japanese soldiers would not surrender until 1947.

STERLING MACE

The general had told us the campaign for Peleliu would last three days. We were there for forty-four.

R. V. BURGIN

When we got on that boat and left Peleliu, really, we hadn't slept for a month. I was wiped out after thirty days of constant fighting. Exhausted. Mentally and physically. We all were. Some were barely able to climb the rope ladder to get aboard the ship to leave.

I don't remember changing clothes for the whole damn time we were on Peleliu. The coral and sweat from the heat mixed together. Everyone's clothes were raggedy, frayed, torn. Shoes were just about gone. Everybody stunk. Nobody was changing his socks. Many men are sick. There was a lot of diarrhea going on. We were a bunch of raggedy-ass Marines.

CHAPTER FOURTEEN

BACK TO THE WORLD

★ ★ ★

Pavuvu

After Peleliu, the 1st Marine Division returned to Pavuvu in early November 1944.

JIM YOUNG

When we pulled in to Pavuvu, the beach was lined with new recruits, but the big surprise is that a bunch of our guys who we thought were killed were here to greet us! There were tears in the eyes of a lot of us. It was a real great feeling.

R. V. BURGIN

This time, Pavuvu looked pretty good to us. At least nobody was shooting at us. They'd fixed it up a bit since we were last there. The rotting coconuts had been cleared away and the tents were new. At the pier when we embarked were half a dozen Red Cross girls standing behind tables. They gave us cups of grapefruit juice to drink in paper cups. It felt strange to me, them welcoming us here. What the hell were they doing in the middle of a war?

Sledge resented this, too. He proved to be a good Marine once we got to Peleliu, and never hesitated to do anything I asked him to. You can't ask much more than that from a Marine.

JIM YOUNG

After marching from the docks to our tents, we found four recruits had been placed in the bunks of our lost buddies. What hurt me most was seeing one of them in Corporal Brown's bunk (who had his head shot off when he jumped from the amtrac). The new boys were all over us asking how it was on Peleliu. They thought we were real heroes.

We all talked long into the night and the boys drank their ration of beer. I didn't drink, so I had a Coke. I hit the sack and got one of the best night's sleep I've ever had.

WAYBURN HALL

Eventually our complete outfit returned. Then everybody was finding out who got back and who didn't. We had a parade or two. I got a Purple Heart pinned on my chest. I'd say the whole outfit was pretty docile for a while. We'd had our fill of what battle was like.

R. V. BURGIN

We didn't do much for the first ten days or so. They let us alone to rest and regain strength. Florence's letters caught up to me. She sent me newspapers. And a fruitcake, which the guys ate while I was out of my tent.

You had to balance the joy of being alive with bitterness of where we had been. Peleliu was a waste. To me, it was the roughest battle of the Pacific War, and it was a battle that should have never been fought. MacArthur wanted the airstrip on Peleliu secured. But we had already bombed that airfield three months before. Hell, we could have gone on bombing it for the rest of the war. There was no way the Japs could have rebuilt it to make it usable again. They were pretty much finished as an air power by then anyway.

It was a damn unnecessary battle. I'll say that to any man today. And what makes it worse is that no one has even heard of it. Since a lot of our top brass thought the battle would be over so quickly, not a lot of reporters and photographers went there. I'd say that pretty much everybody has heard of Guadalcanal and Okinawa and Iwo Jima—the big battles of the Pacific. But the majority of American people today don't know about Peleliu. Many have never even heard of the island.

The 1st Marine Division lost over a thousand men the first day on Peleliu. Thirty days later, when the Army finally relieved us, we had 6,526 casualties by then. The Army had over 250 killed and 1,200 wounded. So that made up more than 8,000 casualties on this island that nobody ever heard of.

JIM ANDERSON

Pavuvu wasn't much different the second time, except we had better food. The guys who had fought in three campaigns left for the States. Pop Haney was on that ship—he'd had enough and said this was a young man's war. I was promoted to corporal but remained a runner for Captain Haldane's successor. Captain Stanley was a fine, fine gentleman and a good warrior. Captain Haldane was our number one commander, but Captain Stanley was a close second. Some officers treated you like a servant, but Captain Stanley, when he was going to tell you to do something, he would say, "Could you do this for me?" He was quite similar to Haldane. Captain Stanley also called me Andy. He must have heard that from Haldane. He probably learned a lot from Haldane.

R. V. BURGIN

Captain Haldane was going to put me in for a Silver Star for securing that bunker on Ngesebus, but he was killed before that happened. Stumpy Stanley took over as company commander, and he never put anybody in for anything. I asked him about that one time, and he said, "Ah hell, I always thought everybody deserved a damn medal, so I never put anybody in for one." I told him, "That's a hell of an attitude to have."

JIM YOUNG

After two and a half years, for me, it was finally over. What was left of us "old salts" boarded a liner, the USS *General William Mitchell*, bound for the USA.

This ship was returning from the China-Burma-India theater of war when Admiral Nimitz made them stop and pick up us survivors of three campaigns and drop us at the San Diego Marine Base. This was lucky for us because it may have been months before another ship was available.

The people on this ship were mostly women and children. There are also about twenty nuns with the largest hats I'd ever seen. These people were rescued just before the Japs were able to trap them. We had a great time with the kids. Many of them were orphans. We kept giving them all the candy they could eat. The nuns gave us heck and said we were spoiling them. I guess we were. The orphans hung onto our hands and walked the decks with us. They were lonely and a lot of them had lost their parents.

At San Diego there was a Navy band playing for us. The Red Cross was there with hot coffee and donuts. Some of the fellows kissed the ground as they left the gangplank. We ate, listened to the band, then boarded trucks for the ride to the Marine base. From the docks we headed right down the main street of San Diego.

Every building was camouflaged, and there were camouflage nets strung from one side of the street to the other. People on the streets were cheering us. It was a wonderful welcome.

The Marine base was a beautiful sight. The cooks at the mess halls threw a big feast for us, with just about anything you could think of and all the ice cream you could eat. Our orders were issued. We got new uniforms and got ready to board trains for the East Coast. I was to report to Quantico Marine Base in Virginia.

At Quantico, my duties were to train FBI agents on firearms. I didn't like this job, so they gave me one training officer candidates in the art of the 81mm mortar. This was a real neat duty. But after five months I became ill and spent twenty-nine days in the Quantico Naval Hospital, an aftereffect of my time in the islands.

Meanwhile on Pavuvu . . .

R. V. BURGIN

They started to work us, and that helped us put things behind us. I was promoted to sergeant. We had a lot of replacements come in. They were raw, straight from the States. So we did our best to get them in shape. They think they're combat-ready, but they're not. Whenever you're going into battle with someone for the first time, you're never sure how they're going to react. Most of them do their duty. I'd say 98 percent do. But you always worry about your new men.

One new Marine assigned to K Company was Harry Bender.

HARRY BENDER

I was born and raised in Chicago. When Pearl Harbor hit, I was about fourteen, I guess. I had been to the movies, and I came home.

My parents were all talking about it. I didn't even know where the hell Pearl Harbor was.

When I was seventeen, I enlisted in the Marines. I was five-foot-three. You were supposed to be five-foot-four to get into the Marines, but because I was seventeen, they figured I'd still grow. So I got a waiver. My father was chairman of the draft board in our area, but he didn't push me in either direction. He had been in the Marine Corps in WWI and approved of my decision.

I was a grunt, meaning I was in the infantry platoon. I was the youngest, the shortest, and the orneriest. You could say it was chosen for me. They asked me what I wanted to do, and I said, "Communication." They said, "Well if you don't do communication, then what?" I said, "Okay, photography." My parents had given me a 35mm camera, and it was really nice. I wanted to be a combat photographer. I thought I'd be good at it. I ended up in the infantry.

After we finished advanced infantry training, we shipped out. We were scheduled to go to Peleliu as replacements. But the division pulled out of Peleliu, so we went right to Pavuvu.

Some people think of Pavuvu as some goddamn country club. That's bullshit. Sure, Pavuvu had been fixed up a bit since the time the guys were first there, but Pavuvu was still bad news. The land crabs were terrible. Pavuvu was a combat area without snipers in the trees. There was nothing there.

Actually, there were two things we did on Pavuvu: There was good swimming there. And they showed a movie damn near every night.

The unit's veterans were not hostile to us. They knew you proved yourself in combat. You didn't prove yourself in training. So I had to wait. My only problem was I couldn't complain too much. Everybody knows you by your serial number, whether you're an enlistee or a draftee. All the draftees' serial numbers started with nine. I wasn't a draftee. My serial number started with five. So if ever I started bitching about something, they'd ride you a little and say, "Shit, you asked for this shit." You get to the point where you don't complain anymore.

WAYBURN HALL

After Peleliu we trained some more and took on some new replacements. All of the old guys were sent home. We were mostly a new outfit. Some of the old sergeants were still around, but I know my platoon sergeant was gone after Peleliu.

I was made corporal and a gun squad leader, in charge of about six other men. We started training the new guys, breaking them in on the guns.

The Marines celebrated Thanksgiving 1944 with all the trimmings . . .

HARRY BENDER

It was Thanksgiving and the officer's mess was roasting their turkeys the night before. I was on guard duty for officer's mess that day. A buddy of mine decided we were going to steal one of the goddamn turkeys from the officer's mess. So he stated that he was going to start a fire in an area a little ways away. And that I was going to react to it by leaving my post. Which he did, and I did. We stole a turkey and quite a few of us that night ate turkey. My buddy and I took the bones and scattered them down L Company's street.

Next day I was called to the XO's office. "Shadow" we called him. Lieutenant Loveday was his name. He was a real prick. He asked me about the turkey, but he didn't believe a damn word I said. Nothing was ever done about it.

Mind you, we were going to have turkey anyway on Thanksgiving. It wasn't like we were going to do without. But we just wanted to eat another turkey the night before as a snack. We were getting a head start on things.

WAYBURN HALL

The scuttlebutt came around that we were going to make another push. Everybody wondered where. At first, they said Formosa, and we made some practice landings on Guadalcanal just to get used to landing on the beach in Higgins boats and all.

HARRY BENDER

I had mess duty. Some older guys told us about making jungle juice. So I scrounged around and found some peaches, then we had these fruit bars that came in K rations. Nobody ever ate the damn things. So I told the guys to give me theirs, and we saved them up. We had dried peaches, and the fruit bars, some yeast and sugar, put it in a five-gallon can, and we started brewing. But we didn't know that you weren't supposed to seal the can, you were just supposed to put cheesecloth over it. We sealed it, and then took off for two weeks in Guadalcanal.

We went up to Guadalcanal and made a landing in preparation for Okinawa. They had us up there maybe two weeks. There's this kunai grass that grows about six feet high. You get in the middle of that and its so hot you pass out. Guys were passing out left and right. Finally a Navy doctor called the exercise off.

They had a PX there, but you could only get into the PX if you had khakis. There was an Army signal unit nearby where we bivouacked. Next day after we saw that, there was a lot of Marines running around in Army clothes. That's how we got in the PX.

When we got back from Guadalcanal, our goddamn jungle juice had fermented all right, but then because we'd sealed the can, it had gone and exploded. Everything inside our tent smelled like rotten peaches. So much for making jungle juice.

CHAPTER FIFTEEN

ISLAND X

★ ★ ★

Iwo Jima

In February 1945, while the 1st Marine Division recovered on Pavuvu, the 5th Marine Division sailed for its first and only fight of the war on the volcanic island of Iwo Jima.

CLARENCE REA

We had no idea where we were headed. They called our destination "Island X" until the day they summoned us noncoms and officers into a room on the ship. There, they had a map of Iwo Jima. That was the first time we had heard of the place. They told us we were going to win Iwo in three days and then board ships to meet the 1st Marine Division. We were supposed to take Okinawa together. This would have been a good deal for Basilone—that was his old unit.

CHUCK TATUM

Colonel Butler came on the loudspeaker and told us we were going to fight on Iwo Jima. It was going to be the closest battle to Japan so far in the war.

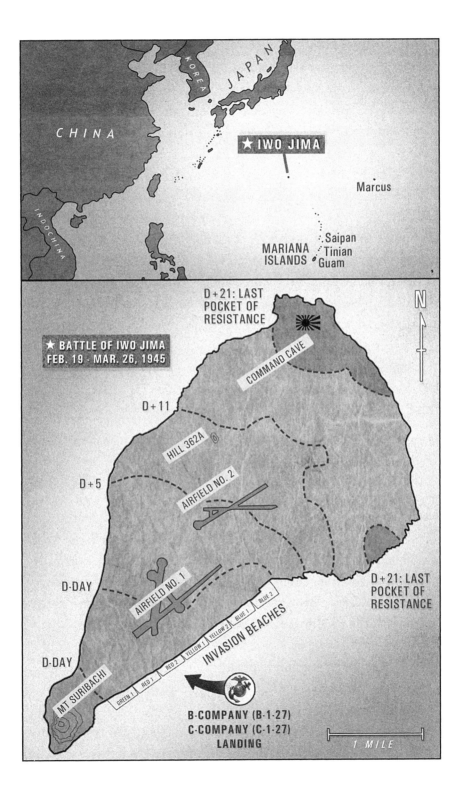

CHINA

KOREA

JAPAN

★ IWO JIMA

Marcus

INDOCHINA

MARIANA
ISLANDS

Saipan
Tinian
Guam

D+21: LAST
POCKET OF
RESISTANCE

N

★ BATTLE OF IWO JIMA
FEB. 19 - MAR. 26, 1945

COMMAND CAVE

D+11

HILL 362A

D+5

AIRFIELD NO. 2

D-DAY

AIRFIELD NO. 1

D+21: LAST
POCKET OF
RESISTANCE

BLUE 2

BLUE 1

YELLOW 2

D-DAY

YELLOW 1

INVASION BEACHES

RED 2

MT SURIBACHI

RED 1

GREEN 1

B-COMPANY (B-1-27)
C-COMPANY (C-1-27)
LANDING

1 MILE

It took forty-two days for us to get there, aboard ship. We were on the LST on the way to Iwo Jima, and I don't know why but they had us on guard duty, guarding the ship's deck, that far out at sea. Anyway, it was my turn. The LST had all our gear on it, including our seabags. I was getting sleepy and lazy and I lay down on a seabag. One of them wasn't very comfortable, and I said to myself, "Golly, that's a bottle of whiskey in there."

Well, I liberated it. Sure enough, it was a fine flask of Old Taylor bourbon whiskey. After I got off duty, I took it up to where the guys in the machine gun platoon were. I hid it until the next day, and showed it to my friend Herb. He had two bottles of Coca-Cola. So we mixed it together and all had the biggest party as long as the whiskey lasted.

Everybody had some anticipation. Some nervousness. But I don't remember being afraid then. It wouldn't do any good anyway. What were they going to do—let me off ship? I didn't know what to do except do whatever I was told to do.

CLARENCE REA

On the way to Iwo, there was some sniper activity on Saipan. So we stopped there. I was assigned to take a team out into the mountains and get the sniper who'd been causing trouble. We were out on a mountain at night and had a dog handler with us. The idea was that these dogs could spot a sniper in the dark by smell. Man, those dogs were great. One of my squads was with me. We were out about two o'clock in the morning. I'd worked with dogs a lot before, back at Pendleton. The idea was that a dog points in the direction he thinks the sniper is, just like a bird dog would. You have to get close to the dog in the dark to see which direction he's pointing.

The dog alerted. I walked up to the handler and pointed to where the dog had alerted to. He was on about an eight-foot leash, and as I turned around and walked back to my squad, this dog came around and bit me in the stomach. I have no idea why the dog did that. It was a Doberman. That was kind of a scary thing that happened. But luckily because of my cartridge belt, the dog didn't hurt me. But if I hadn't had that belt on, my stomach would have been all over that mountain. Oh, and we got that sniper.

CHUCK TATUM

A religious service was held two days before we landed. They had a sailor guy who had some religious training, I guess. He talked pretty good on the Bible. He conducted a service, maybe thirty-minute sermon. My favorite hymn was "Onward, Christian Soldiers." They used to sing it in Bible class as a kid. I didn't tell anyone this was my favorite hymn, but I remember we sang it that day, and I liked that they did. The guy quoted from Psalm 23—you know the one that goes "The Lord is my shepherd," and that's pretty much my favorite passage from Scripture. So that made me feel better, too. All the guys were there for that service. I don't remember anyone being an atheist.

Sure, I believed in God, but I never had any sense that God was going to single me out for protection. You couldn't pray for yourself. You had to pray for everybody. That's how I felt. I had read this book just before joining the Marine Corps, *Magnificent Obsession* by Lloyd Douglas. It's about this guy who needs to use an ambulance right when this famous doctor did. He lives, but the doctor dies. To pay everything back, his obsession becomes to always do better. That's how I wanted to live my life—selflessly like that.

CLARENCE REA

They bombed Iwo for thirty days before we ever got there. Bombed. Shelled. Everything you could think of to soften it up. These battleships were firing these big shells on the island. The bombers flying overhead. You'd think none of the enemy would ever survive. We were supposed to take Iwo Jima in three days then go on and take Okinawa. That was our mission.

Well, it ended up being thirty-two days on Iwo, and a hell of a lot of people killed.

CHUCK TATUM

February 19, 1945, was D-day for the invasion of Iwo Jima. What do I remember? Oh heck. I slept in my dungarees, woke up about 4 A.M., and got my gear ready. Our last meal on board was steak and eggs early that morning. The eggs were powdered. The steak was worse than gasket material. But the coffee was good. One thing I remember—it was morbid—but I kept thinking that a lot of these same people wouldn't be eating tonight. The guys I knew so well. It was true.

CLARENCE REA

We waited as the island was being shelled. As daylight came, we could see the bombings and the smoke from the shellfire coming from the battleships. Everything was firing all around us.

CHUCK TATUM

They lashed wooden boxes full of C rations along the edge of the amtracs. Steve Evanson, the assistant gunner, and myself had the job of operating the big .50-caliber guns going in. Our other job, as soon as we got to shore, was to cut the ropes of the wooden boxes and kick the food overboard.

CLARENCE REA

I was a platoon sergeant by this point, some thirty-two men in my charge. We started getting into our amtracs. I had one assigned to me, Basilone had one, Clint Watters had one. That's where we parted. John, Clint, myself, and our buddies shook hands and said, "See you later." We got in our amtracs. Then we headed for the beach.

CHUCK TATUM

We were in the first landing wave. Going into the beach, there was nothing to shoot at, but Steve and I shot every now and again to bolster our courage. All around us was smoke and noise and confusion. Heavy guns from the ships out at sea pounded the island. Overhead flew Corsairs and Hellcats on bombing drops. The island was really getting hit hard.

Our tractor came into the beach and turned. They lowered the rear ramp, and all the guys ran out except Steve and me. We started to kick the stuff off. But very quickly the guy in the tractor took off while we were still up there. We screamed and hollered at him to stop, but he couldn't hear us. By now we'd gone a long ways down the beach. We were way, way gone from the rest of our guys. Finally, I got the driver's attention. I jumped off the edge of the tractor. Steve tossed me the machine gun and jumped. It was a nine-foot drop off the top, plus we had the machine gun and tripod. Both of us ended up on the sand. Unfortunately we never got all the C rations kicked off.

Ahead, we saw these big sand dunes. We started running off the beach toward these terraces. The first danger we saw was this Marine Corps bomber coming parallel to the beach. The pilot had been shot and was dead at the controls. I could see his face. He was only about a hundred yards away. He was shooting the sand right in front of us. The plane turned and headed out to the ocean. It hit one of those tractors and it exploded.

CLINTON WATTERS

When I landed on Iwo, I didn't feel any fear. That incident with God I'd had at Bougainville had changed my life.

The Japanese had made terracing out of the volcanic ash on the beach, and as we landed the footing was just terrible. Every time you took a step, it filled in with ash. You couldn't run. You couldn't hurry to get up and over the banking. Even when the tanks came to shore, they got mired down and stranded on the beach. The drivers had to wait so grading could be done before they could get up and over the terracing.

CLARENCE REA

People say that the initial landings on Iwo weren't that bad, but don't believe it—it was bad. We hit the Red Beach One under heavy fire. They opened up on us with big guns on Suribachi and others at the other corner of the island. Immediately, there were guys dying all over. My first lieutenant had just gone ashore and had his left arm blown off at the shoulder. He wasn't more than ten feet from the boat. He was evacuated right away. I hated watching the kids of my platoon get hit. That's how I thought of them—as my kids. And I called them that.

Your training tells you to keep moving forward. That's what you've gotta do. It's like if you're in a race car, you don't think about getting killed. You've got an objective before you. That's all you do.

We tried to move up over the black sand bank that was in front of us. We got over it and we lost another man, my squad leader, who was to my left. I heard one of my other guys yell, and I looked around, and the only thing left of my squad leader was his one boot sticking up out of the sand.

CHUCK TATUM

They'd told us to get off the beach as soon as possible. So Steve and I climbed these big terraces. When you're climbing those sand dunes with a machine gun, sixty pounds of ammo, and everything else you've got on you, you're really struggling. We finally got to the top of one, but then there's three or four more to go. We finally got to the last one, and Steve and I were exhausted. We were also all by ourselves. We looked around for our unit, but couldn't see any traces of the rest of our guys. Between Steve and me we only had five hundred rounds of ammo in two boxes. With our machine gun, that meant we had less than two minutes of firing time. Being separated from our platoon was the last thing we wanted just then.

Just then I looked back to the beach and saw the third wave was coming in. John Basilone was leading that wave, and I recognized him. The forward motion of that third wave carried Basilone close to where Steve and I were.

A Jap shell *shwish-shwished* in and hit with a blast off to our right. Up exploded a huge mound of black sand. All hell broke loose. The Japs dropped mortars, artillery shells, one right after another in a huge bombardment. Jap shells cascaded from the sky, and big showers of sand fell all over us. Men tried to dig in, but that's pretty hard to do when you're still on sand dunes. We all hit the deck and hugged the earth.

One lone Marine wasn't digging in. He was running back and forth between soldiers, shouting, yelling, kicking butts. "Move out!" he kept saying. "Get your butts off the beach!" A group of men followed him. It was Basilone.

CLINTON WATTERS

We were taking quite a lot of mortar shells and fire and lost a lot of men right from the beginning. I was maybe three-quarters of the way up the banking, maybe fifty yards up and stalled, when Basilone came running up. By that time, we'd already lost several men. Basilone got us all moving and up on the banking. We fought our way up toward the airport.

We ran into pillboxes with the enemy firing out—concrete bunkers with sand way up over them so even if shells hit, they weren't wiped out. We soon learned there were lots of underground tunnels in that area, too. The Japanese came at you from behind when you weren't expecting it.

CHUCK TATUM

Basilone saw our machine gun and ran right over to me. He whacked me in the head, the signal to go into motion at his command. I couldn't see anything, but by looking down his arm, I could just see the aperture of this big, giant pillbox. Basilone had seen it from behind, while he was still coming up the beach.

"Fire on that target!" Basilone yelled. Steve and I set up the machine gun. But it was so full of sand it wouldn't work. I tell ya— right on the beach in the middle of battle all our training kicked in, and we cleaned the machine gun right there. It only took about thirty seconds, but it felt like a year. The second time we tried it, our machine gun fired. We were in business.

Basilone directed the fire into the pillbox. I can still see our tracers hitting it. Then Basilone found a guy from the demolition squad to run right along our line of fire up to the pillbox without us hitting him. The guy ran to within fifteen feet of the pillbox, and Basilone whacked me on the head again, this time the signal to quit firing. The guy ran the last few yards to the pillbox and threw ten pounds of Composition C in the aperture of the pillbox. Well, this blew things to kingdom come. Big chunks of concrete. When all the debris had fallen, Basilone had me open up again. I shot some more.

Then he found a corporal named Pegg, a flamethrower operator, who ran up to the pillbox and gave it several bursts of napalm. I'd say napalm is one of the most dangerous weapons in war. Basilone made me quit again, hit me on the head, and Pegg got out of the way. I was lying on the ground, operating the machine gun, and Basilone was behind me. He reached down and unhooked the machine gun from the tripod. The ammo belt was still on it. He picked up the machine gun with the bail* on it and screamed in my ear to get the belt. So we ran forward. Basilone carried the machine gun in his hands. And I carried the belt. He's running, and I'm running with him.

We got to the top of the pillbox. Basilone knew those Japanese would exit the pillbox. Sure enough, when we got to the top, here were eight or so Japanese running out the back. Basilone mowed them down with the machine gun, firing from the hip, me still holding the belt. They were on fire, from the flamethrower, yes. It was a mercy killing more than anything.

This is the first up-close kill I've seen. I could give you a pound of adrenaline. It was a hell of a war going on, that's what I was thinking. We've been here less than thirty minutes and already we're right in the thick of things.

We climbed up a slope and found ourselves at the very end of the airstrip, where they turn the planes around. We were still under

---

* The "Basilone bail" was a specially designed device used to carry a machine gun. It comprised of a wooden handle fastened by wire to the barrel of the weapon, and was inspired by Basilone's Medal of Honor engagement on Guadalcanal after he burned his arm while carrying a hot machine gun. Without the bail, it would have been nearly impossible to control the blistering machine gun when removed from its tripod.

intense fire. Later we learned the fire was coming from a nest of Jap gun emplacements on the slopes of Mount Suribachi, about a mile away.

We were also taking fire from our own ships. We'd moved ahead so fast that we'd come right up under our own shells. It was a very bad place to be.

CLINTON WATTERS

When we got up to the start of the airport, we could see a lot of revetments where they parked the planes. I led my people to the first revetments—it was a bank of lava-type stuff, about eight feet high, that wrapped around where the plane would be, except there were no planes because they were smashed up along the field. We went over the banking and down into the flat part of this revetment where the plane would be. We were going south to north, and then crossed over the north bank when Basilone stopped us. He hollered and said, "Bring the men back on this side—you're out too far in front! I'm going back to get a tank or something to see if we can get some artillery in here!" Then he went running to get us support. That was the last time I saw him.

CHUCK TATUM

Basilone turned around and handed me the machine gun. I thought we should get back with everybody else from our unit. But Basilone wouldn't let us retreat. He stopped me right in my tracks and said, "You guys gotta stay here come hell or high water. I'm going back to get more troops. We can fight our way across." Then he took off, back to the beach to get more troops.

Basilone placed Tatum, Watters, and the others on the edge of the airfield strategically. He knew they had come far enough and had to hold this critical terrain with a field of fire across the airfield.

CLINTON WATTERS

I directed my men to go back across the revetment and stay there behind the south bank. I waited until they got back over there before I started back. I was in the flat area in the base of that revetment, when a mortar shell dropped in there. It was just like someone hit me in the base of the spine, with a hammer. The blast knocked me down and felt like it hit my back when actually the shrapnel hit me in my thigh. Grains of coarse black sand also got blasted in my right eye and it was bleeding. That was it for a while. After I was hit, I crawled over the banking and lay there. I couldn't stand.

CHUCK TATUM

I couldn't tell you in real time how long he was gone. But pretty soon I looked back the way we had come, and I saw Basilone and three or four other Marines running back to where we were. He was seventy-five yards from me, less than a football field. I heard this incoming mortar shell come in. That mortar shell hit right near Basilone and the other Marines.

I didn't see anyone moving. I knew they were all dead. That's when I realized we had lost Basilone. Word went down the line from hole to hole. "They got Basilone." It was ten-thirty in the morning.

CLARENCE REA

My good friend John Basilone, who was off to my left with a machine gun platoon, was killed. I didn't see his death, but one of the guys told me later about it. I miss him an awful lot, even now.

CLINTON WATTERS

Soon enough the corpsman came over. He wrapped up my leg and gave me a shot of some dope. "Sorry," he said, "but there isn't anybody to help you get back to the beach. I guess you're going to have to do it on your own." So I started crawling back to the beach. It was maybe a third of a mile away. The ground was sandy, hard to move. I ripped the bandage off my leg and found that easier going. I crawled a long ways, and my leg bled quite a bit.

I was maybe halfway back to the beach when I saw a young Marine. He was just wandering around aimlessly. Shells were landing in his area.

"Get down!" I hollered at him. The shells were flying all around.

"I can't see!" he hollered back.

"Just stay right where you are then," I yelled over the noise. "I'll be right there." I crawled over to him and said, "I can't walk. But if you can help me up, then I'll direct us both back to the beach."

So that's how we got back to the beach, him and me. When we got back to the beach, the Navy guys were there. They took the blinded man right out to the hospital ship. He had to have some fast treatment. A while later they took me out to a barge in the water, because I wasn't considered critical. To this day, I don't know who that man was or what happened to him afterward. I often wonder if he ended up permanently blinded.

CHUCK TATUM

We had what I call "the big Iwo Jima Turkey Shoot." It consisted of us guys that Basilone took up there, maybe eighteen or nineteen guys. We've only got one machine gun between us and half a box of ammo left. With Basilone down, we dug into our holes and stayed put. It would have been safer to get out of there, but Basilone had ordered us to stay and hold our position. Even with him dead, we obeyed his order.

After a while, someone hollered, "Hey, there they go!" We looked down the airstrip, and there was six or seven Japanese running from the beach side to the other side. Well, Steve grabbed the machine gun and mowed them down. Fine with me, but I knew we'd need to conserve ammo. There were no officers or sergeants around. I kinda took charge. I told the guys that the next time we see any Japs, the BAR guys would need to get them. They did. They spent all afternoon shooting Japanese.

The day wore by. I started to get concerned about our longevity, to be honest. About one in the afternoon I ate a K ration. I hadn't eaten since four o'clock in the morning. We were there all day long, fighting, waiting, fighting, waiting. Around four-thirty I looked around at the end of the airstrip. There was Sergeant Windle coming over the end of the airstrip, with the rest of B Company. They came right to where we were. They had an ammo carrier, so we resupplied then.

CLARENCE REA

We fought our way to the airfield. By the time we secured the airfield, it was dark. We holed up for the night. I got my guys all situated on the line where we were very secure.

That first evening, I was sitting with a couple of my squad leaders under a red Japanese meatball painted on the wing of a wrecked airplane on the airstrip. We'd found an old phonograph that had these old Japanese records, you know, and were sitting there playing that thing. All of a sudden, this screaming and hollering came at us. A Japanese soldier was charging our way. The word quickly went out to the guys on the line, and they shot him almost instantly.

CHUCK TATUM

I was promoted that first day. We were getting the lines set up that evening, and my sergeant, Windle, called me over and said, "Tatum, you take the squad." I said, "Why me? I don't want to be a squad leader on Iwo Jima." He said, "Well it just so happens that you're now the ranking PFC in the company." Our company had suffered severe losses during the beach assault. By the end of the day, we had seventeen men killed and fifty-one wounded.

CLINTON WATTERS

That night they took me to the hospital ship, where they operated on me. They operated on my eye and leg the same night. They operated on my eye first and took out all the sand. I could still see out of it all right. They were quite concerned I was going to lose my eye from infection, but I didn't. My eye has never bothered me since, even though I still have one little speck of sand that's visible even today. Then they operated on my leg. The shrapnel had gone into my thigh and lodged there without exiting. They cut a place on the inside of my thigh and pulled the piece of shrapnel the rest of the way through. Then they stuffed a piece of gauze all the way through the inside of my leg. They propped me up on my side and poured penicillin on that gauze. It acted just like a wick. They also gave me penicillin shots in my rear end, every four hours, night and day, for two weeks. I was so sore I had to sleep on my side and stomach. I tell you, my rear end hurt more than my wound.

CHUCK TATUM

That first night on Iwo Jima was terrifying. It's worse fighting at night than any other time. Remember, the Japs knew the island perfectly. We didn't even know where we were. Neither did we know which way they were going to attack us from. To put it bluntly: We didn't know anything.

We surmised there'd be a huge banzai attack, so we set up six machine guns to put up a line of fire. But the first night they didn't come.

I was so tickled to be alive the next morning.

Having landed and secured one of Iwo Jima's three airfields, the Marines began their conquest of the island, by attacking west to east, yard by yard.

CHUCK TATUM

The morning after the invasion it was raining. Cold, too. It made everything muddy and miserable. Word came down the line who had been killed and who'd been severely wounded, out of the action. Lieutenant Dreger, Gunnery Sergeant Kavato, Sergeant Lutchkus, Brookshire, Whaley, Pospical. Those were just in the machine gun platoon. All capable leaders. There were many more.

CLARENCE REA

The next morning we started out again, this time on the left side of the island going north. Shelling was heavy during the night, every night. You were lucky to get fifteen minutes of sleep. I never slept for more than thirty minutes each day, my whole time on Iwo Jima.

From about the third day onward, the Japanese artillery fire got very heavy. Under heavy fire, I'm sure everybody feels different. I had thirty men I was worrying about. You're trying to pick out targets, you're just so busy you don't really think about anything other than what you've got to do. I'm sure you've had dangerous experiences where you don't realize how in danger you are, so that you don't even think about it. At the time, you're just too damn close.

CHUCK TATUM

A lot of fire came to us that day from Suribachi, a mountain that loomed over us on the island's western coast. But the Japs didn't hit us then. The rounds were too short. They tried, all over the island, they tried. We found an empty Jap pillbox and took cover there. We figured they would never direct their fire at their own pillbox. There was just a lot of shooting that day. A lot of action. A lot of noise.

A night or two later we experienced our first banzai charge. Maybe 9 or 10 P.M., shadowy shapes appeared on the horizon. You wonder what it's all about. Then all these enemy soldiers with their bayonets fixed started running right at us. They ran low to the ground and were screaming, "Marine, you die!" and a whole lot of other stuff that was just undecipherable. High-pitched shrieks. Really eerie stuff.

By reflex I opened up my machine gun and just kept it going within my field of fire, traversing it back and forth and back and forth. I kept my finger glued to the trigger and was so tense I forgot to fire in short bursts like you were supposed to. Soon the barrel of my machine gun turned red from heat. In no time flat I'd spent a whole belt of ammo. Steve quickly snapped a new belt in place, and we were back in business. With the second belt, I was calmer and fired like I was supposed to. The whole attack lasted about an hour. No one slept after that.

Meanwhile in the hospital on Guam . . .

CLINTON WATTERS

All that penicillin must have worked, because I kept my leg and it healed up well. I was in the hospital in Guam when I was told that Basilone had been killed. That was a shock. It was hard to believe. He seemed invincible. I don't know when Johnston and Wheeler were killed, but they were in his wedding party, too. And Martini, the other sergeant in the party, he lost his arm and got the Silver Star for it.

You would hear things in the hospital, just rumors from Iwo. I wondered how the platoon was making out. Some of those people still out there were pretty young.

Meanwhile on Iwo Jima . . .

CLARENCE REA

After that first couple of days it was pretty scary. We didn't think we gained anything but a couple of yards on the beach. You didn't know for sure what was going to happen. There was a lot of doubt.

I was standing there when they raised the first flag on Suribachi. I wasn't up on there, I was down below. All of a sudden you heard the ships blasting their horns. Somebody noticed the movement on that mountain, and everybody started looking up there; then you could see them putting up the stars and stripes. It was only a couple hundred yards away. It was absolutely amazing. Guys started yelling and cheering. Most of us had tears in our eyes.

I thought, *At least we've got the mountain; now we've got the rest of the job to do.* Hell, we still had three-quarters of the island to take. There is something about seeing that flag that builds up a courage or something in you, that makes you want to get the hell going, get the job done, and get out of here. It inspired us to go forward as it did for every kid on that island.

I saw the second flag go up later. That's the one you see in the famous pictures and the statue. The first one was the one that got the reception.

CHUCK TATUM

To give you an idea of the big picture: Iwo Jima was a series of daily battles. The fighting was continuous. We advanced one yard at a time. There was no no-man's-land. The enemy could be fifty to sixty feet in front of us. Often we fought all through the night and into the next day with no rest.

CLARENCE REA

The Japanese had what they called these "spider traps." These were fifty-gallon oil drums buried in the sand. The lids on them, they were hinged. There'd be a Japanese soldier squatted down in it with the lid down. They had grass and stuff on top of it, so we'd walk right on over it and wouldn't know it. Then, when we were in front of them, they'd raise the lid, get their rifle out, and fire at us, then quickly close the lid again. Many times, you didn't know they were behind us like this. Sometimes we were able to find the man, if we could find him. But other times not. You turn around and look back, and all you see is level ground and weeds. These traps were everywhere. Eventually we got them all.

CHUCK TATUM

George Van Conkelberg had been the gunner in our squad, but he had a tooth that got infected on the way to Iwo Jima. He came ashore on D plus five or six. Technically, Van should have been made squad leader, because he had two years longer in the Marines than me. But I guess I had more battle experience than he did, after those few days of fighting. He was really pissed because I was the corporal now. He was a couple years older than me and kinda treated me like his little brother.

Once, Van noticed me chain-smoking after a heavy bombardment. I lit one cigarette after another. He said, "Tatum, I need to talk to you about that smoking. You're smoking too much, that's dangerous for your health." I said, "F-you, man. Being on this island is dangerous for my health."

CLARENCE REA

One night we were taking heavy shelling, and we got into this big shell hole for safety, me and a couple guys. These shells were hitting all around us. One shell hit really close to our hole and blasted sand all over us. A second shell hit. We had one young guy in our outfit, a really young kid, maybe eighteen, we called him Chicken, he just lost it mentally and took off running. Well, the Japanese shot him before he got fifteen yards. That's the kind of stuff you remember, and it really hurts.

The fighting took a mental toll on you. The island was only eight miles long by four wide. But the fighting went on, day and night, for thirty-three days. You knew the only way to end this madness would be to kill every human being—every Japanese soldier—on the island.

On the tenth day of fighting, in the northern portion of the island, the Marines encountered a rock wall named "362A" on the map. The Japanese had turned this work of nature into a fortress.

CHUCK TATUM

Maybe a week in we experienced our darkest of days fighting on Hill 362A. It was a horrible place. No place to dig in. No way. The name "362" referred to the height—362 feet high. It was probably the second largest part of the island.

When we first approached it, it was nothing to look at. We were in a flat area at first, and nobody knew anything about the hill. All we could see was this big lump of land ahead. Later, we learned it was the Japs' number one defense line going across the island. So they were going to hold it at all costs. We kinda stumbled into it, honestly. We had no idea how many pillboxes were hidden in the side of that hill. More than three hundred, we discovered.

Captain Jimmy Mayenschein was leading our group then, the XO in our company. Jimmy was very popular. Shorter, maybe five-seven. Maybe not even that tall. But he was all man. He'd been a Paratrooper and had already seen combat at Bougainville. The Japs got us trapped in this area during a bombardment. Finding pathways out was difficult. Captain Mayenschein got us out of harm's way then followed us toward safety. He never made it. The last man out, the Japs used him for target practice, shooting him to pieces.

I was fighting alongside Lloyd Hurd, Steve, and Van. I was the acting corporal of our squad. You couldn't see anything on the hill, but Windle spotted a cave and directed me to put the machine gun on that. So I signaled to Van, the gunner, to make that his target. He ran up and threw the tripod down. Steve came behind him with the machine gun. Before they could get all the way set, a sniper shot Van in the back, shoulder area, while he was still leaning over. They shot Steve in the stomach while he was still running up to help. A gut shot like that is real bad. Steve was bleeding hard.

I got pissed. Both of my friends were down. I ran over to where they were, grabbed the machine gun, and opened fire on the cave from the hip. I fired the whole belt of bullets into that cave. The belt ran out. I have no idea how many I killed, but in my citation it says that I killed several of the enemy. I was afraid that if Van or Steve moved, the Japs would shoot them again.

Then I ran and got a medic, and Hurd and I and the medic carried Steve and Van down out of sight. A corpsman gave the guys morphine.

Steve gave me a thumbs-up signal, very weak, letting me know he was still alive, and maybe I had tears in my eyes. I can't remember ever crying about it. I should have, probably. Mostly I was angry. I'd never been so mad in all my life. Somebody had shot my friends. Hell, they might be killing me next. I hated this island. I absolutely hated it. I hated the Japanese. I hated the war. I hated everything I could think of.

The rest of that day was foggy to me. The stretcher bearers took Steve and Van out. I told Windle I wanted to go with them, but he wouldn't let me go. "We've lost too many men already," Windle said. They took them away, and I never saw them again on the battlefield.

I found out later that Van made it but Steve died during the night. When you're gut shot, you're going to die. Sadly, he did.

The caves in the northeast corner of the island marked the fever pitch of the battle for Iwo Jima and, in many ways, a repeat of Peleliu.

CLARENCE REA

About three-quarters of the way up the island, near some cliffs, we came to a section where all the Japanese were in caves. That was where it got really bloody.

One day I was in a foxhole and my guys were dug in. We were trying to figure out how to move on. The Japanese had us pinned down. We didn't have tanks up there at that time. I was calling for the Corsairs to come in and drop some napalm bombs at the face of the cliffs, which the other companies were doing as well.

I saw a Japanese machine gunner up there in a niche in the rocks. My BAR man was in a hole over to my left. He was a little Italian kid who I had brought through parachute school. I called over to him and pointed the Japanese soldier out to him, to put the fire on him. As I was peeking over the edge of my hole, I heard the sound of metal on metal. I looked over to him. His head was slumped. "Benny, Benny, are you okay?" I asked him. He didn't answer. I lifted up his helmet and the back of his head was gone, blown away. His brains were running out the back of his helmet. He'd been shot directly in the forehead and killed instantly. It was like losing one of my own kids.

CHUCK TATUM

I don't remember a lot of the specifics of Iwo anymore. Days blurred into one another. The whole experience on Iwo was a lot more of the same thing, over and over. Just continuous fighting, the whole time I was there. No letup.

We were on a ridge somewhere, and I was walking behind the company a ways. We walked by this Jap body. He looked dead anyway. But just as we were past him, I saw him move. Just a bit. Maybe he was wounded, because he threw a grenade at us, and it was a pretty weak toss. I jumped back and rolled down the hill. The grenade exploded above me. I felt its blast smash against my back.

Everything was completely black for a few seconds. Maybe it was longer. I don't know. When I came to, I noticed that my carbine was still in my hands. I hadn't let go of it. For some reason, that felt good to think I hadn't dropped my rifle.

The Marine I'd been following was a few feet away. He was okay. Just covered in dirt. But he was yelling at me and I couldn't hear what he was saying. My ears were all crazy. Inside my head it was like a drum beating—I don't know how else to describe it. There was a cut on my leg, maybe eight inches long, and it was bleeding, but it didn't look terribly deep. We just got up and kept going. I felt dizzy and achy and wanted to lie down. I thought my head was going to explode.

CLARENCE REA

One of my squad leaders was a kid from Fresno named Dawson. One day I called him to bring his squad up on line. As he was running to where we were, a machine gun opened up on him. He was running and dodging. And we were saying, "C'mon, Dawson! You can make it!" He was almost to us, but then the machine gun hit him about ten feet from the hole. We crawled out and pulled him into the hole. Dawson was shot all to hell. We all thought he was dead.* So pretty soon the corpsman came, and we had to move on. We couldn't just sit there.

CHUCK TATUM

We were marching somewhere and they called a halt. Anytime you're hungry, you use whatever time you have. I broke out a K ration. Nearby on the path was a dead and bloated Jap body. There's nothing worse than the smell of a dead body. But I kept eating anyway. Pretty soon a tank came along and ran over him. Completely squashed the corpse. Some of the body fluids splashed up and onto my pants. I couldn't get the smell out, so I took my Ka-Bar and cut that part of my dungarees off and threw it away.

Another time, a young guy came up as a replacement, Buckland. He told whoever the sergeant was, "I'm sure glad to get up here on the front lines."

"What, are you f-ing crazy?" the sergeant said.

"I was out on the beach burying people," Buckland said. "I'm glad to join the fight and be up here." He hated burial detail that much.

---

* Clarence Rea would remember, "Later on, I was walking down the street near the hospital in Oakland, and I'd be damned if I didn't walk into Dawson, face-to-face. The corpsman had drug him back to the aid station, and they'd pulled him through. He'd made it. Of course we hugged each other. It was great to see him alive."

Once the Japs buried themselves for us. We were on a ridge above a closed off cave. We could hear the Japs down below. Somebody mentioned that they might blow themselves up, but we didn't think anything about it. We stayed there that night.

We heard a tremendous blast underneath us. The Japs blew themselves up, and us with them, too. The ground just exploded. There was no time to think about it. Rocks, dirt, went everywhere. All the rocks rained down. We were lucky to be alive.

CLARENCE REA

I had thirty-two men in the platoon when we started. A few days later, I'd lost ten. A few days later the number I'd lost was up to sixteen. You can't ever describe what it's like to lose half your men. You're hurt. Really hurt. You've learned to love these kids, you've brought them through training. But it doesn't really hit you until years later. At the time you're so damn busy, you're thinking of things so fast. All you do is call back and ask them to send you some replacements.

CHUCK TATUM

Corporal Angelos Tremulis—now there was a bright spot in the war. What a guy! Before he came to us, he'd been a seagoing Marine and was on the *Yorktown* when it was sunk. He spent eight hours learning how to deep water swim in the Pacific Ocean before he was rescued. He got out of that, and didn't want to be seagoing anymore, so he became a paratrooper to avoid the dangers of being aboard a ship (laughs). When they disbanded the Paratroopers, Tremulis became a regular Marine. He was a corporal when he came into B Company. He was skinny as a rail, Greek ancestry. His folks ran flower stores back in the States, and that's what he wanted to do, too. I thought it was funny that this tough Marine wanted to open a flower shop. But Tremulis figured that after the war a lot of the guys would be getting married, so there'd be big money to be had.

Tremulis was a leader of a machine gun squad. Just like Windle. Tremulis got dysentery very bad. It went on and on. Dysentery is one of the worst things that can happen on the front lines, because you're not keeping any food inside of you. Day after day, Tremulis never got any better. They have a medicine for it, but they ran out of it. It got so bad he couldn't walk anymore, his ass was so raw. But here's what he did. He got a bandage from the corpsman and smeared it all over with a half inch of petroleum jelly, and stuck the bandage between his ass cheeks. He just pulled his pants up and kept going. He couldn't walk otherwise.

CLARENCE REA

I was hit on the thirteenth day, hit in the left arm with shrapnel. I didn't see or hear it coming. There was so much firing going on. I was on the radio, calling for air support, when the shell hit. The sensation I remember was that somebody hit me on top of the head with a sledgehammer. It knocked me out. When I came to, my arm was just hanging useless because shrapnel had severed the radial nerve. I wrapped it with a tourniquet and took off. I wanted to get down, get it fixed, and come back.

I started making my way down a trench, heading toward the aid station. As I went around a corner, here comes this Japanese soldier with a rifle in his hands. I had a .45 pistol in my hand. He had to pick up his rifle to shoot—I had my .45 ready. I shot him before he could get off a shot.

I made my way back to the aid station. It was set up in a shell hole. It was primitive care—you gotta realize there's nothing on the island yet.

I didn't want to go. I wanted to stay, but they couldn't treat me at the aid station there. I lost complete use of my left arm, so they just carried me down the beach and put me on an LST, took me out to a hospital ship, and hauled me down to Guam.

It was tough to leave the guys. You trained all those kids. You got so you knew them so well. They told you all about their families, everything. I had lost a lot of them, almost half of my platoon, and now I had to leave the other half behind. It hurts. It was a brotherhood. Even if the government decides someday there won't be a Marine Corps, it's still going to live.

CHUCK TATUM

The days wore on. It kept raining. We were cold, hungry, tired. Everywhere you looked was a dead body. We were in battle all the time. It all got blurry. My head ached from that grenade blast. The ringing in my ears wouldn't go away. I felt sick to my stomach all day long, every day. I had the craps, just like Tremulis and every other man on the island did, but not quite as bad. My mind was hazy. I felt numb. Guys would say things to me and I wouldn't answer them. I went to a medic and he kept giving me aspirins for my headaches, but that didn't do anything. What else was he supposed to do?

We were given the day off to reequip and resupply. Half an hour into it, B Company got called into another battle. It was D plus fourteen, and we began to take heavy mortar fire. We're deep into it and it's as bad as it ever was. A round hit close to me and I thought to get to some nearby rocks. Halfway there, another round hit and I got knocked down. Fortunately, the barrage stopped as quickly as it started.

All of a sudden I realized I'm sitting on a rock by myself, and I don't know where anyone else has gone. Nobody. I have no idea how I got there or what I'm doing there. That's what was happening in my mind. And then I said to myself, "Tatum, if you sit on this rock, you'll be a good target." We had already had two guys from my squad killed that morning. From my section—that morning!

All of a sudden, here comes Windle out of the rocks. He came up to me. "You're going to be all right, Tatum. Come on, we're going back to the platoon." So he led me back to the platoon.

I didn't know about combat fatigue, but that's what I had, apparently. I kept having these headaches, sure. Sometimes when a mortar goes off near you, you get these concussions from the shock. There's no aspirin for it. There's no cure. I think my mind slipped into a protective mode. You're hoping for the best, but you've already seen so much, you don't believe in the best.

Later that afternoon Windle said, "Tatum, I'm sending you back." Just like that. I was very surprised. I didn't argue with him. What they were afraid of is that I might do something and get them all killed. So that's the reason he got rid of me. I don't know what they were observing in me. I wasn't goofy. I was just sitting alone with a blank stare, I guess, dizzy, with a ringing in my ears. Alone with my thoughts.

Tremulis could hardly walk by then. So Windle sent Tremulis out, too. "You're *both* finished," Windle said. "Get the hell back, both of you."

Tremulis and I started walking toward the beach. We hoped no Jap snipers would get us. The farther we walked away from the front, the more we began to improve. A guy in a DUKW came along and drove us several miles to the rear. I remember we passed this distillation plant and we filled our canteens with some real water. Everything else we'd been drinking since landing tasted like oil. Both Tremulis and I drank as much as we could hold.

Tremulis and I got aboard the first ship we could. Just like that, our war was over.

We'd been fighting on Iwo for fifteen days.

The battle for Iwo would last a further twenty-one days and culminated in a Japanese banzai charge against American airmen in their tents on airfield number 2. The attack would be repulsed and the battle won. By then, Tatum, Rea, and Watters were under medical care.

CLINTON WATTERS

From the hospital in Guam, they shipped me to another hospital in San Francisco, and then to the naval hospital in Newport, Rhode Island. I would be in the hospital for the next six months.

CLARENCE REA

The hospital in Guam was just a little Quonset hut right up against the jungle. Still pretty primitive. So many guys were coming in there so fast, hundreds of them, thousands, from Iwo. The hospital ship had been full, and they were trying to unload all these guys so fast so they could rush back and get another load. The hospital staff didn't have time to do a lot of special work. They just had to patch you up and get you out so they could get other guys in. I'd heard that Clint Watters had been hit. We were friends and more— we were both born on the same day—March 12—but I was born in 1921 and him in 1922. So when I got to the hospital, I tried to look for him. The information they gave me was that he'd died. He hadn't made it.

One of the riflemen in my squad, they took both his legs off right there in Guam. They were going to amputate my arm. I told them I wouldn't accept that. I guess I convinced them, because they decided to send me back to the hospital in Pearl Harbor. I went back there for a week or so then they shipped me to the naval hospital in Oakland, California.

In Oakland, a new young Navy doctor, Lieutenant Cummings, had just started doing experimental work, nerve surgery. I signed permission so they could experiment on me. They cut my arm open, almost the length of it, got the two ends of the nerve, and put it together. Through a lot of therapy, gradually the hand healed. It didn't come back completely, but we hoped that someday it would.

The stuff I saw in that hospital never left me. I can see it now. It was sickening. Pitiful. Kids with no arms or legs. Some with no appendages whatsoever. Some burned so badly they didn't look human. Some of my kids. One had his jaw shot off. The doctors took skin from his side to rebuild his face, but what they would do, they would take a long strip of skin, attach half of it to his face, while leaving the other half dangling. If the graft took, they'd cut off the excess skin. So many kids were walking around the hospital like that, with gobs of skin grafts hanging from them.

CHUCK TATUM

Tremulis and I spent the first evening aboard this old three-stack destroyer. I sold my carbine to the sailors for $20. Tremulis got $25 for his. He was a better salesman than me. I took my first shower in sixteen days. They didn't have any Marine clothing aboard, so they issued us Navy clothes. We ate Navy food. We went to sleep. That first night I slept for fourteen hours straight.

We were transferred to another ship, a troop carrier, and spent several days sailing from Iwo to Saipan, where they put us in an Army hospital. Everyone else there had everything wrong with them, but I felt kinda funny, because I didn't have any wounds that bled. I was labeled *SSCF*, shell-shocked, combat fatigued. They don't have any cure for it, you know.

Combat fatigue is kinda like if you're on a sidewalk, and you're trying to cross a busy street. As soon as you start across, a big semi truck rushes at you. Okay. And that keeps happening and happening. You keep trying to cross, but more and more trucks come, so you get more and more jumpy, more and more scared. If you get away from that busy street, then you start to relax more. If a man has combat fatigue, it doesn't mean he's a coward. It's just that a mind can only stand so much. I was just eighteen years old when we landed on Iwo. I wanted to fight, and I could have gone on, I always felt I could have. But perhaps it was just the graciousness of Windle. He saved me, really. Later in life I thought it through, and if Windle hadn't sent me back, I never would have made it off Iwo alive. I would have been killed—I'm sure of it. I had had so many near misses already.

They sent Tremulis and me on another ship to Hawaii, the island of Oahu, where we went to a naval hospital. That's where we ran into Van and learned that he was still alive. That was good. He was one of my best friends in the service.

In the hospital, there was a lot of evaluations. Doctors asked everything about you. I told one of the psychiatrists that I was okay mentally and I wanted to rejoin my outfit. That's when he decided I was off my rocker. Seriously, it didn't help my case at all.

Eventually, they sent me stateside, to San Francisco. We were aboard a civilian ship that had been converted to transport troops. This was about April 1945, and news came aboard the ship that Roosevelt had died. That was a sad moment for everybody. Truman became the next president.

In San Fran, they took us to another Army hospital. As a matter of policy, we were quarantined for five days. That's when Tremulis and I decided to go on liberty. They wouldn't let us out, but we thought, *The hell with them.*

Tremulis found a place down by the tennis court where a corner of the fence was dug away and you could crawl under and get to the highway. So one night we snuck out through the fence and caught a ride to downtown San Francisco. We had about $4 between us, went to a bar on Market Street, and bought drinks with the money we had. I ordered a 7 and 7, whiskey and 7-Up, because that was the only drink I knew. When I paid for it, Tremulis said in a voice that could be heard by the guy next to us, "We just got back from Iwo Jima." Golly, that brought the whole place alive. We spent the night carousing in San Francisco, getting drunk, with everybody buying us drinks and dinner.

Finally, the Shore Patrol caught us. "Why are you out of uniform?" they asked us. We were in our dungarees and without hats. Tremulis told them a story about how we were here with Hollywood, making a movie with the Marines. He talked them into it, and they let us go. But next we faced a real dilemma. It's easier to sneak out of a Navy hospital than it is to sneak back in. We came back on a different street, and we couldn't find the corner of the tennis courts. So Tremulis decided that he'd hoist me over the fence, and I'd find a place to get him in. As I'm crawling over that, I hear the click of a machine gun. I looked around, and here's this nervous little sailor, with his hands on a submachine gun. So I jumped down and got on the ground. Here stands the Shore Patrol around us. Four of them. Tremulis told them this story about how we just got back. Finally the guys turn to each other and say, "I didn't see anything, did you?" They all agree they didn't, so they open the gate and let us back in.

I was sent to Oak Knoll Naval Hospital. It was psychiatry-related—I could tell from all the talking and interviews I was doing. The whole thing was a psycho ward. I didn't feel like I should be there. The ward is a bunch of wacky people, including me, I guess. A bunch of Marines and sailors. Nobody believed me that I wanted to stay in the service. But it was true—I had hoped to become a Marine officer eventually. I figured that would have been the greatest thing a guy could do for a career.

Then I heard word I was going to be discharged. And they did. Finally it came through, June 14, 1945, and I was able to go home. It was an honorable discharge, but a medical discharge under honorable conditions, which meant I couldn't go back into the service ever. My days as a Marine were over.

CHAPTER SIXTEEN

THE LAST ISLAND

★ ★ ★

Okinawa

On March 14, 1945, the 1st Marine Division sailed from Pavuvu, bound for Okinawa, an island state of the Japanese Empire just 350 miles from Japan.

WAYBURN HALL

We left Pavuvu for the last time, went aboard ship, and sailed out through the bay. A joke went around that as we were leaving, a million of those land crabs had gathered on the beach. They were waving good-bye to us, shooting us the finger.

STERLING MACE

We left Pavuvu on a pretty good ship, a converted freighter, and went up to a gathering point at Ulithi in the Carolina Islands, north of Peleliu. As far as you could look in any direction, there were ships. We pulled into the harbor there and anchored.

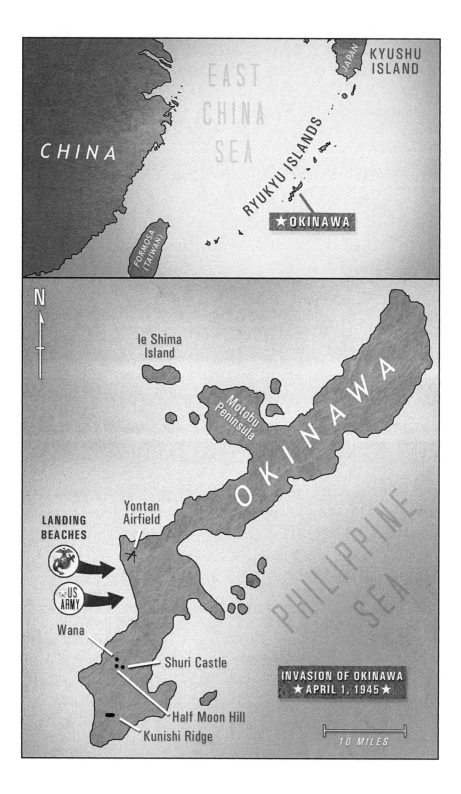

KYUSHU
ISLAND

JAPAN

EAST
CHINA
SEA

CHINA

RYUKYU ISLANDS

★OKINAWA

FORMOSA
(TAIWAN)

N

Ie Shima
Island

Motobu
Peninsula

O K I N A W A

Yontan
Airfield

LANDING
BEACHES

US
ARMY

PHILIPPINE

SEA

Wana

Shuri Castle

INVASION OF OKINAWA
★ APRIL 1, 1945 ★

Half Moon Hill

Kunishi Ridge

10 MILES

JIM ANDERSON

This was the first time I absolutely knew for sure that the United States was going to win the war. As I looked out across the harbor, there was nothing from one end to the other but ships. Literally thousands and thousands of our ships were there.

WAYBURN HALL

One day we got up and went topside. We spotted this aircraft carrier off to our left, maybe five hundred yards away. It was the USS *Franklin*, the one that got shot up so bad by the Japanese. That was a sight to see. It's a miracle it survived. I forget how many men they lost. The deck was just rubble. They finally towed it back to the United States.

R. V. BURGIN

While we were at Ulithi I got a letter from my Dad. It said that my brother, J.D., which stood for "Joseph Delton," had been killed. He was in the Army and had just gotten to Europe when he was killed by artillery. I remember being up on the top bunk, just staring at the ceiling. It was pretty hard but I never did have time to really grieve his death. I still had business to take care of.

STERLING MACE

From the harbor, we headed up to Okinawa. We were in the high seas, rolling. The only excitement came one day when we sat at a mess hall table. The table was wet. The ship rose on the port side, and our cups of coffee on the table slid. The roll went through and the starboard side came up, and our cups came down. That was just the start. The waves got higher, because pretty soon dishes were sliding. Then we slid on our seats. Then one big wave came, and the whole cafeteria was thrown against the starboard wall. Dishes, tables, chairs, everything. We made a joke about it, laughing. But we decided we better get out of there. We didn't want to end up in a cleaning crew.

HARRY BENDER

On the ship on the way to Okinawa, I had mess duty. I actually volunteered for that, the only time I volunteered for anything. I figured the guys on galley duty would have it okay. Turned out I was right. The only showers you could take onboard ship were with salt water. But we got fresh water in the galley. So you'd just strip down, and another guy would pour the water on you. It was a hell of a lot better than taking those saltwater showers. Then there'd always be these fresh loaves of bread or whatever going to the officers. A tray of those would come by the galley and we'd grab it first.

WAYBURN HALL

We got to the East China Sea, close to Okinawa. We pulled up and dropped anchor. The 1st Marine Regiment was in division reserve for the landing on Okinawa. So we were not set to land the first day. For a while all we did was hang out aboard ship.

STERLING MACE

A Jap seaplane came by, one of those observer planes that operates off a battle wagon. The Navy guys started shooting at it. We were ordered to go below deck. So we were below deck, and we heard the guns topside going like a son of a gun. It started a small riot with us, because we didn't like what's going on outside, and we were trapped inside.

So we went to the door. Now, if you turn the dials on the door to get out, there's another guy on the other side trying to stop you. But we overpowered him and opened the door. Some lieutenant was going to arrest us. We told him, "You can do anything you want, but we're coming topside! No way we're going to be trapped!" We made it up to the fresh air.

JIM ANDERSON

Okinawa had been a Japanese possession for many years, although it was not originally part of Japan. The island is seventy miles long and varies in width. The north end is all mountainous. In the south, it's rolling farm country. Just off Okinawa, still at sea, we was told it was going to be a terrible, terrible battle. So we were expecting something similar to Peleliu.

HARRY BENDER

While we were still on ship, they recommended cutting your hair short, even shorter than it already was. If there were head wounds on landing, it was better if a guy didn't have a whole lot of hair. So a couple days before we landed, we started cutting hair.

The morning before the battle, you get steak and eggs for breakfast. Bill Leyden, my buddy who was a veteran of Peleliu, pulled me aside and said, "When you go through the mess hall line, get some extra pieces of bread, and we'll make some steak sandwiches to eat once we're on the beach. Beats the hell out of C rations." So we did.

R. V. BURGIN

I was always very confident I was going to survive. I knew there was a possibility that I could get killed. But I always figured it wasn't going to happen to me. Even being wounded—all the way along I never figured it would happen—until we got to Okinawa, my third battle. Then I started figuring—well, you keep sticking your chin out, somebody's bound to hit it.

April 1, 1945, was both Easter Sunday and April Fool's Day. Together, the 1st and 6th Marine divisions landed on Okinawa's western beaches, along with two Army divisions.

WAYBURN HALL

The military feared that the Japs would attack the transports and try to sink the ships with all the troops aboard, so they ordered us ashore.

We went over the side of the ships about noon on that first day of the invasion. You crawl down these rope ladders with all your gear on.

STERLING MACE

We went down the side of the ship on ropes. You go down on this net and get to a Higgins boat. The Higgins boat is rising and falling with the swells. One minute you're ready to get in it, the next moment it drops five feet. So you've got to watch the swells. Just another little hazard.

WAYBURN HALL

We were in that landing craft probably four hours. We were in a larger boat this time. I don't know how many troops were on there, but it was a lot. We were packed in there pretty tight, but you could still take your helmet off, set it on the bottom of the boat, and rest on it for a while. I was sick to my stomach, I have to admit it. After the experience I'd had on Peleliu, I was scared to death, fearful of what was coming.

Late in the evening we pulled up in the area opposite the Yontan Airfield, the landing area for the 1st Marine Division. We had the Army on our right flank and the 6th Marine Division on our left flank.

We went ashore, wading across the coral reef. It was anywhere from six inches to two feet deep. If you were careful to not step in a chuckhole, you were all right. If you stepped in one, you'd go down under and come back up all soaking wet. The enemy aircraft activity had picked up by then, but we made it onto the beach with no problems, no casualties. The landing went smooth, without opposition, which was a great surprise to everyone.

STERLING MACE

It was a soft landing. We were in the seventh or eighth wave. The Japs were intermittently throwing shells at us. We were told we'd need to use ladders to get over a seawall that was there, but the seawall had been destroyed where we were, knocked down to ground level. This kid from Ohio, Bob Whitby, said, "Boy, this is a piece of cake." It was his first campaign. People were all over the place. We saw this actor, part of a camera crew, and waved to him.

We moved up, through this brush area, to a clearing. There, a sixteen-inch shell that had come in must have hit a whole platoon of Japs and just blew them all apart. Big mess. Bodies. A head here, an arm here, a shoulder, whatever. I called Whitby over and said, "Bob, come here, I want to show you something." He came over. I said, "This is what you call a piece of cake." He couldn't believe what he was looking at. So he got an eyeful of that. We moved on.

JIM ANDERSON

We just fell into columns and marched, without any return fire. The Japanese pulled an April Fool's Day joke on us. There was a reason for this. The 32nd Japanese Army was on Okinawa with about 110,000 men. But they had pulled down to the southern end of the island.

WAYBURN HALL

From the water's edge, we climbed up on this ridge. We hiked up there toward the airfield. A revetment was there, where the Japs had stored their planes, and we bivouacked in there for the night, kind of hiding.

Sometime before dark, a Jap Zero tried to land on the airstrip. It came zooming down there, and all the firing you ever heard took place. They knocked the plane out before it quit rolling. So that was the first close-up I'd ever seen of a Jap plane.

The night got real chilly. We'd been used to heat where we'd come from, but this was cooler. They'd issued us a light jacket and we had our blanket rolls with us, so we were okay.

HARRY BENDER

When we landed, there was no resistance at all. No enemy anywhere. But everybody was still as nervous as a sinner in church. We stopped and dug in for the night and ate our meal. Guys were throwing grenades and shooting off their weapons at any little thing that moved. That shook me up more than anything.

I had turned eighteen on March 8, 1945. I was ready to see enemy soldiers. But there was no way in hell I was ready for what I saw next.

The next morning when we started to move out, we went by a

shack belonging to some Okinawan civilians. In the courtyard were two little girls, maybe nine and eleven, all dressed up in kimonos. They were dead. We had done it, yes. I'm sure of it. There was nobody else around. No adults. Just the two little dead bodies. They were really dressed up, too. I don't know whether it was for some ceremony or what. You could see their wounds, where they'd taken fire. So this was very sobering, right early on. All the guys were feeling the same thing, I think. We weren't prepared for this. Goddamn, I was throwing up that steak sandwich.

The 1st Marine Division had its mission: to race across the island and cut it in half. Meanwhile the 6th Marine Division on their left flank would peel north to clear the upper island, while the Army divisions on their right flank would steer south where the enemy was reportedly waiting.

WAYBURN HALL

Next morning they moved us out. The rifle companies were ahead of us. We struck out to cut across the island and isolate the Japanese on the northern part of the island from those on the southern part. We walked down to a little town called Kolbe and marched down the streets of this little old town. There were two or three dead Jap soldiers in uniforms spread out in the streets. And one woman was there who'd been killed, I don't know how. That was the first dead people I'd ever seen up close like that.

JIM ANDERSON

We walked right across the island. I was still a runner for company headquarters. The biggest combat at first was fighting all the fleas that were there. I don't recall exactly how long it was before we ran into Japanese troops. That tells you something.

Compared with New Britain and Peleliu, Okinawa seemed pleasant to the Marines. Pine trees dotted the hills and Easter flowers bordered the cold streams, filling the air with a clean scent.

WAYBURN HALL

While we were going, we found some horses and commandeered them. We used them to pack our mortar equipment. They were kind of a raunchy bunch, but we slung our equipment on the back of those horses and made out all right.

STERLING MACE

It was too quiet. Guys were getting complacent. When guys are bored, they do anything to pass the time. We'd take a cigarette and blow on it, trying to blow sparks on another guy.

WAYBURN HALL

We set up trip wires for night defense purposes. You stretch out a wire six inches off the ground and put a grenade on the other end of it. Well, one of the guys was messing with one of the horses we had. Riding him or something, and he tripped that damn wire and almost took our lieutenant out. Luckily no one got hurt. That was a scary thing to have happen, right off the bat.

JIM ANDERSON

The Okinawans were peaceful people who had small farms and raised sweet potatoes, chickens, pigs, and ponies. We used some of these ponies, but officers later on took them away from us, because we had pony races at times when there wasn't any action.

On April 4, their fourth day on the island, the Marines reached the island's eastern coast.

HARRY BENDER

By April 6, we were on the beach, on the other side of the island. We were told there was a possibility the Japanese were going to make a landing right where we were. So we dug in, right on the beach, waiting. There wasn't much food, but we'd come across a nice big hog, and we shot it and skinned the sunovabitch. That's when we had our first casualty.

STERLING MACE

The First Platoon found and butchered a pig. They had it strung between two poles to eat later. Two guys were carrying it. The guy in the front was from Indiana. As he walked, the pin came loose from one of his hand grenades.

HARRY BENDER

When you take a grenade out of the canister, what you usually do is take the tape that comes from the canister and wrap it around the spoon to make sure the pin don't slide out. Most of us took our medical packs—where you have your first aid supplies on your belt—you take that stuff out and two grenades fit in that medical pack real good. That's where most of us carried them.

My squad leader had taken the tape off a grenade and had not put it back on. The next morning we started moving out and heard a *Pop!* (the sound of the grenade's fuse lighting). There was no other warning. I guess he knew what was coming because he ran and jumped in a ditch to get away from us. The grenade went off in his pouch. There was a big explosion that killed him instantly. About six guys were wounded.* Some of the shrapnel went into my pack. Fortunately it didn't break any skin or anything. Then it set off some ammunition. He had a Thompson, and some of that ammo went cooking off.

WAYBURN HALL

We spent a couple days there on the other side of the island. Somebody took a prisoner. This Jap was sneaking around and they captured him. They brought him up to our platoon. I guess they were going to interrogate him or send him down to battalion headquarters. But the guy broke loose and started running. He ran across a field into a bunch of houses.

Somebody shot him. But he kept going. So the lieutenant said, "I'll take some men and go down there and get him." Everybody was eager to go. Four or five of us went down there and went looking in those houses.

Two Okinawan women were sitting outside on the doorstep of a house. We spotted some steps going into that house. So one of the guys went in there. A couple others followed him. Suddenly there was a pistol shot. Ours. A pistol shot went off again. We got the prisoner out of there, and he was on his death throes. So we just went ahead and took him out. I'll put it that way.

During the second half of April, the 1st Marine Division patrolled and cleared central Okinawa.

---

* Mace would remember, "A guy, Warren Euber, I met him again on a visit to Parris Island sixty years after the war, he was still being treated from his leg wound from that hand grenade. All those years later."

STERLING MACE

We were soon relegated to patrols. Rounding up civilians at night to ask questions. One day we went out on patrol with the Third Platoon. My squad brought up the rear. The whole thirty-six of us in the platoon were in a column file, walking through a wooded area. Thirty-two of the men went by without seeing nothing. My fire team came up. Will Banks, my BAR man, looked into the wooded area and saw four Japs sitting there. So he swung his BAR around, emptied it out, and killed all four. Then he and this other guy ran down there like kids to have a look-see.

I chewed their asses out. "Good thing you killed all four!" I told them. "But how the hell do you know there aren't more of them somewhere who have got you in their sites?" We saw this happen once on Peleliu when these two Marines went over to this dead Jap and wanted to take his gold fillings out. Nearby was a Jap, not more than fifteen feet away. He killed the two Marines.

WAYBURN HALL

A day or two later we started moving back across the island toward where we'd come. We stayed on the same airfield a couple days. We set up there on a ridge.

During daytime, we'd go out on patrols. We went by this court-yard more than once where a Jap body lay. It was starting to swell up in the heat, and each time we passed it, it had swollen up a little more. After a while a lieutenant called me over and said, "Take a couple men down and go bury that body." So we got some long poles, drug the body outside to a field, and buried it. Talk about holding your nose.

In the evenings, the Jap planes were always trying to attack our new airfield. They'd turn their landing lights on because that's what our planes did, and then they'd come down our runways strafing.

One evening, a Jap Zero did that, and our guys down on the field started shooting at him. The plane came over this ridge where we were bivouacked, and I bet you he wasn't more than twenty-five feet off the ground trying to clear that ridge. I could see the pilot's face clearly. He was looking back, really hauling Jack.

There was a 20mm anti-aircraft gun down on the airfield, shooting at him, and that stuff was flying up toward us, trying to shoot the plane. We could hear—and feel—those bullets coming toward us. Luckily they missed us and hit the Jap. I said to the man next to me, "I swear if I had my hand on my tommy gun, I could have shot him down myself." The Jap pilot cleared the ridge and was gone. But I don't think he made it far.

STERLING MACE

We were up north looking south. Every night the sky would be all lit up, like the sound of a thunderstorm. The Army must have been running into hell. That was all part of the Japs' strategy—first, to let us come onto the beach with no problem. Second, the kamikazes would take care of our fleet. Third, we'd be up north without any big support, and the Japs from the south would come and wipe us out. It was already starting. The kamikazes were coming in every night. Our guys were taking a beating down south. Finally at the end of April, they told us to load on trucks. We were going south into all that shit.

CHAPTER SEVENTEEN

THE LAND OF MUD AND DEATH

★ ★ ★

Okinawa

On May 1, 1945, the 1st Marine Division rushed to the front lines to relieve the Army's battered 27th Infantry Division. "It's hell up there, Marine," an Army soldier warned Eugene Sledge. "Yeah, I know. I was at Peleliu," Sledge replied.

R. V. BURGIN

We encountered a lot of civilians. Most of them were marching out, single file, from the south going north. Mostly old people and really young. Just kids, babies. Some of them would be wounded. We stopped many times, and our corpsmen would treat their wounded. We'd give the kids candy bars.

I saw a wounded baby. He wasn't crying, which surprised me, even though he had a big gash on his leg where he'd been hit with shrapnel. He was in his mother's arms, or at least I guessed it was his mother. The corpsman went over and patched him up.

The Japanese had spread stories about us before we got there. They told the civilians we'd rape the women and murder them all if we landed. I guess some of the civilians even committed suicide when we landed. They'd jump off the cliffs with their babies in their arms. I never saw that, but that's the stories we heard. But it didn't take long for word to get around that we weren't the monsters the Japanese had made us out to be.

HARRY BENDER

The Okinawans speak Japanese and all that, but in their religion they're more closely related to the Chinese than they are the Japanese. There were so many civilians that were killed, too. The Japanese used the Okinawans as shields. They'd be moving out somewhere, crouched behind civilians. We saw a lot of wounded civilians.

STERLING MACE

The Army guys were heading up toward us. They looked beat. You don't say much to them because it's no good.

R. V. BURGIN

The Army's 27th Division was a National Guard outfit from New York that didn't have the greatest reputation. When they passed us by, I heard a sergeant tell a PFC to do something, and the PFC said, "Go f—k yourself. I'm not doing it. Do it yourself."

That type of insubordination showed a lack of discipline on that unit's behalf. Now, I was a squad leader on Peleliu and a mortar platoon leader on Okinawa, and if one of my guys had ever told me that, he'd need to go see a dentist.

Discipline is tremendously important in a combat situation. If ever you get in combat and your sergeant or lieutenant says hit the deck, you don't stand there and ask why. You do it! You know for a fact that he's trying to protect you. Discipline saves lives.

STERLING MACE

We relieved the Army. You throw smoke shells in, then take over their foxholes. They'd been there for two weeks and didn't move two feet.

From their new lines, the Marines could see the ocean to the west. They knew that the south end of the island lay just ten miles distant, obscured by intimidating ridges.

R. V. BURGIN

Okinawa was narrow, just fifteen miles wide at its widest point. A ridge and a valley, a ridge and a valley, from the north end to the south end of it. Some of the ridges were higher than others, but basically that's what it was.

WAYBURN HALL

They loaded our mortar platoon on amphibious tractors and ran us down to the front lines. We were put on the far western flank there. Our lines were spread across the island—two Army divisions and one Marine division at the time.

We moved into this cave that we had cleared of Japs. It had been used as an artillery battery. There were living quarters there, so we settled in, thinking it was safe. The fleas there ate us up. About the second day, somebody saw movement. There was a mound with portholes around it which we felt was part of the gun emplacement, never thinking it could be occupied. But someone thought they saw a Jap in there.

We studied the area and realized it might have been the opening to another section of caves. So we called a flamethrower in and he put a flame to it. Must have been a Jap ammunition storage down there, because it all blew up good. That was scary, but we were lucky and got out of the cave unhurt.

On May 2, in an attack reminiscent of World War I, K Company and other units across the American front would attack across open, muddy ground, under artillery fire, and straight into the enemy's sights.

STERLING MACE

They told us, "Tomorrow morning we're going to take off at eight o'clock, and you go out over that bridge there and keep going. You'll come across those rice paddies, which is dried out. Keep going until you reach an embankment." And that's all they told us.

After heavy shelling, all three platoons started in unison. So the whole company starts out abreast, one, two, three, right across. First Platoon is on the left, the second one is in the middle, and we're on the right. We start out and get up over this one little hill, and a Jap machine gun goes ripping right across the ground in front of us. You could see the dirt shaken up. All they hollered was "Don't stop." The three guys right in front of me went right through it. Didn't even get hit. So I followed.

We get to the embankment and got into position. Then we started to take hits.

R. V. BURGIN

We were pinned down. On the other side of the bank was a small valley, and at the other end another ridge. There was a machine gunner there shooting at us, and I knew the general proximity of where he was, but we couldn't see him. Everyone was just hugging the dirt. We put up with the machine gunner for a while. Whenever we tried to move, we had to throw smoke grenades and people would get hit.

STERLING MACE

We were there just two minutes when the word came, "We gotta pull back out, we're losing too many people!" First Platoon was taking a beating; the Second Platoon had stopped again.

Someone passed the orders. "Team up with somebody. Get a poncho and carry the guys who are wounded." Carrying a guy in a poncho with two people—that was tough. While the wounded guy lay in the center, you were dragging his ass through the mud. So you'd have to get two more guys and each would take a corner of the poncho.

Now, we had to make a strategic withdrawal. There was a little dike there with a road on top. If you ran along that, back toward where we came from, you could keep your head low and the Japs wouldn't see you. So that's what they told us to do. *Keep low, and run one at a time.*

Everybody wanted to get out, so nobody listened. "Keep low and run one at a time" became "four at a time."

R. V. BURGIN

I figured somebody had to do something to spot this guy. So I just stood up and ran out in front of the ridge where the gunner could see me. Facing his direction I walked backwards, slowly. My thinking was, if he fired I would spot it, and we could drop some mortar rounds on him to knock him out. As I walked backwards, sure enough, he opened up on me. I saw the fire pouring from his barrel and knew exactly where he was. It didn't take me long to run out of his line of fire and jump onto our side of the ridge. When I caught

my breath, I noticed he had put two bullet holes in my dungarees, in the same place on both legs, about shin high. But he didn't
hit me.

Anyway, I called back to our mortars and had them fire one
round. I made the adjustment and got a direct hit. The machine
gunner went flying through the air. I'm positive I killed two of
them with that one shell, because a machine gunner always had an
assistant. I never did go over there to check, but I'm positive we
knocked it out because we never did draw any more fire.

STERLING MACE

We got back, then we licked our wounds and said, "Tomorrow we'll
do it different." Our first real battle on Okinawa didn't go so good.

WAYBURN HALL

We set up at night on a ridge with a railway track cutting through
it. Half of our platoon was on one side and the other half was on
the other side. We always slept two to a foxhole, so half of us got
ready to bed down. Random shellfire was going on. My buddy and
I were right on the edge of this ridge looking down on this railway
track.

Before it got light, we heard yelling. I grabbed my tommy gun.
Someone was hollering, "He's down the railroad track, coming toward us!" All the noise came from behind our lines.

People starting firing. I did, too. I must have fired twelve to
fifteen rounds down through that area. Our gunney started hollering, "Knock it off!" So we settled down. When it got lighter, a
Marine who had gone down there to check things out came up and
told us what had happened. His outfit was behind us, and he said
this sniper snuck back there and was sniping on them all night
until they chased him up to us.

The lieutenant said, "Hall, take some men down there and check it out." When we got down there, we found the Jap sniper, sprawled on the railway track with three big bullet holes in his helmet. I moved his helmet out of the way to look at his face and the top of his head stayed in his helmet.

R. V. BURGIN

I fought in three battles—New Britain, Peleliu, and Okinawa—and all three were as different as daylight and dark. New Britain was a jungle. Peleliu was a coral island filled with caves, hotter than hell. Okinawa was cool, open country. But on Okinawa we encountered much more enemy artillery fire than any other island. They had a tremendous amount of artillery on Okinawa. They had artillery pieces on Okinawa from the day we got there until the last day.

JIM ANDERSON

Okinawa was a more organized, predictable fight. We had a defense line set up at night, and in the morning, maybe at seven o'clock, they would shell in front of us, and we would move out in lines and move ahead until we hit some opposition. Then we'd dig in or retreat, but always we came carrying the casualties back.

HARRY BENDER

One of the other real bad things about Okinawa was that you could never get any sleep. There was shelling going off twenty-four hours a day. That's also when the rains came. Right when we got there. You'd dig a foxhole. About three o'clock in the morning you'd be sitting in five inches of water in your foxhole with shelling going on. It was bad news.

Let me tell ya about what the Japanese did. Their hand grenades had a button that they hit on their helmet and then threw. Well, they'd bury those damn hand grenades, too, with the button sticking up, and make it into a mine. You'd step on it, and then the next guy behind you, that grenade would go off. The rains would wash these hand grenades anywhere. We had this path we were using for a couple days. The rains washed those hand grenades right next to that path. So you never knew for certain where you could step and still be safe from those grenades.

STERLING MACE

The shelling went on about two weeks. When these Japs threw stuff over at you, they didn't throw little hand grenades. They threw big stuff that whistled over and explodes right up your rear end.

Soon after the Marines' arrival on the lines, during the night of May 3, the Japanese attempted seaborne landings on both coasts of Okinawa simultaneously. They planned for their forces to link up behind the American lines to isolate and destroy the 1st Marine Division. But on the western beaches, H Company and the 1st Marines were waiting.

WAYBURN HALL

An amtrac picked us up and moved us to a small airstrip on the southern part of the island, maybe two hundred yards from the beach. We set up in a defensive position between the strip and the beach. Night fell. A couple hours later, flares started going up out over the water.

Jap barges were heading down the coast, trying to outflank us with a counter-landing. Our Navy patrol boats began running up and down the coast there, lighting up the area for Navy ships to fire on the enemy barges. The Navy had a turkey shoot with these barges.

While the Navy was firing, their 20mm rounds were coming right at our gun position on the coast. I was down in the gun pit, and I reached up and grabbed the tube of our mortar and brought it down to keep it from getting hit—that's how close the Navy's fire was coming—zipping over our heads. A few Jap stragglers came out of the water and into our area, but some people in our platoon took care of them.

They must have killed five hundred Japs that night.

The Marines resumed their offensive, aiming for the enemy's nerve center at Shuri Castle, a stone fortress on a high hill. Between the Marines and Shuri lay ridge after ridge of Japanese fighting positions. As on Peleliu, the Japanese were on the ridges—and within them.

WAYBURN HALL

The land favored the Japs, who would be dug in on the ridge on both sides waiting for us to come up and get them. You could only get up there with small groups of men, say squad- or platoon-size. We had to use tanks to get small groups up there. The Japs were dug in there and in their caves, and we had to root them out. The fighting was ferocious. The elements favored the enemy, too.

HARRY BENDER

Once, we jumped into a trench, and I came across a Japanese soldier up close. He was right there, running right at me. I hit him with my M1. Shot him. About eight times, I shot him. I know I hit him every goddamn time I shot him, but I guess the momentum must have been so strong, because he just kept coming at me, running forward. Right before he got to me, he dropped.

JIM ANDERSON

To me, the Japanese didn't seem as die-hard as they'd been on Peleliu, although they still had a firm grasp on the island. They were more patient and set up in foxholes, trenches, and caves.

R. V. BURGIN

For a week, we did the same thing again and again. We'd start across this valley and they'd open up on us. We'd throw smoke grenades and retrieve our men. We had to do that a couple times one morning, and never did make it across the valley. By next morning, it was the same damn thing. So we shelled the hell out of the opposing ridge with our artillery, but that didn't do any good. A lot of times the Japs would gather behind and below the ridge, where they could hide while our artillery would pass right over them. Then they'd come out to welcome us when we started across the valley. That's what was happening. Our artillery was arcing over the ridge and exploding too far behind. Only our mortars could drop shells down at a steep angle, on their heads.

So I set three mortars up to fire slightly behind the enemy ridge. I figured the Japs were there in a gully. I registered the first gun to fire down and to the left, the second gun down and to the right, and the third gun in the middle. I fired all the guns at the same time, twenty rounds per gun. We saturated the ridge and slope behind it with mortar fire. When we started to move out the next time, there was no resistance.

You never talked about what you did. You just did it, and went on to the next phase. I never even talked with my lieutenant about it. In 2002 I went and visited him. "Scotty, did I ever tell you how many damn Japs the mortar section killed that morning?"

"Nope," he said. "I never did know. But I know you got them because we moved out after that and didn't have any problems."

"Well I went up there afterward and I counted fifty-three freshly killed Japs," I told him.

"I'll be damned," he said.

As the Marines battled for muddy ridges named Awacha, Dakeshi, and Wana, the rain fell and fell, sometimes for ten days straight. This made a miserable task even worse.

HARRY BENDER

It rained and rained, and just kept on raining. By mid-May, it was difficult to get supplies up to us. They used an amtrac to bring up water and rations. Sometimes when the guys came up with the half-tracks to bring up the chow, we got to hear the radio. They talked about Tokyo Rose, the Jap's propaganda tool. We loved to listen to her. The music was really great, you know. She'd say things like, "Hey, American GI, wouldn't you rather be with your honey tonight, having a hamburger and fries and all that good stuff?" And we'd say, "Yeah, we would." It didn't do anything to hurt our morale. If anything, it picked it up. We all laughed at Tokyo Rose, that's about the size of it.

We'd been in this area for about four days, on the top of this hill, and one of our amtracs came to the bottom of the hill and hit a mine. We got the driver out. He was wounded pretty bad. We were right there. I took his .45 off him. Then we unloaded whatever we could from the amtrac. Whatever we could still use.

STERLING MACE

They brought up bread to us. We thought it was seeded rye bread. It wasn't rye bread—it was goddamn fleas.

WAYBURN HALL

Everything was at a standstill for a while because of the weather. The rain slacked off, and we got some supplies by airdrops. No vehicles could move for a while still, because of all the mud. So we got supplied by air. One morning some guys found some ammo cartons, made a table out of them, and we started playing cards, all sitting in six to eight inches of mud.

Three Corsairs flew over, heading to drop some bombs on a ridge nearby, we guessed. So we knew they were able to get off the ground now. Anyway, this one Corsair released his bomb too soon. It fell down and hit below us, on our ammunition dump. Then he strafed us—our own planes! Cards and people started flying, hitting the mud hole. I guess the pilot realized his mistake, because he pulled up real quick, and the other two planes with him never fired a shot. They must have been embarrassed.

JIM ANDERSON

When we were fighting on New Britain all the way through Peleliu, we never ever had anybody turned in for battle fatigue, that they couldn't stand the front lines, the firing and so forth. But in Okinawa we did have some people from K Company turn themselves in for battle fatigue. We had one man come up, he was a sergeant. He had been in the service a long time. He wasn't on the lines roughly a week and he turned himself in as a battle fatigue case. He just couldn't stand the constant barrage from artillery. We didn't know if he was faking it or not.

On Peleliu and New Britain we never got any replacements while in the fighting. But on Okinawa after a month or two of fighting we started getting replacements. Some of them were turning themselves in fairly regularly when things got tough, saying they couldn't stand combat any longer.

Some guys actually did have battle fatigue from all the time on the front line. They deserved to be turned in, deserved to go to the rear for rest. I felt very sorry for them. Everybody has a breaking point, but some people could take more than others.

R. V. BURGIN

Early the morning of May 20, we were dug in on Wana Ridge, and Jim Burke and I were scouting, looking for targets. An artillery shell came in. I told Jim, "Let's get the hell out of Dodge!" We started running down the ridge. He jumped in one shell hole. I jumped in another. Just as I hit the bottom of the hole, a shell landed right beside the hole. It buried me for a few seconds. I couldn't see. Couldn't breathe. I dug my way out with my hands. That was about ten in the morning.

Later on that afternoon, maybe two o'clock, all hell was breaking loose. Our Corsairs were strafing and bombing, artillery was going both directions. It was one hell of a battle. We were out in the open, in the middle of it. Artillery was going on both sides. An artillery blast went off, and a fragment hit me in the back of the neck. Our corpsman patched me up, right on the spot.

Later, I felt a bit light-headed so I headed to the aid station where the doc patched me up. I don't know how I ever lived, to tell the God's truth, or how I kept from getting wounded on the way over to the aid station. The battle was raging, and it was machine gun fire and artillery all the way.

I got to the first aid station and sat around 'till dark. Then we left in an ambulance. I held a glucose bottle for a guy who was in really bad shape. I don't know if he made it or not, but he was still alive when we got him to a field aid station. They didn't have any cots, just stretchers on the ground. I lay down on a stretcher on the ground. They gave me three to four shots of morphine that night, until I asked them what the hell was going on and they stopped giving me shots.

The next morning they sent me by ambulance to an Army field hospital. As I walked in the front door of the tent, I was given the second bunk on the right. I imagine there were eighty to a hundred Marines in there, wounded. The nurse come and gave me a sponge bath. I'll never forget it. The dirt and dry skin rolled up on my belly like never before. None of us had changed clothes since landing on the islands.

My stomach was so sore, I couldn't bear to touch it with a powder puff. Turns out it was a concussion from the previous day's explosive. In a few days it didn't hurt as much.

The doc took good care of me, and my neck healed up okay. I stayed in the hospital twenty days before I left and hitched a ride back to my company. I wasn't wounded enough to go home; I never even thought of it. Sure, I wanted to go home, but I wasn't really thinking about it. If you did, it would run you nuts. I knew it wasn't going to happen.

CHAPTER EIGHTEEN

THE WASTELAND

★   ★   ★

Okinawa

By late May 1945, the Marines had fought their way to a series of muddy hills opposite Shuri Castle. From hills named Sugarloaf, Horseshoe, and Half Moon, they besieged the ruined castle. Eugene Sledge would call his foxhole opposite Shuri "a ghastly corner of hell."

HARRY BENDER

It was about May 21 when we got Half Moon Hill. It had rained so damn much there was water lying around the hill. We referred to it as the sea of death, because there were dead Marines laying down there in that water. Graves Registration hadn't had the chance yet to come and get them out, which is one thing the Marines pride themselves on and usually do real well. It was real sobering, seeing those bodies. The hill had the smell of death all around it—a sickening sweet smell, like something was rotting. Seeing those goddamn maggots in the bodies, boy, that was hard.

WAYBURN HALL

We'd moved to a ridge closer to Shuri Castle, the Japs' main stronghold. The rains set in, and it bogged down everything and it all stopped to zero. No vehicles could move. We sat there for days in a mud hole.

Me and my buddy found some old boards from an ammunition crate or something and spread them out in the bottom of our foxhole. We covered ourselves with ponchos, but we were soaking wet all the time. You're soaked all the time. Of course, it's cold at night. We had jackets and blankets, but they were wet, too. You can kind of wrap up in them and try to keep warm, but it's just miserable. I don't think I took my boots off for ten days. When I did finally take them off, the skin came off, too.

The fighting had been heavy on that ridge before we ever moved in. Right in the middle of all that rain and mud, I woke up one morning. Over to my right was a human elbow sticking up out of the ground. It was about six feet from our foxhole. What we'd done was move up in an area where they'd buried a bunch of Jap bodies in a hurry. All that rain had started uncovering them. What was I thinking? Oh, by then it was just another Jap body. We'd all seen lots of Jap bodies by then, and plenty of them hadn't been buried.

JIM ANDERSON

At times, they couldn't get food to us. Sometimes we went four, five, six days without food. But we did not suffer very much. We found chickens and pigs, and dug sweet potatoes out of gardens and ate them. Airdrops got food to us sometimes.

HARRY BENDER

We were getting C rations that were made in Australia. Meat and beans and hash. Goddamn mutton. I think Australia was paying their war debt by making C rations. The Army got a new ration with spaghetti and ham, but we were getting the old Australian rations. One time an Army truck was in our area and it had all these rations all on it. We stopped the truck and started unloading rations. They said, "You can't do that." We said, "Watch us." So we got some of their new C rations.

The Okinawans had these big Chinese-style burial vaults—tombs—and inside these vaults they had a big bowl of sea salt. They'd use the salt for ceremonies, I guess. Sometimes we'd get in there, scrape the dust off, and borrow that salt to use on our food. It made the food taste better, anyway.

JIM ANDERSON

Half Moon Hill was shaped like an upside-down half moon, and the Japanese were still hiding in caves below us. They'd come out under darkness.

At night we'd set up a circular defense line. One night we was on guard duty and *bang, bang, bang, bang!* Somebody called out, "Halt, who goes there?" And *boom! boom!* We tried to figure out what happened. One of the men who'd been on guard duty had fallen asleep. He woke up and saw two figures in front of him on the path. He shot at them, both Japanese, and they ran into the circle. The *boom, boom* we heard was that these two Japanese held hand grenades. They pulled the pins and killed themselves.

STERLING MACE

The Japs had cut the lines between the 5th and 7th regiments. I got called over to the captain. We were to go out and find out what we could about the situation. Now, Major Paul Douglas (the future senator from Illinois) wanted to go out on patrol with us. In other words, the mission was "Take the Major and go get lost."

I took my fire team and Major Douglas. He was a brave one, so he's going to lead the patrol. Sure, I let him. I'm a corporal at the time. Every time he saw a little hole, he thought it was a cave. So he came up to this hole. Maybe six foot deep. He took his .45 and shot into the cave. Word was that Douglas got nearly killed on Peleliu inspecting a cave. Then he wanted us to go in with him.

This guy, Whitby, I went to see him in Florida sixty years after the war. We're sitting in Whitby's living room, and he said, "Do you remember what you told Major Douglas when he told you to go into the cave?"

"Yeah," I said. "I think I said something like 'You got to do more than shoot a .45 in a cave. Throw a hand grenade in there.'"

"No, that wasn't it," Whitby said. "You told him to go f—k himself."

We laughed. Did I actually say that? Nah, maybe I thought that, but I wouldn't actually say that to an officer.

Anyway, there were no Japs in the cave.

HARRY BENDER

When we were on Half Moon my platoon got all the shitty details. Bucky Pearson led us out on patrol to find out what was out there. We knew what the hell was out there. The goddamn Japanese were out there!

So we went out, nine of us. We went out so far that the Japanese were behind us on this little knoll. They started shelling us.

Well, for that patrol I was the guy on the walkie-talkie. It wasn't me usually, but the regular guy couldn't go on the patrol that time. So it was on to Bender. I was in the rear, and Bucky yelled for the walkie-talkie. The corpsman I was with said that every step I took running forward, he could see a shell landing behind me on my heels.

I got to Bucky and he got to Stumpy and he said, "Get out the best way you can." So we threw smoke grenades and just started running forward into the smoke. That's how we got out.

There were nine of us on that patrol, and only one of us got hit.

JIM ANDERSON

The Okinawa people had burial vaults in their hillsides. Inside them were urns, maybe two feet high. It's rumored that those were the remains of their relatives. We wouldn't go in there unless we were receiving artillery fire. We didn't go into them because of curiosity or anything like that. It was a good place to be when you were being shelled.

STERLING MACE

I was sitting in a foxhole when I took a sniper's bullet right through the poncho. I don't know where the hell that Jap was who did that, but he had to be well over a hundred yards away because I didn't see anybody around at first.

More fire came in. We sat there a bit longer, and I heard Major Douglas calling for help. He was up at the lines helping to bring the wounded back and two of his guys were hit.[*]

"We can't, Major," someone hollered back. "We're taking fire."

---

[*] Days later, Douglas would himself be shot by a machine gun and his left arm forever disabled.

We sat there awhile longer, still taking fire. Pretty soon about six of our guys were hit. Nobody was doing anything. Everyone was afraid to move.

I spotted this jeep sitting in an open field, stuck in the mud. I though, *Geez, if I could get to that jeep, I could load these wounded guys on it and take them back to the battalion aid station.*

So I ran out to the jeep, hopped in, and hit the starter. It turned over but didn't start. I was so nervous I'd forgotten to turn the ignition on. I started the jeep up and drove back to where these wounded guys are. We put the six on the jeep—one in the front with me, two in the backseat, two hanging on the back, and one clinging to the side.

I wanna tell ya, we went through about thirty yards of mud about a foot deep. I still don't know how we did it. I must have shifted twelve times to keep the momentum going. Shifting, clutching, shifting, clutching, but I'm doing it. I think the weight of all the guys in the jeep gave us the traction we need. We get through this mud and hit hard ground, came up about a foot and cruised straight to the aid station.

The greeting I got, you wouldn't believe it. This lieutenant came over to me and said, "Where the hell did you get that goddamn jeep? It's mine." He chewed my ass out.

I'm looking at the wounded guys—the corpsmen are running around getting them out, but this lieutenant was only interested in his jeep.

So that was my big heroic thing. The wounded getting to safety. And me getting my ass chewed out.

On May 28, under the cover of darkness, the Japanese evacuated Shuri Castle and fled southward to regroup and resist to the bitter end.

HARRY BENDER

When we were moving toward Shuri Castle, the Navy was shelling it, using those big sixteen-inch shells. You focus your eyes, hear those things, then look up. It looked like a garbage can floating in the air toward the castle. All it did was chip the wall. It wasn't doing any real damage to it at first.

From where we sat, Shuri Castle just looked like one big wall. The Japs had their headquarters in there. Compared with Half Moon Hill and Sugar Loaf, the battle for Shuri wasn't nothing. We just blasted it for a while and eventually it fell.

JIM ANDERSON

We were close to Shuri Castle but never actually went in it. I was within a half a mile of it. To me it looked like partial ruins on the top of a hill. I guess it was a monastery or something like that.

WAYBURN HALL

When the rains stopped, we pushed on. The Japs evacuated Shuri and started heading to the southern end of the island. We had spotter planes up as soon as it got daylight, and they spotted a column of Japanese headed south. The planes started bombing and strafing that column.

This stopped a lot of Jap artillery fire, too. They knew they couldn't expose themselves because we had spotter planes up a lot and they would record the gun flashes, then our return fire, our artillery, and especially our aircraft would get them. So they'd fire off a few rounds and then hide in a cave.

R. V. BURGIN

I was in the hospital when most of the bad rains came on Okinawa, when the unit fought for Shuri Castle. When I came back, we'd lost thirty-six men in the fighting.

Just after I got back to K Company from the hospital, I explored a cave with a Sterno can on the end of a stick. I was all by myself. The cave was four to five foot in diameter. I thought maybe I'll get some souvenirs. It was about the stupidest thing I ever did.

I went about thirty to forty steps back in there and you couldn't see three feet in front of you. I came upon a cot on my right and reached down and touched it. It was still warm. I thought, *Oh shit.* I stood real still and listened. I heard a clock ticking. So I backed out of there as quick as I could. I just backed out all the way. I called a demolition squad and they closed it up. If that Jap had killed me in that cave, nobody would have ever known where I was at. I would have just disappeared off the face of the earth. That was the last cave I ever went in.

WAYBURN HALL

We started moving rapidly then, pursuing the Japs and trying to get down there quick before they could get set up in the south and create defensive positions. We had them on the run, was the idea. So we were moving real quick down from Shuri to the southern tip.

R. V. BURGIN

We moved out one morning going single file on both sides of a dusty road. A sniper picked me out. I felt the bullet zing right by my ear so close, but it didn't hit me. Somebody got the sniper, and he didn't fire a second round after that. I thought, *Those sons of bitches are still trying to kill me.*

JIM ANDERSON

As we pushed on down toward the end of the island, I went into a cave and picked up a Japanese flag. It was white with a red sun with Japanese writing all over it.*

DAN LAWLER

One day we were looking for Japs and came upon a cave. We could hear talking in there, so I took out my pistol and shot three warning shots right over the top of the cave. Nobody came out, so we figured there weren't any Japs in there. It was undoubtedly just civilians. In Japanese I said, "Come out, we'll give you food and water."

Sure enough, a few people slowly came out. About four or five adults, Okinawans. Along with the parents was a little boy, maybe five years old, and a little girl, maybe two or three. At first, they were quite a ways away and very cautious of us.

I motioned for them to come closer, and slowly they did, little by little. Other Marines took care of the adults, but the little girl came closer to me. Her hair was all messed up. She didn't have any shoes on, and she had blood all over her. As far as I could see, she hadn't been wounded, but somewhere along the line someone had been shot in close proximity to her, and the blood had spread all over. She was shaking 'cause she was so scared.

I broke a piece off a candy bar and held it out to her. She wouldn't eat either end of the bar. I guess the Japs had told stories of us poisoning food, but finally she ate from the middle of the bar.

She was still shaking then, so I picked her up and set her on my

---

* Anderson would remember, "A few years back, a friend of mine took a picture of the flag and got it interpreted. I wrote to the Japanese consulate in Chicago and got in touch with the owner's son, fifty-six years old, who lives in Tokyo. I gave the flag back to him and he sent me a photo of him and his wife holding it."

knee. That's when she put her arms around me. Well, I broke right there and started crying. It was terrible to see civilians caught in the middle of war.

A captain come along and asked me, "You all right?"

"Yeah, I'm all right," I said. "But why do these innocents need to be involved?"

"It's war," was all he said.

HARRY BENDER

Okinawa was eighty-two days of fighting. Only one time did we get pulled off the line to get to change our clothes. It was early June. We got a hot meal that day, and dry socks. Goddamn. You can't appreciate how you like dry socks until you've worn wet socks for days on end.

CHAPTER NINETEEN

THE LAST MILE

Okinawa

With disappointment, in June 1945, the Marines realized that one last battle lay beyond Shuri, a ridge as vicious as any other, and worse—within sight of the sea.

WAYBURN HALL

We never knew where we were in Okinawa, never got that info from above, but we knew about Kunishi Ridge, that's where we were headed. It was part of the defensive line south of the Shuri Castle area.

We set up in a valley. Our rifle companies started attacking this ridge. That was some of the worst, most vicious fighting we ever encountered on Okinawa.

R. V. BURGIN

We knew the Japs would never give up. They were down to their last holes now, their last men, and they were fighting to the very end. We knew we'd need to beat them here, then go onto the

Japanese mainland next. It was going to be real bloody fighting the Japs on their home ground. That was nothing to look forward to.

STERLING MACE

It was a bad twenty-four hours. First I got caught in the middle of a shelling, running between holes on the line, out in the open. A shell came in, I heard it coming, and hit the deck. The thing landed right behind me. It was a goddamn dud. They scare you just as well as a live one. The noise they make. It hits the ground and muck and dirt comes flying over you. It just sizzles there and you smell its metal.

A burst of nearby Jap bullets encouraged me to move. As I run, another 8mm shell falls from the heavens. You hear it, look up, but only see rain. This one is not a dud; its explosion knocks me down. The concussion from its blast bursts my eardrums and knocks my vision silly. I look up and see three horizons, not one.

I stumble back to my foxhole to sleep it off. I crawl under the poncho into my hole, and who is there—some new kid, a replacement just fresh out of boot camp named Piazza. The rain is coming down, and he's telling me about him and his girlfriend in a car, and how the rain reminds him of how it sounded on the roof of the car. Like I needed to hear that.

The next morning I'm sitting along my foxhole, holding my head. My busted eardrums and concussion gave me one hell of a piercing headache. Then Bill Leyden comes over, and I said to Bill, "Look what I got here!" as I point to Piazza, "Another freaking kid!"

Bill looked away and I knew something was wrong. Even though I gave them hell, I had made friends with another of the new guys, Hudson. We called him "Junior." Bill says to me, "You don't want to hear it." Turns out Junior caught one of the shells that missed me. He got evaporated, a direct hit on his hole.

That was all in one day.

A day or two later my head was blistering and eyes were blood-shot. So I went back to see our corpsman, Chupps, hoping he could give me some pills or something. He took a look at me and said, "Mace, don't even bother. Go back to battalion, let their people check you out." So I went back to battalion, and this one guy puts a tag on me that says, "Psychoneurosis Anxiety." Then I walked around the sand and another guy comes up, takes the tag, and writes on the other side "Combat Fatigue." I've got "Psychoneuro-sis" on one side and "Combat Fatigue" on the other. I didn't know what psychoneurosis is, but I liked the sound of that better than combat fatigue.

I'm sitting there, and the next thing I know a doctor says, "I'm going to give you sodium pentothal." So he gives me the shot. It's an anesthetic that relaxes you. Then he starts talking to me. I was talking my ass off and don't know what I must have told him. The next thing I know I was walking to a big tent. I lied down in a bed and fell asleep.

The next day the guy next to me says, "Geez, do you know what was going on while you were sleeping?" I says, "No." He says that a USO group came to play in the tent for the wounded—trumpets, bugles, all that stuff—and they played at the foot of my bed and I slept right through it.

I was like that in the hospital, in my own world. I stayed by myself. I just didn't want to listen to anyone's bullshit stories. The next thing I know, a guy calls out eight names and I'm one of them. They drove me to the beach, and next thing I know I'm on a ship. That night the kamikazes came in and attacked our fleet. While these freaking kamikazes are coming in, the ships all broke and ran. The captain of our ship sneaked us out—and all the way to Guam. After Guam we went to Hawaii and from there to San Francisco.

R. V. BURGIN

We got into a lot of trouble fighting to take that Kunishi Ridge. We fought for two days to get up and take that ridge.

HARRY BENDER

I was wounded the night of June 17. We had made a nighttime move, up through a sugarcane field, up to a big coral ridge, Kunishi Ridge. And we'd gotten some replacements in. One was a sergeant, a banana marine who'd been in Panama but hadn't seen any combat. He was the odd man. I was assistant BAR man, Bill Tyler was the BAR man; we shacked up together, and we took the sergeant into our hole. Actually, it wasn't a real hole. Since it was all coral, you couldn't dig in. There was a pillbox there that was ours, so we stacked up pieces of coral around the side of the pillbox, and that was our foxhole.

It was my turn on watch. So I was sitting there in our foxhole, against the pillbox. Tyler and the sergeant were on the other side of me, both sleeping. I had my helmet on, but neither of them did. It was more comfortable to sleep without your helmet and fairly common for guys to do that.

Jap artillery started coming in. I guesstimated right, because the way the Japanese fire their shells is different than the way Marines did. The Marines hit four corners and then fill in the square. The Japanese make a half moon pattern.

The artillery started landing, and the pattern was coming our way. It was going to be real close. Sure enough, one shell came right at us, exploded above us, and shrapnel splattered down on us. The sergeant was killed outright. Tyler was alive, but he was hit in his skull. I was sitting up and took shrapnel in the upper front part of my legs. My back. My arm. It blew my helmet off, too, and I was combing tiny pieces of shrapnel out of my hair for a while, too. Hot metal. Burning metal.

I could still get up, so I did. I started running for the command post. I spotted a corpsman, and I yelled at him to go take care of the other guys. One thing I'd like to mention is that some of the real heroes were the corpsmen. They were really something else. When somebody got hit, everybody else would try to dig in deeper, but the corpsmen, they'd go running toward the trouble. They were exceptional men of valor.

The corpsmen took us to the aid station, then they put Tyler and me in the back of an ambulance and took us to a field hospital.

Tyler was a big guy, about six-two and 220 pounds. He's wounded in the head and out of his mind, ranting. They have him tied down, but he's getting loose. I'm in the stretcher right across from him. I said, "This is no place for me." So I crawled up front to the passenger side of the ambulance. When we got to the hospital, they said, "You're supposed to have two wounded, where's the other at?"

I said, "Me, up here in the front seat." So they took me in and lay me down on a table and started dressing my wounds. I don't know where Tyler went. I never seen Tyler again after that night.[*]

The thing that pissed me off was that this Army nurse came by and said, "How are you, little boy?" I looked rather young anyhow, so I guess she was just trying to be funny in a stupid way. I told her, "I'm no goddamn little boy, I'm a goddamn U.S. Marine!" She shut up. I didn't take too kindly to that shit.

---

[*] Harry Bender would remember, "About ten years ago I tried. I sent a letter to every Bill Tyler I could find. But I never got an answer back."

R. V. BURGIN

The Japs were on the sides of the ridges, on the top, in caves—anywhere you look, they could be. We had to root them out. I tell you one thing—I carried my M1 rifle all the way from New Britain to Okinawa, and I used it a lot those days. It never failed me one time.

JIM ANDERSON

K Company run up against a pillbox there with Japanese in it, and we couldn't get them out of there. This was near the end, so an interpreter was brought up, but he couldn't talk them out.

So they brought up a demolition squad who had satchel charges. A satchel is about a foot square and full of explosives. Now, a good friend of mine was Ted Barrow, who was first cousins with a famous outlaw, Clyde Barrow, as in "Bonnie and Clyde." He was a very forward-fighting man; he carried a tommy gun and was always on the front lines. Anyhow Ted crawled up on top of that pillbox with me. When they threw that satchel charge through the porthole, six Japanese came rushing out. Ted and I cut them down, but Ted got most of them.

I went over to one of the dead Japanese. One of the .45 bullets from Ted's Thompson submachine gun had hit the scabbard on the man's hip and dented it. I took the bayonet off the guy's rifle, slid it back into the dented scabbard, and then took it as a souvenir. It wasn't grisly. We earned it. I respected Ted but never said a word to him about Bonnie and Clyde. Rumor was he didn't want to talk about that.

While moving to attack Kunishi Ridge in the dark, K Company was nearly annihilated when friendly artillery began exploding amid the company.

JIM ANDERSON

We had some of our own artillery firing harassing fire at the enemy, five shots about every ten minutes. But it was landing extremely close to K Company. Now, in battle, ninety-nine times out of a hundred, you do not move at night. The Japanese move at night, but we stayed strictly in our foxholes.

That artillery was coming in within fifty yards of our front yards. The company commander said, "You think you can get back there and get that stopped?"

I said, "This is night, you're not supposed to move. But I'll give it a whirl." Our artillery was about a half mile away from the front lines.

I crawled on my stomach through the water and all that filth. I got challenged a few times. Luckily none of our guys shot at me.

Finally I got back to where our artillery was coming from, and I told the lieutenant, "Your artillery is falling on our front lines."

"Oh, you're crazy," he said.

"No sir," I said. "With all due respect, you're going to kill someone if you continue firing."

Well he just didn't see how that could be happening.

Finally I used some pretty strong language and used some pretty dirty words that today if you used them you'd be court-martialed.

Finally, I said, "If you don't stop it, then somebody's going to die, and it's not going to be us dying up on the front lines—it's going to be you dying back here."

"Just a minute" he said. "Don't get excited."

He checked around, and sure enough, his artillery group was shooting at us. So they stopped. When I got back to the company the next morning, the company commander put me in for the Bronze Star.

R. V. BURGIN

That was our last big fight. K Company lost thirty-three men during those days, five of them killed. We didn't know it at the time, but the war was practically over. No one wanted to be the last one to die.

WAYBURN HALL

In June, toward the end of the battle, a truck pulled up to deliver mortar ammunition. A dozen of us went down in this grove of trees to pick up the ammo. The truck driver looked familiar. Would you believe it was Bayling—the ex-boxer who had defended me in boot camp? Here he was in Okinawa, driving a six-foot truck! We had a good time with each other, like you do when you haven't seen a buddy for a long time. It was real brief but a real joy.

Then the Japs dropped in mortars on us. Did we ever scramble. We went running clear up the ridge we had come down from, and I never saw Bayling again. His truck was gone. I hope he drove away and didn't get hit.

DAN LAWLER

There were still skirmishes. At the end of Okinawa we had some Japs cornered down at the end of the island. We were on high ground, a ridge. They were out near the water. A few of them came up toward us with white flags. They still had weapons with them and their uniforms on. But white flags? Why didn't they surrender before? Why were they waiting until the end? *The hell with those bastards.* We were firing down on them. With my machine gun, I took most of them out.

We had a new captain, who was hollering, "Cease fire, Cease fire!" Of course he doesn't know shit. Our captain was patting me on the shoulder, hollering at me, and I didn't pay any attention to him.

When it was all done, he said, "I'm going to give you a general court-martial!" I said, "You know what, sir, I couldn't hear a damn thing you were saying over that machine gun, and it's going to be ten or fifteen minutes before I can hear ya." I was bullshitting him, you know.

He just walked away. Everybody was for that deal we pulled. I believe it was on Wake Island where the Japs cleaned out everyone they captured.*

WAYBURN HALL

About the 15th of June we were pulled off the line. We left the Kunishi Ridge area and moved into this valley near the coast. Late in the evening we settled into a wooded area there near a little town. We got a little concerned when we found it was a rocky area and we couldn't dig foxholes. Anyways, we told ourselves we were just safe by then and that the fighting was all over.

After we gave up digging, near dark the Japs poured mortars on us. They must have spotted us moving in. They had the range, and that night the shells were coming close. Didn't they know the battle was almost over? This ole boy was scared, I tell ya.

---

* When the Japanese seized Wake Island they captured 450 American service personnel and 1,150 civilians. The Japanese beheaded five prisoners on the ship en route to a prison camp; then in October 1943, they blindfolded and machine gunned 98 of the civilians after keeping them on the island as laborers. Before one prisoner was killed, he carved "98 US PW 5-10-43" into a rock that remains today and is known as "the 98 rock."

R. V. BURGIN

We got pulled off the line on June 18, relieved by the 8th Marines. We were sent out on burial details, shoveling dirt over enemy dead. A few Japs were still alive in caves, and we got them out or shut up the caves. I watched one small group creep out of a cave, maybe three of them at the most. They wore only their jock straps. One carried a white flag. It was the only Japs I'd ever seen surrender.

WAYBURN HALL

On the 21st of June they officially declared Okinawa over. There were still some Japanese stragglers running about, trying to infiltrate our lines, and once in a while we'd get one. That was eighty-two days total on Okinawa. Some of it was good days. Some of it was not too bad of days. And some days was the most hell you've ever been in.

DAN LAWLER

When Okinawa was over, we were a real sight to see, all spattered with blood and matted hair. We stunk. I had a hard time hearing because of all the machine gun fire.

When we were heading back through the rear-echelon guys, they were all clapping and saluting us. We were just dragging our asses at first, but our commander stopped us and said, "Let's show these guys we're still goddamned Marines." So we picked up our cadence. Eyes right, forward march. There was a general there, and he was saluting us, clapping at the same time. I'd never seen that before. A general saluting us. So that felt pretty good.

R. V. BURGIN

After the battle was over, we were down there for a week, ten days or so, on the south end, policing the place and burying the Japs, picking up brass, cleaning things up a bit. Around July 10 we went by trucks to the north end of the island.

WAYBURN HALL

Our division was sent to the northern part of the island, where we started building a training camp up there. The idea was to start training for our next big push, which was going to be the main island of Japan.

We had a typhoon blow in there, while we were still building the camp. We got down behind a seawall, and that protected us from the wind, which was blowing pretty good. That's where we spent the night of the typhoon, behind that seawall, with a quart of sick bay alcohol: about 190 proof. One of the guys finagled it from a corpsman or something. We cut it with grapefruit juice. Wasn't too bad.

R. V. BURGIN

We were there in that last camp for weeks. Nothing to do now but wait. A little road ran through the camp and was used frequently by a Piper Cub airplane that would come in and out to deliver messages and pick people up. It was smooth enough and long enough for a Piper Cub to take off from. It don't take very much runway for a Piper Cub.

Me and Jim Burke, and maybe three or four more of us, would sit out there along the road and watch the Piper Cubs come in. We used to make bets on when the Piper Cub was going to lift off. How far one would taxi after it landed. All that kind of stuff. I bet you a dollar, I bet you a dime, I bet you a quarter.

We would see a Corsair fighter fly over every once in a while, and he would do a victory roll for us. When they would do that victory roll, it was our impression that they had shot down a Zero. The war wasn't over then, of course.

One day I looked up and there was a Corsair coming in from the west, roaring down at our little road in a dive. Just a little bit before he got to ground level, he flipped the Corsair upside down and flew down that little road upside down and close enough that if he stuck his hand out of the canopy he would have touched the ground. He did a victory roll then went out a little ways, came back around, and did the same thing going the other direction. Upside down. The whole length of that road. He did another victory roll and flew away. I'll never forget that if I live to be a hundred. That's not very long from now. I still don't know what that pilot was celebrating.

JIM ANDERSON

When we was on the northern end of the island, they dropped the atomic bombs and Japan surrendered. One morning we heard a tremendous barrage of artillery. It was our own. Later on word came through that the war was over, and they'd fired a big barrage in celebration. In December 1943, there were 235 men in K company. The amount who ended up alive and well at the end of Okinawa was 19.

R. V. BURGIN

We didn't celebrate much when we heard over the radio that the atomic bomb was dropped. *An atomic bomb, what's that?* we thought. Same with when the war ended. We didn't celebrate like the people did back home. It was quiet and somber. If anything, you think of the buddies you lost. We were pretty stressed out by the end of the war. Flat numb. I slept with Florence's picture underneath my pillow.

When I figured out what an atomic bomb was, I thought it was the best thing that ever happened in World War II, as far as I'm concerned. Some people say it was awful us using it. But if they think that was awful, I don't think people have a damn clue what would have happened if we'd hit Japan. The war in Europe was over. We had all our planes. All our manpower. All our Navy. Tanks. Artillery. If we'd have hit Japan, we'd have bombed it 24-7 and shelled it with naval guns from offshore. We would have killed *millions* of Japanese, and there's no telling how many of us would have been wounded or killed, too, going in. The Burgin family lost one son in Europe, and maybe those bombs saved them from losing another in the Pacific.

Meanwhile in America . . .

SID PHILLIPS

On V-J Day, I was at the University of North Carolina. There'd been a rumor that the Japs were going to surrender. It was announced that the Japs had surrendered, but nobody believed it was actually over, until it became true. We turned on the radio, and they talked about how the war was truly over. We just went wild with joy.

We came pouring out of the dormitories we were in and ran down to the main street at Chapel Hill. Somebody started a bonfire right there in the middle of the intersection. People were running up and down behind the stores, finding boxes, anything they could. They kept adding to the bonfire until it became gigantic. It must have been thirty feet across. It burned up the traffic light in the middle of the street. Everyone was jumping up and down and cheering.

The Chapel Hill fire department came and started pumping water on the fire. Then the police arrived. I think there was one police car in Chapel Hill. We told the guys, "Go on, everything's all right." We picked them up and put them back in their police car. But oh, we were happy.

We were thrilled that the war wasn't going to go on and on, forever. A ground war in Japan would have meant many, many killed.

CHAPTER TWENTY

COMING HOME

★ ★ ★

On Opposite Sides of the Pacific

During the summer of 1945, the wounded Marines and "old salts" with three battles to their names came home first, while veterans with less time on the line received a new assignment—occupation duty in China.

HARRY BENDER

They shipped me to a Navy hospital in Guam. The hospital in Guam was all right. I was there about three months, and then they put me on a hospital ship back to San Francisco. I remember going under the Golden Gate. It felt real good to be back in America.

For four days I was in a receiving hospital near Geneva and Moscow streets. Then they shipped me to Oak Knoll Naval Hospital in Oakland, where I finished out the war.

STERLING MACE

We landed in San Francisco on June 10, 1945, and stayed there a couple days. On the ship I had met a Marine from Pennsylvania,

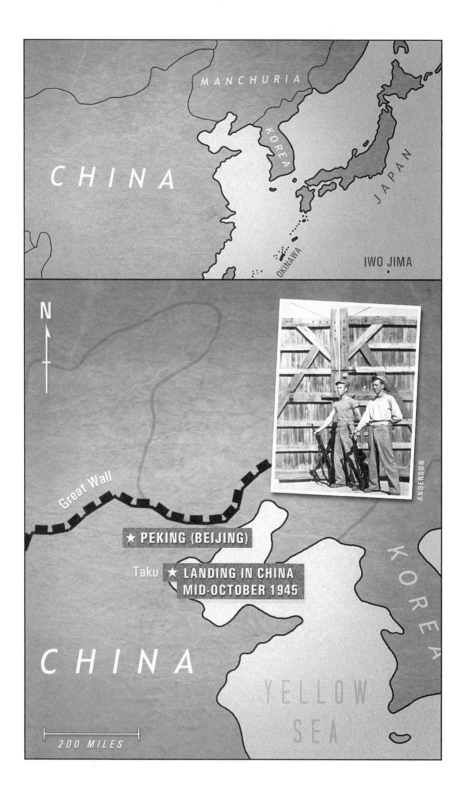

MANCHURIA

KOREA

CHINA

JAPAN

OKINAWA

IWO JIMA

N

Great Wall

ANDERSON

★ PEKING (BEIJING)

Taku ★ LANDING IN CHINA
MID-OCTOBER 1945

KOREA

CHINA

YELLOW
SEA

200 MILES

which was close enough to New York that we became pals. While I was getting checked out at the hospital, I continued my friendship with this Marine. He comes to me and says he received some money from his family so we quickly secured a liberty pass and hit the streets. My mind was working pretty good by then.

We walked to a barbershop and got the works. So we're walking down Market Street, with our uniforms on and new haircuts. This car pulled up, a guy gets out, dressed nicely, and two gorgeous young girls are with him, both about twenty years old. They saw the 1st Marine Division patches on our arm and asked us if we know a friend of theirs who's a Marine. We say, "Sorry, we don't know him." There's, like, twenty thousand Marines, you know. The man invited us along with them.

He took us to the Mark Hopkins Hotel, one of the best luxury places on the West Coast. Turned out he was the manager there at the Top of the Mark Lounge atop the hotel. He got us all this free food and drinks. The girls were very pleasant. Just a very nice time. It was amazing to think that a month ago I was in the middle of the mud on Okinawa, and now here I'm in the States, celebrating in style. The big joke was that Eleanor Roosevelt had decreed that Marines needed to be quarantined in bases in San Francisco after their return. She felt we needed rehab because we were "over there too long."

After a week of rest and evaluation at the hospital and some outings in San Fran, I was sent on a train to Maryland via Memphis, Tennessee. The trip took about five days, and I saw the guys do something clever. Someone got ahold of some chalk and scrawled on the side of the train the names of the battles he had fought in. I borrowed that chalk and wrote "Peleliu" and "Okinawa." As the train raced through the American heartland, you should have seen the people stop and stare as we passed. At the crossings, through the towns, at the stations. No one knew how to react. They just watched with their mouths open. That chalk was a really good idea.

R. V. BURGIN

While I was still on Okinawa, I had started the paperwork to bring Florence to the States. We had an understanding that we would get married, first chance we got. But it would be another year before she could get to the States. The reason it took so long was that getting the troops home was the first priority. Then the military was bringing over Australian women who had married Americans and had children. Next came married women without children. And last were the fiancées.

One day I started shivering. Then I started sweating. Chill. Fever. I'd caught malaria. I walked down to the camp doctor's office, my knees so wobbly I could hardly walk. The doc started me on quinine. In about a week the symptoms subsided. But malaria never really goes away.*

After fighting on New Britain, Peleliu, and Okinawa, I had enough points to go home. I arrived in San Diego on November 9, 1945, and was discharged fifteen days later.

STERLING MACE

I got to Bainbridge Naval Hospital in Maryland. I was put in a special ward. All the guys I saw around me were there for combat fatigue. There was this little hallway with little private rooms, maybe two on each side, and windows you could look in. There was a kid, maybe eighteen, nineteen years old, he was in his room, and every time we would pass by on the way to the cafeteria, he would be doing ballet dancing. We would snap our fingers and he'd never even look back. Man, I wanted out of there.

---

* R. V. Burgin would remember, "After the war, I had malaria on and off for years. Spent time in the VA hospital with it. I think I had my last attack in 1947. A lot of men had that malaria fever. They still won't take my blood donation, even today."

You go before a survey board, they call it, and you sit there and there's maybe four guys, medical officers. They talk to you to determine if you're ready to go out into civilian life. After that they'll say, "We'll let you know." The next thing I know, they say, "Mace, you're getting discharged—you're all finished." I was out, that was it.

You go home with your uniform on and the ruptured duck sewed over your right lapel. It's a gold patch of an eagle that meant you were honorably discharged from the service.

WAYBURN HALL

After the Japanese surrendered in August, they sent our division up to north China to accept the surrender of some of these Japanese troops up there.

JIM ANDERSON

On September 26, 1945, we left for north China on LSTs. Our ship got into a typhoon and the ship rolled really bad.

DAN LAWLER

I had enough points to go home. But we had to wait for replacements to relieve us, and not enough showed up, I guess, so I ended up going to China.

On October 17 we arrived at Taku harbor. We got off the ship and there was a big field there. While we were waiting, some of the nationalist Chinese soldiers came over and met us. We gave them some tobacco to chew. They swallowed it and threw up all over the place.

We boarded a train and went to Peking, the city now called Beijing. We were some of the first ones there. Our main job there was to round up any Japanese that were still there and send them home.

We arrived in Peking and filled up the French Legation then the American Legation, so we stayed at the British Legation. Of course there was so many of us, and these legations only held so many people.

On the first day there, we had some of these MPs coming in from the States. They took over. They thought they were the greatest thing in the world and that policing after a war was their job. We fought the damn war, not them.

WAYBURN HALL

They moved us into some old British barracks. They held some official ceremonies, to accept the Japanese surrender. Some of our guys were in the ceremony, and they selected the tallest guys, I remember, guys over six feet, fifty or sixty of the biggest Marines we had. The Japs looked kinda short next to them. I thought that was funny.

JIM ANDERSON

We were busy putting them on trains and sending them to the harbor for a ship ride home. They were happy to get out of China, and we were happy to be sending them away. It was strange to go out on liberty and see Japanese soldiers in their uniforms, just without guns.

DAN LAWLER

I was on guard duty at the front gate soon after we got there. Our colonel came down and said, "I want nobody out those gates!" I said, "Yes, sir." I had a young greenhorn kid with me, fresh from the States, so I said, "Something's wrong, put your bayonet on." He put it on and we guarded that gate.

A few MPs—they were miserable bastards—they walked in there with their sticks swinging around, and one of them tried to walk out the gate, so I pinned him up against the wall. I said, "When I tell you to halt, you halt!" He said, "I'm an MP!" I said, "I don't give a f—k if you're Jesus Christ, when I tell you to halt, you halt!" I had an order from the colonel that nobody was to go out that gate. Nobody.

Come to find out the goddamn Japs had killed three Marines that day. They had shot them. That's why the colonel didn't want anybody going out the gate. The Japs weren't even prisoners, they were free. The war was over for two months by then. They were just waiting for a ride home and still had to be killing Marines like they had since 1941.

That started it. We never said a word. The next night a bunch of guys and myself went out on liberty into the streets of Peking. We had pistols and carbines under our jackets. We went to where this group of Japs was staying and cleaned them out. We shot every goddamn one of them. Now they could send them home—in wooden boxes. We did that on our own. They couldn't order us to do that because the war was over. We probably weren't supposed to do that. The Japs wanted war, so we gave them war.

WAYBURN HALL

We were there a few days, then they moved us to the Chinese sector of the city. The Chinese Communists were attacking no telling who, so we were purposely isolated in the city, for our safety. We stayed in a girls' two-story schoolhouse, all brick. We were confined to that schoolyard unless we had official reason to be outside. To go on liberty, you had to get on a truck where they took you downtown. You had to catch a truck back at a certain time at night, or you'd be stranded.

DAN LAWLER

One day I decided to go wandering a little farther, so I took my pistol with me and headed off base. I didn't like what I was seeing. A little Chinese man came walking toward me along a wall. He had a hurt leg. When he saw me, he just leaned up against the wall. Another guy came along who spoke English, and I said, "What's that guy doing?" He spoke to the man and translated. He said, "He's waiting for you to shoot him."

You see, the Japanese would just line up Chinese and shoot them. They'd get a line of them, shoot them all, and, like a contest, see which one hit the ground first. This Chinese guy got a big smile on his face when he understood I wasn't going to shoot him.

JIM ANDERSON

At that time I was K Company's supply sergeant. I didn't have hardly anything to do, and they assigned me two privates to help me do . . . nothing. So I could go out anytime that I wanted to. I spent a lot of time talking with Eugene Sledge, just reminiscing. We had a lot of back pay, and could go out and have a big dinner for 50 cents. Everything was reasonable. China was pretty easy duty.

I carried a Japanese rifle for a time, a bolt-action rifle, but I got sick of carrying that, so I gave it away. One day they told us we could go down to the old Japanese arsenal. The guys who'd been overseas the longest got to go in first. You could pick out sabers, bayonets, rifles—and I picked out this brand spanking new Nambu 8mm pistol, still in Cosmoline and a holster.

DAN LAWLER

I saw the Great Wall of China and the Forbidden City. But it wasn't over yet. The Chinese Communists attacked us. We were aboard a steam engine going someplace. They put logs across the track, stopped the train, and got two of our Marines. Shot 'em. They were still shooting at us even after we cleared the tracks, so we said, "Okay, shit with that." Instead of getting back on the train and leaving, we took two water-cooled machine guns and put them up front on either side of the engine, on the walkway where people taking care of the steam engines would walk. We cleaned the commies out, piled them right up. Had to wait a day just to get the bodies off the damn tracks. After that they never touched us again.

WAYBURN HALL

It was maybe December 1945; a buddy and I were able to get a seventy-two-hour pass into Peking. We rode this old train up there; the windows in the boxcar were all busted out. It was freezing. We visited all the historic sites of the city.

They started rotating us home on the point system. I had two years overseas by then and had double the amount of points required to come home.

I landed in San Diego in the middle of February 1946. I had a good trip all the way home. Landed in the same pier I left from two years ago. Sure enough did.

JIM ANDERSON

I left China on December 21, 1945, and was aboard a ship for Christmas. When we landed at San Diego, I'd been gone from home for almost three years. I came back partially crippled for life from my wounds on New Britain. But I was proud of my flag and the small part I played in keeping the United States free.

DAN LAWLER

After four months in China I was shipped home. I brought a ton of souvenirs with me. I had pictures of Japs that I got, the pictures off the bodies. None of the people in the pictures I have are smiling. It must have been cold country, because some of the people are wearing winter clothes. I took some bigger souvenirs, too. I had two Japanese flags that they wore around their necks, a bugle, a samurai sword I picked up on Okinawa, two rifles with bayonets, and a naval officer saber that I got in China.

We could bring all this loot home as long as we had clearance slips, which I got for my stuff. But when I got into Grand Central Station back home in New York, two Army MPs grabbed me and took me into this room. The chief was there, and they brought in the state troopers. "Are you trying to be a wise guy, trying to bring all this stuff into the country?" one said to me.

"You think I'm a wise guy?" I said. "Listen—if you try to take any of that, I'll have your asses in jail by tomorrow morning. I guarantee it. You want to try?"

They went to check things out more, then came back apologetic. "We're very sorry, we never knew about this."

So that's how I got it all home.

WAYBURN HALL

They sent us to Pendleton to get discharged. I got a clean, starched uniform—first new clothes in two years. Everybody was standing around the train depot, and a Marine pulled up in this little old Ford touring car. "Hey, anybody want to go to Texas?" he called out. So I jumped on it. He was going to Fort Worth, so he took me there and then I took a bus to Houston.

I got home to Sugar Land on a Greyhound bus about five o'clock in the afternoon. I got off in front of the little old drugstore there, shouldered my seabag, and walked home about three-quarters of a mile up the hill to my parents' house.

They knew I was coming home, but they didn't know when. I didn't want to promise them something in case something would happen. So I just took it cool.

I went to the back door and walked in. There my mama was, sitting in the kitchen. Ah boy. Man, I tell you, we were just both overcome. Dad came in. It surprised the heck out of my parents. It was a wonderful time. It'd been two years since the last time I'd seen any of my family. I was home for good.

CHAPTER TWENTY-ONE

THE LIVES WE LIVED

★ ★ ★

Stateside, After the War

JIM ANDERSON

The Veterans Administration sent me to a mechanic's school for six weeks' training. So I became a mechanic. That's what I did for a job.

Two or three years after the war was over and we got things a little bit straightened out, I visited Eugene Sledge down in Alabama. I got a picture of him and his wife and me. He was a courageous guy, a good Marine. He did an outstanding job on his book. I couldn't find one thing in there that I felt different about. He captured it all.

I haven't seen *The Pacific* TV series. Combat in the Pacific was a terrible, terrible experience for a human being. I don't watch Hollywood productions about any of the battles. I do enjoy reading the experiences though, from the men who were there.

DAN LAWLER

When I got home, I found my old friend from training, Jimmy Butterfield, and we went out to visit the family of Harold Chapman, who'd been killed on Peleliu. He was the guy who got outnumbered in a bayonet fight.

We walked up on the porch, and this gal ran out to greet us, a good-looking gal, and threw her arms around my neck. It was one of Harold's sisters. I never even knew he had sisters. I walked in, and Harold's Purple Heart was sitting there. Course, his mother was taking it pretty hard. I don't remember all we talked about, but that was kinda hard. Butterfield did most of the talking. Later on I wrote a poem for the family. It was the only poem I've ever written.

I went back to high school and got my diploma and finished that off. Then I got a union job in a bakery. I got married a few years later. My wife, Virginia, was beautiful. When she wore heels she was six foot. I'm about six-foot-two or -three. She was the only girl I knew who could ever put her chin on my shoulder when we were dancing. We have two sons together.

A lot of guys never talked about the war when they got home, but I always did. Right away, I put together a scrapbook, pretty much right when I got home. It's all beat up today. But anyone who ever wanted to see it, I showed it to them. That's one thing that got me talking about the war, that scrapbook.

I live near the foothills of the Adirondacks, and I got mountains all around me. These mountains go right into Canada. I've got a camp in the Adirondacks right on the end of the lake. It's a 150-foot lot right on the end of the lake. Everybody who lives around me are doctors and lawyers.

My wife Virginia died a few years back. I miss her greatly.

I have a girlfriend today, Nancy. When she first came up to my place on the lake, my wife's picture was still there, and I turned it down before she arrived. But Nancy turned it back up again. "Don't you ever turn your wife's picture down again," she said. Nancy's picture is right next to Virginia's today.

I go into the local high schools and colleges and talk to the kids today. They're very interested. The school administrators keep bringing me back in to talk. Of course you have to be awful careful because they're kids. They ask good questions, and the big one is always "How many did you kill?" You know how kids are? They want to know the number. My answer is: "All that were in front of me." That is one good answer.

I tell them what made the Marine Corps—the discipline. How we learned to fight alongside each other, on the line. How we had a job to do and we did it. How they started it and we finished it.

STERLING MACE

When I got home, I went to see Levy's mother. Levy was my friend, the kid who was holding my cigarettes in his pack when he got headshot on a ridge at Peleliu.

Levy had lived in Brooklyn, so I hopped on a train and went down there, knocked on the door. I walked in that apartment, typical Brooklyn apartment. Levy had given me a picture of himself once, no bigger than a postage stamp. In the living room, here was an oil painting done of that picture. Beautiful picture. Christ, it must have been four foot by five. His mother was teary-eyed. We had a chat. When her son wanted to go into the Marines, she wouldn't sign for him because he was seventeen. He kept asking, and finally she signed for him.

She asked me to stay awhile. All the cousins and uncles and aunts came over. They were feeding me and giving me drinks. What was I going to say to them? Well, it wasn't going to be any details about how he got it, you know. But I just said that their son went out quick without any pain or suffering. He was a good soldier. That was it. I went out that door and said to myself that was the last time I'd ever go see a dead soldier's mother like that. I never visited anybody again.

I went to work for a clothing store, first for a tailor upstairs and then down on the floor selling clothes. While I was doing that, I kept thinking of commercial art school. A friend of mine who'd been in the mortars was there, so I signed up for a course in commercial art. I went to school days and worked evenings and did pretty good. I married and we had a son and a daughter.

I got another job, at the Jones Beach Theater, so I did that instead. For five years I drove a barge for them. Then I became manager of the theater. That job was the greatest and I did it for eighteen years. Then, just recently I wrote a book with a talented young writer, Nick Allen. *Battleground Pacific*. It's sorta my manifesto of what I saw over there. I figure the survivors owe it to the guys who didn't come home to speak the hell up.

HARRY BENDER

For fifty years I worked for the Army. I was actually a civilian, working for the Army Corps of Engineers. I went back to Okinawa and stayed there from 1951 to 1956. Then I went to Taiwan until 1958, and then I was transferred to St. Louis for one year.

When I was in Okinawa, I married a girl from Hawaii. Her name was Sin Wai, and she had Chinese ancestry, but she was born on the Big Island. We worked in the same office. She was a maintenance clerk. I was working in the inventory section. We started having lunch together. Eventually we got married.

In those days, mixed-race marriages were not that big, pretty much everywhere you went. It was hard for us to live in St. Louis. My parents lived in Memphis. My wife and I would be driving down to Memphis, and we'd stop at a service station. The bathrooms were white only and black only. My wife says, "I'm not black, I'm not white, where do I go?"

After St. Louis, my wife and I moved to Hawaii. An old buddy from Okinawa got me an interview for a new job. I landed it and worked there in the same Army headquarters for forty years. When

I retired, I was director of logistics for the U.S. Army garrison in Hawaii. All the motor pools, the laundries, the supply depots, the maintenance depots were mine.

So we made Hawaii our home. We liked the islands real well and the people there.

When I hear stories today about how a lot of the guys coming home had problems adjusting, I consider myself real lucky. I never suffered any long term effects from the war. I never had any nightmares. Nothing. When I came home, it was over.

My wife passed away in 1994. We had a real good marriage—never went to bed angry. We had two girls together and a whole bunch of grandchildren and great grandchildren.

R. V. BURGIN

Ever since I was a kid, I had dreamed of working for the post office. I was considered a disabled veteran, but I wanted to work and knew I could.

When I first got out of the Corps, jobs weren't all that plentiful. I couldn't get on at the post office right then, so I went to telegraphy school, to become a railroad stationmaster.

After a while the post office sent me a letter saying a space had opened up. So I started working for the post office as a letter carrier with a pouch on my shoulder, making 84 cents per hour. It was hot summers and cold winters and bad dogs.

The last time I saw Florence was on September 25, 1943—until she left Australia and we met again on a train platform in Dallas on January 27, 1947. We were married two days later, on the 29th, so we didn't lose any time. We already had reservations at the church and the cake on order. Her father handled it real well. He gave her his blessing and wished her well. He told her he would come to see her if he had to work his way over on a ship. He never made it—he died in 1948 from the harm of the gassing in WWI.

My uncle, Romus, the guy that I was named after, my dad's brother, he was also gassed in WWI and he didn't live to be old bones either.

I worked at the post office for thirty-one years and climbed my way up the ranks. The Marine Corps teaches you how to get along with people and to handle situations. It went a long way with me in my post office career.

Little stuff doesn't bother me. One time at the post office one of my employees shot another and killed him out in the parking lot. A guy come running in there white as a sheet and said so and so shot so and so out in the parking lot. I said, "Okay, I'll be out there in a minute." I walked on out there. The nurse was out there, and of course the guy was as dead as a doornail by the time I got out there. That's not the first dead man I ever seen. It didn't excite me or frustrate me that one of my men shot the other one in the parking lot.

Another time, one of my employees told me that he was going to "kick my ass." I looked him square in the eye, and said, "You might want to bring your lunch because it's going to take a while because I don't wup easy." He just looked at me and that was the end of it.

I was pretty tough on my employees, but they liked working for me because I treated them like human beings and didn't roughshod 'em in any way, shape, or form, and never yelled at them. If I had a person that was goofing off and screwing up, I'd just bring them in the office and set 'em down across from me and in a very calm voice tell him what he could expect from me and what I expected from him or her. If I chewed a guy's butt out today, I looked him up the very first thing the next day when I came to work and spoke to him. I wouldn't let any awkwardness fester. My boss told me one time, just because you have to get somebody straightened out is no sign you dislike them.

"Fair, firm, and friendly" was my motto. I retired as a superintendent at age fifty-five. It was a good run.

Florence and I traveled extensively, all over the States. We did a lot of sightseeing for a long time and even went back to Australia and lived there for ten months. Marrying Florence was the best move I ever made. We had four beautiful daughters together. After sixty-four years, six months, and twenty-seven days, I lost her to a heart attack on August 25, 2011.

After the war, I never talked about the war to anybody. I mean, nobody—not my parents, not my wife, not my kids, not anybody. There were four combat Marines I worked with for thirty years, and we never talked about the war. We might tell something funny that happened sometime, but that was it.

In 1980, thirty-five years after the war, I went to my first reunion ever of the 1st Marine Division, in Indianapolis, Indiana. There were twenty Marines out of K Company there, and I had done foxhole duty with every single one of them. We'd be sitting around in the hospitality room, and they'd say, "Burgin, you remember so and so?" and I wouldn't. But they'd start telling what happened and who was involved, and it came back to me just like it was yesterday. The more I went to the reunions, the more I could talk. Each year that I could go, it got a little easier, until I could talk about the war with ease.

Finally in 1991, they had five of us K Company men go to Minneapolis, Minnesota, and do a documentary on Peleliu. That's about the time in my life when I decided that these stories should be told. They should be written. They should not be forgotten. So I wrote a book of my own, *Islands of the Damned*, and dedicated it to the men in K Company who fought so valiantly in World War II.

Now, Jim Burke, he has never talked about the war to anybody, period, to my knowledge. Whenever the war was over, he and his wife came down to Texas a couple of times, and Florence and I spent three or four days with them in Iowa. But Jim has always been tight-lipped. He was a damn good Marine, one of the best. I guarantee you.

WAYBURN HALL

I went to school at the University of Houston. Finally got my education. After that I went up and worked in the main office at the local sugar refinery. My dad worked for them, and I had some sisters who worked for them, so it was easy to get a job. My boss in the office, he was a good friend, and he put me out there as manager of one of the service stations.

I managed that for several years. When they sold, I was able to buy that place. I got a real good deal on it, and I operated it for myself for seven or eight years. Somebody came by and wanted to know if I'd sell, too. "I'll sell anything I got except my wife and kids," I said. So we made a deal. I made some money on it. We'd bought a nice home in a nice subdivision by then.

My father-in-law had a little ranch going. So when he and his wife got in bad shape, me and my wife helped take care of them. I bought some of the property from them. Then my wife inherited some that was left over. So we ended up with 143 acres of land. We're running some cows on it. I got about forty-two head right now of cattle.

We live out in the country, just off the main highway. We still run the cattle. Or they're running me, I'll put it that way. My wife and I have four boys, and I've divided the land four ways, and I'm turning the ranch over to them. The boys all have good educations and good jobs, all for schools or school districts. They come on the weekends.

I'll be turning eighty-seven years old soon. My hearing comes and goes, and it's getting worse all the time. Those mortars during the war didn't help none. Hearing aids don't do me any good. I can hear sounds, but sometimes the words don't come out. That's the problem that hearing aids don't correct. My wife's wheelchair-bound, so I'm taking care of her. We're getting by, and we'll last a few more years, I'll put it that way.

All the things that happened, I'm lucky I'm still alive.

CHUCK TATUM

In the years that followed the war, I decided to have all the fun I could take. For a job, I did everything under the sun. If I couldn't be an officer in the Marine Corps, I was going to become a famous race car driver, which I did for a while. I hung around tracks and finally built a car, became a driver, and won some races with it. In California I was famous, regionally, as a race car driver. Eventually I ran car dealerships and went all over the world—Philippines, Saudi Arabia, Germany. A company hired me to build an automobile dealership in Saudi Arabia, selling Cadillacs and Mercedes-Benz.

In my retirement years, I realized that nobody had ever heard about the death of John Basilone on Iwo Jima. He never had a story about him anywhere. So a friend suggested I write it. So I got a computer and wrote the story of the death of John Basilone, and sold the story in October 1988 to a magazine. My sister Audrey read it and encouraged me to write a book. "You just write a page a day for 365 days, and you'll have a book," she said. So that's what I did. It was titled *Red Blood, Black Sand*, and I self-published it at first, and it did quite well for being self-published. Many good things happened because of the book, and I traveled all over and gave a lot of talks. I even got to address the officer's class at Quantico one time. This last year my book was professionally published by Berkley Caliber. It's been more successful than I ever dreamed. And it accomplished what I started out to do.

CLINTON WATTERS

I was discharged in August 1945. By then, I'd been in the service a little less than four years. When I first got out of the service, I used to have some problems with nightmares, but not anything serious like you hear about. I went out on 50 percent disability for several years due to my leg wound, then I was reduced to 10 percent, then zero.

In 1946, I attended Boston University and majored in business administration. Between my sophomore and junior year, I married Joan, a lovely young lady whom I had met back in the CCC [Civilian Conservation Corps]. Joan worked as an airline stewardess for TWA when we first married, but they fired her right afterward, because in those days you couldn't be married and be a stewardess at the same time. We had a daughter in 1950 and a son a few years later. I worked in finance all my life, and started off at North American Aviation and ended up at Rockwell International, in California, in personnel and payroll. I was corporate payroll manager my final years with them. When I retired, we moved from the hustle of LA to the quiet of Oregon.

I saw Lena Basilone just one time after the war. She lived in Long Beach, California, and my wife and I called and made arrangements to get together and take her out for dinner. We met her at her house and saw that she was living in the past—she had all these things of John's all over the place and just wasn't interested in getting married again.

Dinner wasn't comfortable. I didn't feel that she was enjoying having us visit her. I don't know if she felt that she had been cheated out of a lot and here I was living it up, I don't know. She said she was going to cook an Italian dinner and invite us down again sometime, but she never did. She wasn't the same person that I knew before we went overseas. She probably didn't want all the memories being brought back, so close to home. I tried really hard to keep the relationship going, but it didn't seem she was interested. I never saw her again.

Lena died in 1999 and is buried in Riverside, California. It's true, she never remarried. John is buried in Arlington Cemetery in Washington, D.C. I visited John's grave years ago with my children. That was kind of closure. I felt like I needed that.

CLARENCE REA

In July 1946 I was discharged after a year and a half in the hospital. I didn't want to leave the Marine Corps, but because of my wounded arm I wasn't able to make a career out of it.

I came home to Bakersfield, California, and started going to a gym. I had a special glove made that held my hand open, because at the time I couldn't open it. I went there on my own and worked three days a week. Through therapy and working at the gym, I got so where I could open my hand up again, although I still couldn't use it. I'd played football and baseball in high school; I was always an athlete, so my motivation was simply that I wanted to be able to use my hand again.

After about fifteen years, through the use of working it and working with it, I got so where my hand wasn't noticeable by anybody. Today, almost seventy years later, it looks normal, but it's still weak. Since the day I got out of the Marine Corps, I've never worn a short-sleeve shirt because of the way my arm looks, but I'm a very lucky man. The guys who didn't make it home are the heroes of World War II.

I was married about six years after I was discharged, and my wife said I had nightmares once in a while, but I don't remember them or dwelling on them much. She said that a couple times she'd wake up, and I'd be up, still asleep, wandering around the house. One night I was up under the venetian blinds hollering at somebody. But I don't ever remember fighting any battles in my sleep. My method of coping? Working. Raising kids. Getting on with life.

At first I didn't know what happened to Lena Basilone. Then I found out she was living down in Long Beach. I went down to see her and she wasn't home. I heard she wasn't interested in rekindling those memories. That's the last time I attempted to see her.

I was a deputy sheriff in California for a number of years, then

I bought some rentals and went into the property management business.

I loved the Marine Corps, and I still do. I'm thankful for everything I've got out of the Corps. It's still the number one thing in my life.

CLINTON WATTERS

I knew Clarence Rea way back at Pendleton. We were great friends, born on the same day (just a year apart), and we used to go on liberty all the time together. I have pictures of me and Clarence and Basilone all out on liberty together.

On Iwo, I was heading in on the first wave, and Clarence on the second wave. Just before we landed, we shook hands and said, "Well, see ya when this is all over." I ended up getting wounded the first day. He stayed on the island thirteen days before getting wounded.

He went to a hospital in Guam where I had been, but they moved you out of that hospital so fast, I'd already been shipped out to San Francisco. When Clarence entered the hospital in Guam, he said to the doctor, "I understand that Clint Watters came through here. How did he do?" The doctor said, "Oh, I'm sorry to tell you, Clint Watters died of his wounds."

Sixty-five years later, almost to the day, my son, who's a chiropractor down in California, had a young man come in for treatment. The young fellow said, "I'm going to see my uncle tomorrow. We're pretty close. He's a survivor of Iwo Jima."

"Is that right?" my son said. "My dad's a survivor of Iwo Jima!"

Now, you got to think that this is in California, with millions of people around.

The young fellow said, "I wonder if your dad knew my uncle."

My son said, "I don't know, but we can find out." So he called me and said, "Dad, there's someone here who wants to talk to you."

So I got on the phone with the young fellow. He said, "I understand you're a survivor of Iwo Jima." I said, "Yes, I am." He said, "Did you ever know a fellow named Clarence Rea?" I said, "I sure did! He was one of my good friends. I think he's dead now." He said, "No, he's not, I'm going to see him tomorrow. Boy, he'll be surprised to hear from you!" He wrote down my phone number.

CLARENCE REA

Sixty-five years after the war, I was in Southern California at a party for my grandson. My nephew tapped me on the shoulder, handed me a slip of paper, and said call this number. It had the name "Clint Watters" on it. I hadn't heard that name since the day we started to go ashore at Iwo. I thought, *My God, it must be his kid.*

I took the paper. A couple days later I called the number. It was in Oregon. On the other end of the phone was Sergeant Clint Watters, who I had last shook hands with on the LST offshore of Iwo Jima. I couldn't believe it. And he couldn't believe it. I'd been told he'd been killed.

So we decided to get together. We arranged to meet at a hotel halfway between Medford and Southern California. He and his wife, and me and my wife.

I tell ya, when we met up there at that hotel, and he knocked on the door, and I opened the door of the room, I tell ya, we both just about cashed it in right there.

We had just a wonderful, wonderful reunion. To this day we keep in touch by phone and e-mail. It's one of the most wonderful things that happened to me after World War II, knowing that Clint was still alive.

CLINTON WATTERS

Since then, Clarence and I have become very close again. I'd say we send five or six e-mails per day between each other. And we call each other on the phone and talk all the time.

It's wonderful to have such a good friend.

T. I. MILLER

I got a job in the coal mines. If you stayed in West Virginia, that's where the money was. After two years of general labor, I worked on the maintenance crew as a mechanic and electrician. I worked for the mines for thirty-two years. Twenty-five years of those were underground.

Civilian life was pretty rough for about the first ten years. Nightmares. Rage. Hepatitis. Malaria. I had forty-two separate malarial attacks. Malaria never really gets out of your system. It camps out down in your spleen. Sometimes I could hardly believe the fevers, chills, and shakes that came with it. I had some problems with my stomach, too, and got so I could hardly eat anything except dry toast, skim milk, and oatmeal.

One day down in the mines I was doing a belt-cleaning job, heavy work, and I swear I saw a dead Japanese soldier ride by me on the belt. Another body came by, then another. I had to shake my head and blink my eyes. When I got to the surface and saw the sunlight, the ghosts went away. The hallucinations were caused by a malarial fever. I was in the veteran's hospital after that for twenty days.

My wife, Recie, and family were a big help. Recie and I had three children together—two boys and a girl. We were married sixty-two years before she passed. At the same time, getting better is something you gotta just do yourself. The secret, I found out, is just to stay busy. There were no government programs to help back then. No therapists to see. Nothing like that. I was born and raised out in the country. So after I came back from the war, I built me and Recie a house out there close to where I'd grown up. I got out there and roamed around in the mountains. That's what helped.

One time they closed the mines down for three months. Someone said, "Where you gonna go look for a job?" I said, "I ain't. I'm gonna spend the summer out in the sunshine." And I did. I took a two-pound double-bladed axe and walked a half mile up above where I lived. We had a field there, and I cut down big trees and cut them into fence posts. I got me a half acre of ground, plowed it up, and had a field. That summer I grew potatoes, corn, and beans. The whole summer I spent growing things I wanted to. I'd be out in the woods at daylight. I just worked like that and built myself back up.

Faith helped, too. I was never a Christian growing up or throughout the war, although a chaplain gave me a New Testament once and I used to read it sometimes during lulls in the combat. I'd say there aren't any atheists when you're getting shelled. I always did like to sing, from the time I was young. My cousin and her husband and my sister were singing around in the churches, and one day they heard me singing and asked me to help them. I got to singing with them and we sang at various gospel conventions and even on the radio. I guess those spiritual songs got me thinking about the hereafter and all that. I decided to start living a Christian life, and so I did. I've been a Christian for about sixty years.

Today I live in the same house as my daughter and son-in-law. I just turned ninety-two last November.

ART PENDLETON

After the war, my wife and I went to Quakertown, Pennsylvania, to visit John Rivers's parents. There, I found they had long died and he had been adopted as a kid. So there was no one to accept my condolences. I did find the brother of the man who had adopted him, and he took us into his home. It was a worthwhile stop because I found out that they did in fact celebrate John Rivers every year at Memorial Day. I think they even put a monument up to him in the town.

I think a lot about how I missed Peleliu. My closest friend, Stretch Campbell, who was my gunner, took over my squad when I went to the hospital on Banika. I later learned that on Peleliu, Stretch got hit in the head and had gone on a hospital ship. Stretch was bandaged up but insisted on going back. Finally they let him go back because he became a pain in the neck.

Stretch was a basketball player for the University of Pennsylvania. When he went back, his leg was badly injured. When they talked about amputation, he said, "No, I will not have my leg amputated. I'm going to die." So he wished himself dead and it happened.

They all got killed on Peleliu. My whole squad, including Stretch.

After the war, somebody recommended I get checked out for PTSD. I had no idea what they were talking about. Years later, I went to the White River Junction Veterans Affairs medical center in Vermont. This middle-aged woman did an interview with me for about an hour. My wife was with me and it was a pleasant interview.

As we're walking down the hallway on the way out, the interviewer stopped, turned around, and said to me, "I understand completely what you're saying and going through. I'd lost a job one time and it really messed me up." We looked at each other and that was the end of that.

After the war I went back to school, got a degree, and became an occupational therapist. I worked in the mental health field and even ran a couple of private businesses that I started.

RICHARD GREER

I studied business administration in college. My folks had been furniture manufacturers, so I set out to learn that and had some of the top jobs in furniture managing all over the country. When I was sixty-two, I retired from management and went into consulting, and that took me all over the world. I did that until I was seventy-six. It was good living. If you were a big corporation or a country and had a big forest and didn't know what to do with it, I could tell you.

I was married and we had two children. My son is a minister today, and my daughter is a trustee of Emory and Henry College. She's well educated and spent time at Oxford and Cambridge universities. Neither one of my children ever gave me a nickel's worth of trouble.

After I retired, I got involved in a lot of stuff, the National WWII Museum, reunions, working for the State Department. I started doing volunteer work, nation building projects. I did several in South America, several in Central America, Africa, and Asia. I hate airplane travel anymore, because you're so packed in like sardines, but anytime somebody calls, I see if I can make it.

I was used as a consultant for the series *The Pacific*. They wanted to put me in as a character, but the thing they wanted me to sign, hell, I wasn't going to sign that for anybody. Too much legal-speak. So they slipped me in as "Manny Rodriguez" instead. And then they killed him off. That's where our stories go their separate ways.

Last year, the National WWII Museum presented me with a silver service medal for a lifetime of service to the nation. I have it and it's a beautiful thing. I noticed the year before, Elizabeth Dole got it.

I'm in good shape, but I'm coming up on ninety-five, and I've got enough sense to know that when you're ninety-five you don't have that much longevity. My health is good and I'd like to live to a hundred. That'd be nice.

JIM YOUNG

About five months after I came home, I became ill with something I picked up in the jungle and spent twenty-nine days in the Quantico Naval Hospital.

After the war I worked at a cotton mill in Pennsylvania as a weaver and then for the government as a civil servant at an Army shipping facility. Ultimately, I ventured into business for myself. I stuck my neck out and bought a small motel/hotel/restaurant and bar in Pennsylvania. My wife worked as the head of the kitchen. I worked on that for eight years. It was a heck of a mess and I ended up bankrupt.

I moved down the road and retired. I'm done working. Now I'm kind of comfortable. I never fully recovered from the illness I picked up during the war so am on disability benefits from the VA. I give talks about World War II on occasion and even reunited with Roy Gerlach and Sid Phillips recently at a local air show. Seeing my buddies reminded me, if I had to do WWII all over again, I would do it. I don't regret one minute of it.

ROY GERLACH

I had exactly four years in the Marines when I was discharged. I had no ill effects of being in the service. I never got in any firefights and never was in hand-to-hand combat with the enemy either, which I'm glad about.

I started farming for a tomato farmer. I was a sharecropper. The man who owned the farm bore the expenses, but I worked and got a share of the crops. I signed a three-year contract with him when I started. We raised a lot of tomatoes, but they weren't paying a thing. So after three years, why, I gave it up and bought a house in town for me and my wife Florence, who I married in '44. I got a couple of jobs. I delivered milk to homes then I wound up delivering something else—oil. I became a home delivery oil man. I worked by the gallon. The more you sold, the more you made. For every gallon delivered, we got three-quarters of a cent. We made 75 cents for every one hundred gallons sold. When we would complain about the wages, they would say, "Well, get another customer and you've got yourselves a raise!" (laughs). I made it work and did that for the next thirty-one years.

SID PHILLIPS

I married Miss America—Mary Houston—on April 15, 1946. Eugene Sledge had just come home from China, and he was my best man.

I was determined that the war was not going to whup me, and that I was going to go on with my life. Some of the boys seemed to have that attitude, and some didn't. I know Eugene seemed to be so haunted by the war afterward. We'd sit out on the porch at night, and I'd tell him, "Gene, just forget about all that crap. You got to put it aside and forget it." And he never really could.

Sure, I had nightmares after the war. Mary told me I did. My nightmare was always that the Japs were overrunning us, and I couldn't find my damn weapon, and didn't have any ammunition. That was the one I had over and over again. I'd wake up, and she'd be beating on me to wake up, wake up, wake up.

I laugh about it now. I have to. It doesn't do any good to whine about it.

I went on to study medicine and became a doctor. Mary and I eventually had three children together, twelve grandchildren, and I don't know how many great-grandchildren anymore, it's in the teens.

After the war, Shirley and I still exchanged Christmas cards and things like that. Maybe one letter a year, just like we pledged. We both got married to other people and had families. I'd always tease my wife, "I got a letter from Shirley!" Shirley married an Australian Spitfire pilot named David Finley, who was a very fine man.

One day, years later, oh I was probably in my forties by then, I was at the office, and my wife Mary called me on the phone. She said, "I've got some news for you, are you sitting down?"

"Okay, let's hear it," I said.

"Shirley is here."

I said, "Shirley? Shirley who?"

Shirley and her family were visiting the United States, unannounced to us. They'd rented a car and were driving all around, and they popped into our home in Alabama for a visit. Mary wouldn't let them leave. She kept them with us for two weeks.

Well, during that visit, my daughter met Shirley's son, when they were just children. Then, years later, when my daughter was in her twenties, she and Shirley's son reconnected. They hit it off and were married shortly after. They have three children today—my grandchildren—and they live in Florida, where Shirley's son is a doctor. So my former Australian girlfriend is my daughter's mother-in-law.

Shirley and I will still write to each other every so often, even now. Her husband died a few years back, and of course my wife has also passed. In fact, I need to write Shirley a letter.

I stayed in touch with my buddy W.O. but his story is tragic. He survived the war, married a real fine registered nurse, and had four little boys. We stayed good friends. About fifteen years after the war, W.O. was going to North Carolina, to a church conference, with two of his little boys and was driving a Volkswagen bus. Some drunks came over a hill and hit him head-on and killed everybody on board, W.O. and his two sons. It was rough, of course, on his wife. We had an all–1st Marine Division pallbearer crew. There were still a lot of us around. It was a bad event.

I tried to reach our squad comedian Carl Ransom. I had his mailing address and sent him a Christmas card shortly after WWII but received a notice that said, "Moved, no forwarding address." About ten years ago, O'Leary, who was in our mortar platoon, said he happened to meet Ransom's sister, who said he had died. I made a lot of attempts, but there was no Internet then, no easy way to trace people.

After the war, my wife Mary and I hosted reunions at our home for H Company. She would cook for all the men and their wives, and that's a tall order, but they loved her cooking. Everyone loved getting together, and we saw the old gang.

Now, Eugene Sledge didn't have as much fun at reunions. I went to a 1st Marine Division reunion in Washington, D.C., with him. He would come up in my room and stay because no one could find him there. He had become such a celebrity that everyone wanted to talk with him. Everyone wanted him to sign their book. Everyone wanted their wife to meet him. Of course he was polite to them all. He said he didn't have any fun at those reunions at all and should have just stayed home.

Before Eugene wrote his book, he'd shown me the manuscript and I'd given him some feedback. One of the most treasured things I ever received was a five-page handwritten letter from him. It's dated January 17, 1979. In this letter, Gene thanked me for my notes and explained how he came to write his yet-unpublished manuscript—the one that eventually become *With the Old Breed*.

In that letter he made a startling statement. He said he'd written a lot of academic articles by then as a professor at the university but claimed that writing this book was far different than anything he'd ever written. Even the process of writing was different for him. It was mysterious, almost bordering on the divine. He felt the book was dictated to him from above. I believe him. (Author's note: This letter by Eugene Sledge appears on the author's web site).

Today I'm in my late eighties, and in some ways I don't think I've ever been happier than I am right now. I love being the age I am now. You never get any criticism. People open doors for you.

They go out of their way to be polite to you because they think you're old. As long as the Lord gives me good health, I intend to keep this thing going.

I have a piece of property I live on—sixty acres—and I spend a lot of time working around that. I have a lot of woods, and I'm always planting trees, cutting down trees, Bush Hogging. I had cattle a while back, but we gave those up because the hurricanes around these parts gave us so much trouble with our fences. Mostly today, I just keep up my property. But I'm truly enjoying my old age, I really do.

My sister Katharine and I are closer than ever. We're only fourteen months apart. We live maybe fifteen miles apart and see each other two days a week at least. We have a brother, John, who's seven years younger than me, and we're still close, too.

Katharine and I were both featured in Ken Burns's 2007 documentary *The War*, and Katharine became the real star of that. Then two years later, HBO's *The Pacific* heated up.

Bruce McKenna, who wrote much of *The Pacific*, was searching for information about the main characters in the series—my lifelong childhood friend Eugene Sledge, and then Robert Leckie, who was in my company. He also wanted to know about Basilone. I knew Sledge very well, and I had spent two years with Leckie in the Marine Corps. I did not know Basilone personally. I had seen him from a distance, but that was it.

The young man who played my part in *The Pacific*, Ashton Holmes—he looks more like me than I do. I met him on several occasions, and we had a wonderful time together. He was perfectly cast to play me—handsome, brilliant, charming (laughs).

CHAPTER TWENTY-TWO

THE LAST WORDS

★ ★ ★

Present Day

A message from the Marines to the generations of today . . .

WAYBURN HALL

Every young guy ought to put a hitch in the Marine Corps so he could learn and grow as a young man. I am prejudiced toward the Marine Corps. I told my sons if they got any military training whatsoever they would be in better shape out in the world than most other kids. Two of my boys went in the military and did very well. I'm appreciative of kids today of all races, minorities, especially, knowing how tough some have it. I had hard times growing up in the Depression, so I can relate to them. I know the Marine Corps enabled me to move up out of the situation I was in. I learned to work effectively with people, and when I got out, I got with a great company, moved up the ladder, and eventually owned my own business. I think all young people, in some capacity, should serve the country. It'll help the country and help their lives as they grow.

I am not a true Texan—I moved here when I was eleven—but I guess I'm a die-hard Texan now. I'm proud of the Texas history.

Texas is a leader in the nation. We're fortunate because of what we have here. If everyone in the U.S. loved America the way Texans do, we wouldn't have any problems anywhere. We have a hodge-podge here, lots of different people, and I love all of them.

JIM ANDERSON

To be in combat is a terrible, terrible, terrible thing. It puts a permanent mark on your life and it's hard to shake. A politician would never declare war if he went through it. It's always the old-timers who have never seen war or who forget what war is who send our boys off to fight. Every politician who gets to vote for a war should be a veteran first.

A couple of months ago a friend of mine taped a special on the History Channel about the battle of Peleliu. He gave me the tape, so I sat down here one evening and started to watch it. After about ten minutes I had to shut it off. I can't hear very good, but boy, those sights were getting to me. That about says it. We went over there, did it, but can't even watch what we once lived through. Too many bad memories.

JIM YOUNG

I always listened to my mother. I never wanted to do anything to hurt her feelings. That's what you've got to always think of. What would your mother say?

You've got to pick your company. If you're going with a group of guys, you don't do what the toughest guy says, you do what your mind tells you is right. Stay away from the temptation of booze and narcotics. I never hung around with guys who wanted to do something destructive.

In the Marines I found real friends, good friends. We were kids that played, played hard, had our own games, but we didn't have anybody who stole or hurt other people. We avoided guys who were uncouth and troublemakers. Most of them didn't amount to nothing. They just stayed down as privates. In and out of the brig.

Anytime a kid asks me about the military, I tell them, "If you want to see the world, you're going to see it with the Marine Corps or the Navy." The reason the Marine Corps still seems like a good idea to me is because everybody seemed to really like each other. Everybody. Everybody was worried about you. And you wouldn't do nothing to jeopardize them. We were very close, a brotherhood.

HARRY BENDER

I never pressured my father to tell me any stories about the First World War, but I wish I had. He was in five of the six major battles of WWI. But he never talked about the war.

I don't think today's generations can appreciate anything. Some of these kids just don't realize what they've been given.

CLINTON WATTERS

Some of my Marine buddies talk about how they've never forgiven the Japanese and bear them animosity to this day, but I've never felt that way. They did a terrible thing with Pearl Harbor, yes. But I believe that the majority of the Japanese soldiers were doing what their officers and government told them. That's where the problem was. After the war I never really had any feelings that we should never deal with the Japanese anymore. I drive Toyotas, and some of my buddies think that's terrible. But it's a good car.

There's a college here in Ashland, about fifteen miles from here, where a number of foreign exchange students attend. Our church used to sponsor potluck dinners for the exchange students, to make them feel welcomed in America. I went to many of those and met many Japanese students. They were always polite and very nice. Several times, we hosted the potlucks at our house and we had Japanese students in our house.

I have real difficulty with some of our young people today. I guess it's because I'm a crotchety old man. When I see all of these people gathering and protesting and making all the noise and disruptions, all they are really looking for is attention for no good reason. Something for doing nothing. I have a really difficult time when I see the college kids of today. I wonder how many of them are really serious about getting an education and wanting to work? I don't think they need to go in debt like they often do. I don't think they all need iPods. I don't think they all need luxury goods. They ought to find jobs, even if it's nothing but washing dishes, if it helps them support themselves. So many don't want to do dirty jobs or work at all. I wonder if they're just putting in their time. It's an awful attitude to have, but I feel that way.

I feel really sorry for the kids coming back from Afghanistan and Iraq. We never encountered, in all my time over there, any civilians. The enemy was anyone out in front of you.

These poor souls fighting today, they don't know who the enemy is. Every child, every woman, every person a soldier sees is potentially a threat. They're all around them. Our guys are under stress constantly. They're never out of danger. I think that would be a tough, tough deal to serve over there. I tip my cap to them.

CHUCK TATUM

I generally tell young people that freedom is not free. Somebody paid for us. It's beholden on everybody to accept their share when danger comes.

T. I. MILLER

I look at my grandson, Jeffrey, who joined the Marines, he turned out to be an A-1 Marine, he turned out great. When I see young people at a football game in the band or playing on the field, and they are gung ho, that restores my confidence in America's youth.

When I see crackheads going around with their butts showing and their pants below their knees, ragged and dirty-lookin', I just call them a poor specimen of Americanism. Look at kids with tattoos; one or two I have no problem with, but dozens? Or when I see boys with rings in their ears and girls with rings in their lips, I think, *What are they doing?* I just call them a little bit odd and let it go at that. Maybe they are lacking self-respect.

The Marine Corps is the world's greatest school for self-respect. You learn to respect superiors as well as the new recruit when he comes in. You learn to respect the flag for what it represents. You respect others who serve, like the police, fire officials, and so forth. They teach you independence. That stays with a man when he gets home. He has a certain kind of discipline for life. You look and act like a Marine. You've learned to respect yourself. You're an individual.

The way our military works, each individual is expected to perform at different levels. If every noncom is put out of commission, some PFC could automatically stand up and take control. This didn't exist in the Japanese Army. I learned this firsthand; if they lost their leader, they didn't know what to do. They would do a banzai charge or take their own lives. They didn't know how to surrender. They worried about their reputations they would have back home. They were not strong individuals.

The new generation needs to know this. Get these skills and you've got it made. Becoming a strong individual is key to it all. You'll look and act the part. If you maintain a great degree of self-respect, it automatically helps you to maintain respect for others.

Our esprit de corps in the Marines was reflected in how every man in the squad had pride in himself and his buddy next to him. That made for a strong unit that couldn't be defeated. That pride in the American way is central. But now there are elements in this nation that do not respect America. It threatens the preservation of our way of life. My message is respect America. Love it or leave it!

ART PENDLETON

In all of the history of war, we have learned several different things. It can be created by one man. It can be created by a lot of men. It can be created for many different reasons. Many of them don't make sense at all. But the reality is, you don't have to have war. It's not absolutely necessary to exist on this planet.

As a kid in the United States you are taught a religious belief. That belief stays with you for the rest of your life. How about a belief that you can solve problems without killing each other? I believe the human mind can be consciously aggressive as well as consciously forgiving. I just don't understand, with people as smart as they are, that we can't change the system a little bit. We can get to the moon and back.

I think if an old war veteran started saying to kids, "Hey listen, guys, you've got to change your thinking," that's a start. But it's not going to happen overnight because the whole world has to be involved. It starts with kids. Now, in saying that, kids and teenagers are not going to understand a word of what I'm saying and they'll probably care less.

R. V. BURGIN

I'd want today's generations to know that there was a war fought, not only in Europe during WWII but in the Pacific as well. We got very little publicity out there. Most of the media was in Europe.

People today don't know of all the islands in the Pacific that we had to take back from the Japs. Sure, they've heard of Iwo Jima and Guadalcanal. But nobody has ever heard of the Battle of New Britain. Or Peleliu. Just so many little islands that our military needed to go to and spill our American blood. And nobody ever heard of them.

I had an opportunity in April 2007 to go back to Okinawa. Harry Bender and I were guests on a twelve-day cruise full of history buffs. On Okinawa they have two modern museums we toured, but very, very little information about the war. We wound up in Japan and caught a plane out of there. You can ask young Japanese now, and they don't know anything about WWII or the brutality their people did. It's one thing for American kids to not know their history. It's another thing for the Japanese to be that way. I don't know which is worse.

Personally, I don't think the Japanese have ever reformed as a country. I think they're just biding their time. The civilians, maybe they've had a change of heart. But not the military. I think they'll gradually build up and then get back into it again. They'll pull the same stuff, if the world will last long enough.

Quite frankly, I'm glad I got to fight in the Pacific. Sure, the horrors never leave you. But I can say until my dying day that I fought with the United States Marine Corps. I fought the Japanese on the islands. The men I served with were outstanding Marines. They were great men. Maybe the best warriors the world has ever seen.

RICHARD GREER

I do a lot of speaking, and I make sure they understand we didn't start the war. We were pulled in. Roosevelt had no choice.

I read a lot about the history of man, and I wonder if wars will ever stop. Maybe they never will. I don't know. We had despots in

Europe then, and we have them in the Middle East today. Plenty of countries want to be the big dog in the world, and they just keep pushing, pushing, pushing.

I've been all over the world, and as far as I'm concerned, the United States is the greatest country ever. This place is worth doing everything you can do for it. When I finished working, I set about doing things for the nation. That was my definition of success—to keep serving.

ROY GERLACH

Some call us heroes, but I would say we just did what we had to do. I don't know if we were heroes or not, but we were survivors.

The fighting we did in World War II was for a good cause. A few years back my wife and I were on a bus trip to a historic farm near Philadelphia. The tour guide said a couple from Melbourne, Australia, was on the tour. I said to my wife, "Melbourne! I got to talk to them!" So after the tour I hunted them up and told them who I was and so forth. The lady got tears in her eyes. "If it wasn't for you Yanks," she said, "I would be speaking Japanese today." I'd never thought about it before then. The work we did stood for something. We might not have always realized it here in this country, but the folks who stayed free in other countries sure did.

SID PHILLIPS

They teach so little history now. I talk to young people, twenty-five to thirty-five years old, and they hardly know anything at all about WWII. I spoke with one intelligent young lady who had never heard of Adolf Hitler. This is bad. We need to know the history of our country, and teach it. There's so much history that isn't taught anymore. Freedom isn't free, and we need to repeatedly fight for our liberty.

Governments need to be controlled. People expect too much from the government, but that only promotes inactivity. A government can't give you anything. They've got to take it away from you first. The amount of freedom a people has is directly related to the amount of government it has. Smaller governments mean more freedom.

We need to revive patriotism. It's a serious thing, and if we don't do it, we'll decline and become a has-been nation.

I have heard the reference to our generation as "the greatest generation." We were a great generation, no doubt about it. We were patriotic, we had a job to do, and we needed to do our duty. Yet I think the greatest generation is still a generation to come. It's a generation that will turn our nation back to God.

CLARENCE REA

I'll be ninety-two soon, and I've got everything to be thankful for. A great family, a great wife, a bunch of great friends. I thank God that I'm still here, and still able to get around and take care of myself.

I'm one of the luckiest men on earth. I was in the right place at the right time, it seems like all the time. I loved the military, and I've got a lot of good memories.

My message to anyone is care about your country. America is a great country, and it's worth taking care of.

That's my story.

USMC

BONUS CONTENT

VISIT AUTHOR ADAM MAKOS' WEBSITE,
VALORSTUDIOS.COM FOR NEW STORIES,
PHOTOS, AND ART TO COMPLETE YOUR
VOICES OF THE PACIFIC EXPERIENCE!

Witness the homefront
through the eyes of
Katharine Phillips!

Discover Marine flyboys like
Sam Folsom who conquered the
Pacific skies!

Examine poignant
letters & art of
the Pacific war!

"Off the Beach!" by Matt Hall

ACKNOWLEDGMENTS

I'd like to extend deep thanks from me and Marcus Brotherton to the following people for their help with *Voices of the Pacific*:

To the Marine veterans who reached deep into their memories to awaken the stories for this book: Sidney Phillips, Jim Young, Roy Gerlach, Art Pendleton, Richard Greer, R. V. Burgin, T. I. Miller, Jim Anderson, Chuck Tatum, Clinton Watters, Clarence Rea, Dan Lawler, Sterling Mace, Wayburn Hall, John Marmet, Jesse Googe, and Harry Bender. To our belle of the home front, Katharine Phillips Singer, and the Marine fighter pilots whose stories can now be found on the author's website: Lyle Bradley, Sam Folsom, and Gene Morrison. *Thank you all* for mentally returning to World War II so that we might learn from your sacrifices.

To my editor at Berkley Publishing Group, Natalee Rosenstein, a tremendous advocate for this story who believed these Marines' voices needed to be heard. To my publisher at Penguin Group, Leslie Gelbman, and her team, thanks for giving the green light to share this book with the world.

To the veterans' relatives and spouses, thanks for sharing photos, stories, and your loved ones. Special thanks to Jerry Cutter and Diane

Hawkins, to Vera Leckie and Joan Leckie Salvas, to David Marmet, David Miller, Steve Moore, Charles and Sue Phillips, Sid Phillips III, Audrey Phillips, Jeanne Sledge, Henry Sledge, John Sledge, and Evelyn Tatum. To the historians, experts, and friends who supported this book, Robin Barletta, Dana Caudle, Dwayne Cox, Richard Frank, and Joe Gohrs.

To my dad, Robert Makos, whose deep friendship with the Marine veterans opened doors for Marcus and me. When we needed help with our interviews, we called upon you. To my brother and right-hand man, Bryan Makos, who designed this book's maps, photos, and cover, turning a body of literature into a work of art. To my mom, Karen Makos, and my sister Erica Makos, thanks for serving as my focus group, reality check, and proofreaders. To my sister Elizabeth Makos, thanks for pitching in where you can and mostly just making us laugh.

To my great-uncle, the late Bob Castelli, a World War II Seabee who served in the islands and gave me his treasured photo album when I was a boy. Your stories brought the Pacific to life. To my grandfathers, World War II veterans Mike Makos and Francis Panfili, one of you served in the Pacific aboard PBY seaplanes and the other was destined to storm the beaches of Japan until the war ended first. Thanks for telling the stories that lit a spark in me.

Last, thanks to you, the reader who purchased this book. You chose to discover the Marines on these pages and in doing so, to honor them. Now, the Marines of the Pacific have passed the torch to you. Keep the flame alive. The legacy of great men lies in your hands.

INDEX

Adam Makos is a journalist, historian, and coauthor of the *New York Times* bestseller *A Higher Call.* In his fifteen years of work in the military field, Makos has interviewed countless veterans from WWII, Korea, Vietnam, and present-day wars. He has flown a B-17 bomber and a T-38 fighter with the Air Force, and was one of the few journalists privileged to examine Air Force One with its pilots. In pursuit of a story, Makos has met with presidents, had tea with Prince Charles, and toured the DMZ border in Korea with American troops. The high point of his work occurred in 2008, when Makos traveled to Iraq to accompany the 101st Airborne and Army Special Forces on their hunt for Al Qaeda terrorists. Visit him at his website, www.valorstudios.com.

Marcus Brotherton is a journalist and professional writer known internationally for his literary collaborations with high-profile public figures, humanitarians, inspirational leaders, and military personnel. He is the author of *We Who Are Alive and Remain, A Company of Heroes,* and *Shifty's War,* and the coauthor of *Call of Duty* with Lieutenant Buck Compton. See his website at www.marcusbrotherton.com.